Capitalism and the Dialectic

CAPITALISM AND THE DIALECTIC

The Uno–Sekine Approach to Marxian Political Economy

John R. Bell

PLUTO PRESS
www.plutobooks.com

First published 2009 by Pluto Press
345 Archway Road, London N6 5AA and
175 Fifth Avenue, New York, NY 10010

www.plutobooks.com

Distributed in the United States of America exclusively by
Palgrave Macmillan, a division of St. Martin's Press LLC,
175 Fifth Avenue, New York, NY 10010

British Library Cataloguing in Publication Data
A catalogue record for this book is available from the British Library

ISBN   978 0 7453 2934 5   Hardback
ISBN   978 0 7453 2933 8   Paperback

Library of Congress Cataloging in Publication Data applied for

This book is printed on paper suitable for recycling and made from fully managed and
sustained forest sources. Logging, pulping and manufacturing processes are expected
to conform to the environmental standards of the country of origin. The paper may
contain up to 70 percent post-consumer waste.

10   9   8   7   6   5   4   3   2   1

Designed and produced for Pluto Press by
Chase Publishing Services Ltd, 33 Livonia Road, Sidmouth, EX10 9JB, England
Typeset from disk by Stanford DTP Services, Northampton, England
Printed and bound in the European Union by
CPI Antony Rowe, Chippenham and Eastbourne

Contents

Preface

This work aims to provide social scientists and social philosophers in the English-speaking world with a one-volume introduction to the Japanese Uno approach to Marxian political economy and social science, pioneered by Kozo Uno (1897–1977) and substantially refined by Thomas T. Sekine. Moreover, it does so from a Japanese–Canadian perspective, given that Professor Sekine taught for many years at York University in Toronto, where, with the assistance of Professor Robert Albritton, he formed a small group of local professors and graduate students who shared an interest in exploring and developing the Uno approach. That group, which I joined at its inception, has continued to meet for three decades, though members have now dispersed to academic institutions around the world.

The Uno approach is best known for its distinctive *levels of analysis* approach to the study of the political economy of capitalism. Unoists claim that capitalism can only be comprehended by an approach that increases its theoretical grasp of that economic system by moving sequentially through three distinct levels of analysis: the dialectical theory of pure capitalism; the stages theory of capitalism's historical development; and empirical analyses, informed by these two theories. This book will focus on the first two levels of analysis.

The Introduction and the first three parts of this book are devoted to outlining the first or primary level of analysis within the Uno system: the dialectical theory of pure capitalism. As an Unoist, I maintain that Marx's *Capital* was the first (and regrettably unfinished) attempt to develop such a theory. Drawing on Uno's *Principles of Political Economy* (1980) (this is Sekine's English translation of the abridged 1964 edition) and more heavily on Thomas Sekine's imposing two-volume masterpieces, *The Dialectic of Capital* (1984) and *Outline of a Dialectic of Capital* (1997), I demonstrate how Marx's theory of capitalism can be corrected and completed to provide a rigorous scientific account of the logic which capital employs in its attempt to autonomously and impersonally manage material economic life.

My book may demand somewhat more of the reader than Uno's text, which was itself a primer, but it makes far less demands upon the reader than Sekine's masterful but somewhat daunting two-volume works, which are aimed at scholars who already have a good background in mathematical economics. I have eliminated much of the mathematics that is a feature of Sekine's tour de force, but I have maintained enough to demonstrate that a more rigorous approach to reproducing the Hegelian-style dialectical logic that capital employed in its attempt to regulate economic life in British liberal capitalism will allow us to eliminate theoretical problems that have plagued Marxian economics from the beginning. Once capitalism is theorized in a more rigorously dialectical fashion, the *law of value* and the *law of relative surplus population* will be seen not only as defensible, but as indispensable to the full comprehension of capitalism and its logic, while the seemingly insoluble 'transformation problem' will be overcome with relative ease. Indeed, it will be recognized that there are actually two transformations – a dialectical one and a mathematical one – that take place as we depart the doctrine of production and enter the doctrine of distribution, to employ Unoist terminology.

The eighth chapter of the book outlines the stages theory of capitalism's historical development. In this chapter, I draw on Sekine's as yet unpublished English translation of *Types of Economic Policies* (1971), Uno's most fully elaborated contribution to the development of stages theory, and on Robert Albritton's *A Japanese Approach to Stages of Capitalist Development* (1991). The logic of capital can autonomously manage the production of the light cotton-type use values which were dominant in liberal Britain. Yet a range of other commodities are always required as well. Thus, the economic policies of the bourgeois state in the leading capitalist nation in each major historical period of capitalism's development (mercantilism, liberalism and imperialism) must be examined so as to determine why these policies were most successful in taming the resistance posed by the more intractable use values, thus making it possible for capital and its market to manage their production as well.

I concur with Sekine in believing that our contemporary society is in a phase of ex-capitalist transition, because capital can no longer manage an economic life of such complexity, even with the support of bourgeois economic policies. Nevertheless, I maintain that the dialectical theory of pure capitalism and the stage theory of capitalist imperialism, together with the *general norms of supra-historic* (material or substantive) *economic life* (that is, the norms that any viable and sustainable economy must observe to survive over an extended period), which are necessarily demarcated from the laws specific to capitalism in the course of the development of the theory of pure capitalism, are very useful for ascertaining not only how far we have traveled from a viable capitalism, but also how far we would have to travel to establish a viable and ecologically sustainable socialism. These are topics I cover in my final chapters.

I wish to express my deepest gratitude to Professors Sekine and Albritton, who have been sources of inspiration to me for over three decades, but I should also mention all who were members of the Toronto Uno group over the years. I wish to mention especially Nchamah Miller, Colin Duncan, Richard Westra and, finally, Stefanos Kourkoulakos, whose brilliance impresses us all. I would also like to thank fellow Unoists John Simoulidis and Joe Wheeler for their invaluable editorial assistance, endless patience and penetrating insight.

Introduction

Karl Marx realized that it was neither a trivial nor a simple task to attempt to determine what it was about the nature of capital and its society-wide competitive market that allowed it to reproduce real economic life successfully, including the material requirements of the two major classes, when the state adopted increasingly non-interventionist economic and social welfare policies, as it did in liberal Britain. It was Marx's intuition that capitalism's survival in the laissez-faire era could only mean that the competitive market must be operating according to a rigorous logic, indeed, a dialectical logic. The major task Marx set for himself in *Capital* was to uncover that logic in its entirety. It was a monumental undertaking that Marx was unable to complete. Nevertheless, Marx did not merely flirt with Hegelian terminology in *Capital*. Neither did his employment of Hegelian language, concepts and methodology compromise his scientific project therein. The structure and argument of *Capital* are quite properly dialectical and should be more rigorously so, as they might well have been had Marx's health not deteriorated, such that he was unable to refine, correct and complete that work during his lifetime.

While respecting Darwin and Newton, Marx recognized that it is not possible fully and accurately to comprehend capitalism's laws of motion or inner logic by natural scientific methods. He tells us that 'in the analysis of economic forms neither microscopes nor chemical reagents are of use'. Marx adds that the 'force of abstraction' must replace these; but that enigmatic comment is not particularly helpful when considered in isolation (1969, p.8). Elsewhere however, Marx tells us that, as capitalism matures, it develops its own capacity for self-abstraction:

> Indifference towards any specific kind of labour presupposes a very developed totality and real kinds of labour, of which no single one is any longer predominant ... [T]his abstraction of labour as such is not merely the mental product of a concrete totality of labours. Indifference towards specific labours corresponds to a form of society in which individuals can with ease transfer from one labour to another, and where ... labour in reality has here become the means of creating wealth in general, and has ceased to be organically linked with particular individuals in any specific forms. (1973, p.104)

Thus, labour may be as old as humanity itself, but, before the modern concept of 'abstract labour' can be grounded objectively or scientifically, it is necessary that the development of the capitalist labour market, which achieves

1

an indifference towards specific labours, has already taken place. Although productive activity is essential in all societies, it is the chrematistic form of capital that simplifies productive labour to the maximum degree compatible with the prevailing level of technology and, in so doing, establishes the labour theory of value both as a scientific concept and as the organizing principle of the commodity economy. As Marx astutely recognized, the conceptual abstractions we use to correctly comprehend capitalism were first generated as real abstractions by the self-abstracting, self-defining and self-purifying nature of capitalism itself.

Marx mentions in a number of places that, before we attempt to understand or theorize the functioning of capitalism in history, it is necessary that we arrive at a full comprehension of capital's logic (its power of self-abstraction, its inner laws of motion) by theorizing a purely capitalist society in thought. In the theoretical space of *Capital*, Marx assumes that the laws of capitalism operate in their pure form (1969, p.175); thus, individual capitalists, workers and landlords appear only as agents or personifications of the economic categories that capital itself generates (1969, pp.10, 233, 316, 546; 1969b, pp.373–4). He informs us that, 'a scientific analysis of competition is not possible before we have a conception of the inner nature of capital' (1969, p.316; 1969b, pp.373–4), and that this, in turn, entails 'evolving the different forms' of capitalism 'through their inner genesis' (1969, pp.101, 108).

Marx's controversial statement that the laws of capital operate as 'natural laws' or 'tendencies labouring with their own necessity towards inevitable results' (1969, p.8) appears far less controversial if we think of these laws as working with 'iron necessity' only in his theory of pure capitalism. In any historical capitalist society, these laws are reduced to powerful tendencies by the less than ideal conditions that capital must contend with in such environments. It is unfortunate that Marx would speak of the laws or logic of capital as equivalent to the empirical regularities we observe in the natural world, but it is true that, once reification becomes widespread, as in mature liberal capitalism, capital's commodity-economic logic does tend to exercise a form of impersonal, external, quasi-natural, and thus seemingly unchangeable, coercion over economic agents in all classes. Of course, capital's laws of motion can be suspended by collective human action, but, because they appear to be equivalent to unchanging natural laws, such an eventuality becomes just that much harder to bring about.

In the *Grundrisse*, Marx insists that to theorize capitalism's inner logic or laws of motion 'it is not necessary to write the real history of the relations of production' (1973, p.460). As unsettling as this statement might first appear, Marx tells us that

[t]he question why this free labourer confronts him in the market has no interest for the owner of money, who regards the labour-market as a branch of the general market for commodities. And for the present it interests us just as little. We cling to the fact theoretically as he does practically. (1969, p.168)

Marx did not attempt to incorporate a complete history of labour or labour power into his general theory of mature capitalism, firstly, because 'human labour power is by nature no more capital than are the means of production. They acquire this specific social character only under definite, historically developed conditions' (Marx 1969b, p.35). Secondly, Marx could not focus on such important topics as how labour power originally became commodified and simultaneously theorize how capital autonomously and impersonally managed and reproduced material economic life in mature capitalism after the commodification of labour power had already been achieved. Of course, the laying of the foundation for capitalism's management of the labour-and-production process is a worthy topic of Marxian historical investigation in its own right, but this rich tapestry, which constitutes capitalism's making, belongs

> to the history of its formation ... not to ... the [capitalist] mode of production ... The conditions and presuppositions of ... the arising of capital presuppose ... that it is not yet in being but merely in becoming; they ... disappear as ... capital arises ... which ... on the basis of its own reality, posits the conditions for its own realization ... [C]apital as such ... creates its own presuppositions ... by means of its own production process. These presuppositions, which originally appeared as conditions of its becoming – and hence could not spring from its action as capital – now appear as results of ... its presence. It no longer proceeds from presupposition in order to become, but ... is itself presupposed, and proceeds from itself to create the conditions of its maintenance and growth. (Marx 1973, pp.459–6)

According to Marx, free competition, and not an economy dominated by finance capital in collusion with the state, offers the most solid basis for the reproduction of capitalism by means of capital's logic or laws of motion. In the mercantilist period, capital's laws operated only as weak tendencies, whereas in mature liberal capitalism, Marx tells us that

> [t]he inner laws of capital – which appear merely as tendencies in the preliminary historic stages of its development – are for the first time posited as laws; production founded on capital ... posits itself in the forms adequate to it only in so far as and to the extent that free competition develops, for it is the free development of the mode of production founded on capital; the free development of its conditions and of itself as the process which constantly reproduces those conditions. (1973, pp.650–1)

Marx also asserts that the further free competition is developed, the 'purer' 'the forms in which [capital's] motion [will] appear' (1973, p.651). He then qualifies his remark vis-à-vis the operation of capital's laws as laws, and not merely as powerful tendencies, in mature liberal capitalism. He acknowledges that, in history, capital's laws never operate 'in their pure form'. In reality, 'there exists only an approximation; but this approximation is the greater, the more developed the capitalist mode of production and the less it is adulterated and amalgamated with survivals of former economic conditions' (1969b, pp.23, 175).

FROM MARX TO UNO AND SEKINE

Kozo Uno (1897–1977) was one of the first Japanese economists to conduct a serious and sustained study of Marx's *Capital*. He eventually concluded that the bulk of the content of the three volumes of *Capital* constituted a self-contained, logical system or *genriron*. In order to strengthen the economic analysis in *Capital*, Uno found it necessary to rearrange the order of its exposition such that the structure of the argument came to closely parallel that of Hegel's *Science of Logic*. Uno isolated the first two parts of Volume I, which treat the three simple circulation forms of the commodity, money and capital, and reconstituted them as the doctrine of circulation, a structure which happened to closely correspond to Hegel's doctrine of *being*. Next, he integrated the rest of Volume I (apart from the last chapter on primitive accumulation) and the whole of Volume II so as to generate the doctrine of production, which corresponds rather closely with Hegel's doctrine of *essence*. Here, the production process of capital, the circulation process of capital and the reproduction process of capital are investigated. Thus, this doctrine first treats the process of the production of commodities as value inside the capitalist factory; secondly, as it continues outside the factory; and thirdly, as the macro-interaction of these two processes in the accumulation process of the aggregate – social capital. Finally, all of Volume III of *Capital* becomes the doctrine of distribution in Uno's reconstruction of Marx. The tripartite structure of this final doctrine, with its division into the chapters on Profit, Rent and Interest, may be observed to correspond much more closely to the tripartite structure of Hegel's doctrine of the *concept* than it does to Marx's arrangement in *Capital*; but this innovation allows Uno to launch a much more effective defence of Marxian value theory than Marx was able to muster.

While Uno believed that Marx had laid the foundation upon which the dialectic of capital could be completed so as to expose the inner logic of capitalism, he was convinced that Marx's pure theory of capitalism and, more specifically, his defence of the *law of value* would have been more convincing if Marx had not only been more explicit about the nature of his method, but also if he had himself adhered to it more consistently. Had he done so, *Capital* would not only have reproduced the structure of Hegel's *Logic* more closely, but, more importantly, it would have reproduced capitalism's inner logic with greater accuracy. Indeed, Marx makes many errors in his attempt to copy, retrace or reproduce in thought the method which capital employs in its attempt to regulate the material economic life of a society, because of his altogether too casual and intuitive employment of the dialectic. By adhering more rigorously to Marx's method than Marx himself, Uno was able largely to complete and correct Marx's explanation of the laws of operation (or logic) of capitalism, so as to produce a reconstruction of *Capital* and a defence of *value theory* that is impervious to the kinds of criticism which have traditionally been made of them. With its micro- and macro-theories based on the *law of value* and the *law of relative surplus population* respectively, Uno's theory of capitalism lays bare the inner logic of capitalism, which may be thought of as akin to its 'software' or 'programme'.

Uno's reputation was established with the publication in Japanese of *The Theory of Value* in 1947 and *Principles of Political Economy* in 1952. The latter was later translated into English by Thomas T. Sekine (Uno 1980). Sekine has also made a decisive theoretical contribution to Unoist political economy in his own right by making explicit the Hegelian dialectical method employed intuitively by Marx and, more rigorously and consistently, by Uno. Sekine demonstrates that Uno's account of the logic of capitalism is not just another partial or one-sided (in the sense of both incomplete and ideologically biased) Marxist interpretation of the nature of capitalism, but a complete and objective definition (or specification) of capitalism by capital itself. The dialectic of capital is a method of theorizing or synthesizing a subject–object 'from within'. The object of study is the subject, which, when questioned, must be capable of giving a full account of its operating principles without distortions being imposed upon it by the interrogator. Sekine has also introduced significant mathematical and methodological refinements into the Marx–Uno dialectical theory of capitalism. His contributions are best viewed in the context of his major works, *The Dialectic of Capital* (1984) and *Outline of the Dialectic of Capital* (1997).

While the Uno–Hegel correspondence may have been an entirely fortuitous consequence of Uno having adhered more consistently to Marx's method than Marx had himself, Sekine has convincingly demonstrated that that closer correspondence has strengthened rather than compromised the economic argument in the theory of capitalism. Yet when economic reasoning dictates that Sekine part company with Hegel, he does not hesitate to do so. Indeed, the Uno–Sekine dialectic is the most rigorous one we have available to us, if only because capitalism makes a better fit for the dialectic than does metaphysics.

Unoists believe that the signal contribution of *Capital* to economic theory is the theoretical model of pure capitalism that Marx consciously began to develop therein. As Marx first recognized, capitalism carries within itself a tendency towards the realization of its abstract or idealized image as a purely capitalist society, making it possible both to envision such a society in thought and to reproduce its necessary inner connections as a dialectic. The core of Marxian economic theory thus ought to be nothing other than the dialectic of capital or, in other words, the definition of capitalism by capital itself. Uno and Sekine follow Marx's (1969, p.648; 1977, p.90) lead in acknowledging that late liberal capitalist Britain is the historical society which most closely approaches this pure capitalism.

A REIFIED AND INVERTED SOCIETY

The presence of chrematistic or profit-seeking activity in a society is not sufficient to guarantee the emergence of a viable capitalism. Commodity exchanges originated in the mercantile trading of goods that took place outside of and between what were often widely separated communities. For capitalism to establish itself, these mercantile relations had to penetrate hitherto autonomous communities from the outside. As commodity exchanges became widespread within a community, the human relations in it had to change from personal to impersonal (from person-to-person to reified or thing-to-thing) and from familial or communal to mercantile or commodity economic.

For capitalism to continue to develop, the direct producers had to lose any access to productive land and their own means of production by which they had hitherto produced their own subsistence. They had to be rendered free to sell their labour power to capital, but they could not be free to do otherwise. Indeed, for capitalism to emerge from more limited forms of capitalist activity, human labour power, the ultimate source of productivity, had to be transformed into a commodity of a special type. Capitalism required not only that economic agents in the major classes increasingly surrender control over their real or substantive material economic life to the operation of capital, its impersonal society-wide competitive market and attendant logic, but also that the logic of capital should prove itself capable of managing the production of the range of useful products or use values as commodities that society required to reproduce itself. By the time the Industrial Revolution began in late eighteenth-century Britain, capital could purchase as commodities the production inputs it needed, including the special commodity of labour power, to produce the light use values demanded with the technologies then available. The expansion of the market and the strengthening of capital's logic enabled capital to extend its dominion over the traditional uncommodified and peripheral regions of economic life.

Up until the last quarter of the nineteenth century British capitalism tended increasingly to objectify or reify economic relations as anonymous commodity relations and, in so doing, demonstrated a unique and considerable capacity among the things humans have created to largely transcend us so as to be able impersonally and autonomously to regulate our activities as economic agents 'from the outside', whatever our social class. The goods produced as commodities, the money commodity generated by commodity exchanges, the society-wide market and modern mechanized machinery, though originally human creations and our helpmates, not only mediated between, but also subjugated, economic agents in this inverted society.

Although commodity relations tended to prevail in an increasingly universal way, British society did not collapse or break down. Rather, it experienced unprecedented, albeit uneven, economic growth. Social reproduction was thus no longer guaranteed by the direct human relations of dominance and subservience that had characterized earlier societies, but, increasingly, by the anonymous, impersonal and reified market. The capitalist market could regulate price, profit and wage levels such that the principal classes of capitalists and workers received the revenues, wages and commodified use values required to ensure the reproduction of both capital and labour power. Moreover, the workers, who supplied labour power to capital, did not collectively offer the kind of organized, sustained resistance to capital that would have posed a serious threat either to capital's management of the economy or to the capitalists' management of individual factories.

British liberal capitalism increasingly displayed an innate capacity to move towards or realize a purely capitalist economy, but since there was always some use-value and human resistance that capital's impersonal market could not overcome simply by applying its 'dull compulsion' on capitalists and workers alike, the study of history will not fully or precisely expose capital's logic or the precise limits of its powers.

THE NECESSITY OF PURE THEORY

Only in the capitalist era does the economy tend to 'disembed' itself from the society that hitherto enveloped it (as Karl Polanyi might have put it) so as to become self-defining, self-regulating and self-expanding; thus allowing us to conceive of the 'economic' as distinct from the concepts of the 'social' or the 'political' in a manner that pre-modern scholars could not. Indeed, the modern social sciences developed because of the largely autonomous functioning of the economy in the liberal capitalist era. The market's commodity-economic management of real or substantive economic life made it easier to recognize that the material foundation, not only of capitalism but of all historical societies, is provided by economic relations, whether or not the economic realm is autonomous, as it is in capitalism, or merged with the political and religious realms, as in traditional societies.

If we adopt this perspective and so make capitalism the referent to all other societies, it is incumbent upon us to ensure that our knowledge of how that economic system operates is as accurate and complete as possible. We need not settle for one-sided definitions, models or ideal types of our economy because we both require and can have an objective, complete and scientific knowledge of the operating principles of the capitalist economy, which was not the case for feudalism or other forms of traditional economy or society.

To lay bare the inner logic that allows capitalism simultaneously to self-synthesize and to reproduce material economic life, we cannot rely on a facile method borrowed from the natural sciences. Even if the capitalist economy were still functioning in a largely autonomous fashion today, we could hardly study it in the laboratory, as is possible when one is investigating certain objects in the natural sciences. We must find an environment in which to examine capital's capacity for self-regulation and self-definition. Fortunately, although a purely capitalist economy never emerged, liberal capitalism did overcome use-value restrictions to a sufficient degree that it became possible to conceive of or to synthesize such a society in theory and, thereby, to reveal the goal or telos that capital was striving to reach through the operation of its logic. If, indeed, mature, liberal capitalism was largely governed by a commodity-economic logic, it should indeed be possible for us to reconstruct that logic in thought by what may be referred to as 'method copying'. Our theory does not attempt to copy its object of study directly; rather, it reproduces or follows capitalism's method of self-abstraction or self-synthesis (Sekine 1975, p.85).

A synthetic concept, such as capitalism, cannot be formally defined once and for all in a few sentences. To define capitalism fully we must contrive an 'idealized use-value space' in theory, wherein capital can perform its own abstractions without being impeded by external contingencies (such as intractable collective human, use-value or natural resistance) which would be sufficiently powerful that capital could not overcome them by its autonomous and impersonal operation. We then may reactivate and copy capital's logic or laws of operation without in any way interfering with them. Only when an object like historical capitalism manifests a real tendency to approach its abstract or idealized image by a process of self-abstraction, can a valid theoretical abstraction or image of it be derived by 'method copying'.

Capital's dialectical logic or inner laws of motion only operate in their pure form in this idealized use-value space, and only those use values appear there that capital, its market and logic would be able to produce without active economic or social welfare policy intervention on the part of the bourgeois state. Thus, only in the pure theory do we see (1) capital's laws as laws, rather than as tendencies of varying strength, as they would appear in any historical setting, due to the presence of varying degrees of intractable use value resistance that capital cannot autonomously overcome; (2) the full extent of capital's capacity for autonomous self-regulation and self-reproduction; (3) the limits of capital's capacity to maintain labour power in commodity form, assuming that workers do not collectively resist capital, as they would do, to varying degrees, in any historical capitalism.

The theoretical and idealized use-value space of pure capitalism, which reproduces the unfolding of capital's commodity-economic logic to arrive at a synthetic definition of capitalism by capital, is akin to the space that Hegel provides for the *absolute* in his *Logic*. The absolute exposes himself in the realm of pure thought prior to the development of the philosophies of nature and finite spirits (Sekine 1984, pp.64–5). The dialectic of capital also allows capital, its subject/object, to self-develop or self-abstract in the realm of pure thought, so as to expose its logic as a synthetic abstraction rather than as an axiomatically detached one. Capitalism is thus confirmed, not as a subjective, arbitrary, one-sided and, therefore, dubious formalization of our historical experience, but rather as the only valid theoretical abstraction of a historical capitalism, which existed to the extent that it was self-abstracting or self-defining and self-purifying.

We obtain the idea of capital as a Hegelian-style absolute, by rendering our economic motives infinite. We first 'one-dimensionalize' human beings, reducing them to *Homo economicus* (or to the capitalist as the personification of capital), and then we imagine such a being doing infinitely – pursuing profit or abstract wealth and capital accumulation, single-mindedly and unceasingly – that which we humans can only do finitely (Sekine, 1999b, p.104–5).

Once capitalism reached its mature liberal phase, capital did indeed attempt to promote the pursuit of abstract wealth/profit/capital accumulation without limit, but could never quite achieve the status of a Hegelian absolute in any historical environment. Indeed, the emergence of capitalism, with its concomitant commodification of labour power, was a contingent historical development, due to the fact that our social lives have historically involved use values of incredible variety, most of which were not easily commodifiable. Capitalism developed because of its suitability for the production of light, relatively simple use values, such as the woolen goods of the mercantilist (and formative) era of capitalism or the cotton goods of the mature liberal (and industrial) capitalist era. It existed only to the extent that it was able to maintain a reified, inverted (or upside-down) and 'unnatural' society and, for this, the use-value environment or space in which capital operated had to remain such that capital's grasp over substantive or material economic life could be maintained. This largely self-regulating economy thus had a comparatively brief span as a historical institution.

By the time the liberal era drew to a close, capital and its society-wide market could no longer overcome the resistance posed by an increasingly complex use-value life so as to maintain the momentum it had previously established, even though the state intervened by developing economic policies to support the market by 'internalizing externalities' (for example, by dampening use-value and collective human resistance). Rather, throughout the imperialist era (1870–1914) and beyond it, capital progressively lost its grip over material-economic life – so much so that in the era of the Great Depression, capital and its by then atrophied market no longer had the ability either to successfully regulate or to revive the economy by themselves.

The dialectic of capital successfully theorizes capitalism as a unique, logic-governed mode of production. Capitalism exists historically only to the degree that this logic operates. The pure theory does not aim or claim to know historical capitalism in all of its empirical detail, but only that which appeared as a necessary consequence of the operation of capital's commodity-economic logic. An abstract conceptual theory, which allows us to grasp the limits of capitalism's capacity for self-organization, when it is confronted by only the most tractable of the use values it found in various historical contexts, does not exist to make predictions with regard to the future course of capitalism. Rather, it provides us with a suitable reference point or a framework of necessary economic relations, which we may use to evaluate or determine whether a stage of capitalism still prevails in history in the face of varying degrees of collective human and use-value resistance, or whether these contingencies have undermined capitalism's logic and moved us away from a viable and sustainable capitalism.

The operation of capital's logic does not automatically lead to the system's breakdown or to revolution. Collective human resistance to capital is a manifestation of human freedom and not a product of dialectical laws. The

Unoist stages theory of capitalism's historical development must, therefore, give due weight both to the force of capital's logic as it operated in a given historical period and to the major forms of use-value and collective human resistance to its operation that it contingently confronted.

The dialectical theory of pure capitalism is such a significant advance over neoclassical economic theory precisely because it maintains clear distinctions both between the general norms of supra-historic economic life that all viable economies must observe and the commodity-economic principles specific to capitalism, and between the reproduction in (pure) theory of the logic inherent in capitalism and the subsequent theorizing of how that logic plays out in capitalism's historical stages of development, where its operation is always impeded by use-value and collective human resistance.

THE LIMITS OF SOCIAL SCIENCE AND NATURAL SCIENCE

Marx insisted that abstraction must replace experimentation in the study of capitalism. Sekine (1975, pp.852, 854, 857–61) adds, however, that it is crucial to distinguish between (a) an arbitrary or subjective abstraction, such as an *ideal type*, and (b) a dialectical abstraction that copies or reproduces in theory a process of self-abstraction that was inherent in the object under investigation.

The dialectic of capital need not and ought not to import into its field of investigation the empiricist, positivist and instrumentalist methods, commonly employed by natural scientists and enthusiastically imitated by neoclassical economists. The positivist belief that there is only one scientific method, which is typically taken to be derived from physics and then subsequently applied to the study of not only the natural sciences generally but of the social sciences as well, is an extreme form of methodological reductionism.

It would be ludicrous to suggest that any society is irrevocably given to us 'from the outside' as a quasi-natural order that we must conform to. Nor must any society retain a 'thing-in-itself' that forever remains opaque or unknowable to us. It is we humans who create and recreate societies, including capitalism, no matter how natural and eternal it may appear. The partial and proximate knowledge of the natural sciences may indeed be nothing more than 'so far, so good' and, therefore, tentative hypotheses, convention-ally accepted for the present and subject to refutation or falsification by the further progress of natural science (Sekine 1984, p.20), but it does not follow from this that social science will be unable to entirely divulge or to lay bare the inner logic, laws of motion or operating principles of a social institution such as capitalism.

Because they are mentally straitjacketed within their positivist-inspired metaphysics, bourgeois economists cannot entertain even the possibility that a human-created historical subject/object such as capital might develop a considerable capacity both to self-manage and to manage human economic activities, and, thus, for a finite period, to be able to largely transcend us in its impersonal regulation of those activities. It is the method of dialectic that is appropriate for the objective and scientific comprehension of such a subject/object.

That said, it can be readily conceded that the dialectical method of uncovering complete knowledge of a self-revealing, self-abstracting subject/object cannot be legitimately employed in the natural sciences. Nature reveals no teleology to us. We cannot see or reproduce its logic 'from the inside' and come to know definitively that complex and ultimately unfathomable reality, because we did not create it. In short, we cannot grasp the 'concrete logical idea' or noumenal 'thing-in-itself' of nature as we can with capitalism, which we put in place. Because nature will not completely reveal its operating principles to us, as capital does, a dialectic of nature (or of matter) is an impossibility (Sekine 1993, pp.25–6; but see also 1998, p.436 and 1984, pp.18–20).

THE STAGE THEORY OF CAPITALISM'S HISTORICAL DEVELOPMENT

Unoists claim that Marx was not only the first to recognize the necessity of theorizing pure capitalism, but also that he recognized that capitalism operated differently in its formative and mature industrial periods and that each period must thus be theorized differently. According to Marx, in the formative period, 'trade dominates industry; in modern society, the opposite' (1969, p.330; 1973, p.858). The consequence of this is that while capital always engages in chrematistic pursuits, mercantile capital operates in a manner that is 'directly contradictory to the concept of value'. Prior to the development of the putting-out system, 'to buy cheap and sell dear [was] the law of trade' (1973, p.856). Consequently, 'where commerce rules industry, where merchants' capital promotes the exchange of products between undeveloped societies, commercial profit not only appears as out-bargaining and cheating, but also largely originates from them' (1969b, pp.330–1). During this formative period, when primitive accumulation took place, force and fraud were routinely employed. According to Marx, force is 'the midwife of every old society pregnant with a new one. It is itself an economic power' (1969, p.751). However, in mature liberal capitalism, 'direct force, outside economic conditions [was] ... used ... only exceptionally'. Rather, economic actors were subject to the 'dull compulsion of economic relations' (1969, p.737). Similarly, moneylending capital, the antiquated form of interest-bearing capital, also depended on 'robbery and plunder' (1969b, p.593) in a way that the latter could not typically do, given the maturity of the market economy.

For Unoists, Marxian economics is a discipline that studies real economies in the light of the commodity-economic laws established in the theory of pure capitalism. A stage theory (*dankairon*) aims to be a meaningful and necessary intermediary or crucial link between the singular, abstract-general and deterministic theory of pure capitalism (*genriron*), which represents an extrapolation of an increasingly powerful reifying tendency that prevailed in modern western economic life up until the late nineteenth century, and the concrete-specific empirical realities of diverse capitalist societies that could never be made totally subordinate to this tendency. Because use values are never, in fact, as tame as they are supposed to be in the abstract world of theory, stage theory must bring the logic of the pure theory together with the more realistic use values, which dominate a particular historical stage, before evaluating the working of an actual capitalist society in history. A levels-of-analysis approach is, thus, indispensable for comprehending capitalism.

To characterize each stage, I draw primarily on an unpublished English translation of Kozo Uno's *Types of Economic Policies Under Capitalism* (*Keizai Seisakuron*, 1971) and on Robert Albritton's, *A Japanese Approach to Stages of Capitalist Development* (1991), which represents a critical appropriation of Uno's basic approach to characterizing the stages of capitalism's historical development.

Sekine (1975, pp.859, 861, 870–1; 1984, pp.64–5) explains that the Unoist stage theory of capitalist development plays a mediating role between theory and history, which corresponds to Hegel's *Realphilosophie*. Hegel believed that his dialectical logic corresponded with metaphysics. When Hegel applied his logic to the material world of Nature and Finite Spirit, he expected that the cunning of reason would ultimately prevail there too, but not without some distortions due to omnipresent contingencies. Similarly, the dialectic of capital exposes capital's essence (capital as such) in a purely capitalist society, which exists only in the theoretical realm, while the Unoist stage theory of capitalism examines the unfolding of capital's logic in historical environments, where not all use-value or collective human resistance can be overcome by capital's autonomous operation without undue strain.

Sekine conceives a historical stage of the development of capitalism as a 'material' rather than an 'ideal' type because the characterization of a stage is made in light of the dialectical and, therefore, deterministic pure theory. The stages of mercantilism, liberalism and imperialism in Unoist theory are, thus, Hegelian-style 'alienations' or 'corporeal manifestations' of the inner logic of capitalism in given historical and technological environments and use-value spaces. The characterization of the 'material type of a stage' (Sekine 1975, p.854) is, thus, objectively unique rather than one of many partial (that is, one-sided and necessarily biased) ideal types, which are arbitrarily constructed, subjective images of capitalism, as it is observed from the outside, much as we would observe a natural scientific object.

Sekine (see, for example, 2001, pp.37–9; 2003, pp.127–8) uses the term 'use-value space' to refer to the concrete-specific context within which the material economic life of a historical society evolves. An enormous variety of use-value spaces have existed throughout our history, but few could have been organized successfully by the logic of capital. Only those spaces in which many key use values are capitalistically producible as commodities can be subsumed under the logic of capital and are, hence, amenable to its control. All capitalist use-value spaces in history are less than ideal for capital. In any historical capitalist society, there will always be some forms of use-value, human and natural resistance, which capital's logic will not be able to manage. The capitalisms we experience in history result from specific combinations of the logic of capital and particular, less-than-ideal use-value spaces. This resistance may distort the shape of business cycles or obstruct the operation of the laws of value and average profit. However, so long as the market still tends to achieve an optimal allocation of resources in its sub-phase of average activity, without having to rely on the planning principle of the state in any other capacity but an auxiliary one, capitalism will remain viable. Nevertheless, Unoists recognize from the outset that the cunning of capital will not indefinitely be capable of overcoming human, use-value and natural resistance, even if it has the support of the bourgeois state.

Since capitalism in history only arises when the dominant use values that a society requires are readily producible as commodities, the development of a stage theory of capitalism's historical development must originate in a consideration of the relationship between the operation of capital's logic and those crucial use values which it must manage in a particular stage. To say that historical capitalism must contend with varying types and degrees of use-value resistance in the different stages of its maturation is to say that the extent to which all use-value production is undertaken as the production of capitalistically produced commodities by means of commodified labour power also varies from stage to stage. Each of the three stages is thus characterized by the typical use-value space that prevails within a stage. Thus, the types of use-value production that actually dominated each of the world-historic stages of capitalism must be introduced. In this context, systematic disturbances in the operation of the law of value occur because capital is attempting to produce use values which are not the idealized, cotton-type light use values that appear in pure capitalism, with technologies that are harder for capital to manage than the light technologies that appear in pure theory.

In the context of stage theory, the capitalist is no longer simply the personification of the motion of capital in the abstract, but is rather the organizational form with the modus operandi most suited to the production of the dominant use value in that stage. In the period of mercantilism, the dominant form of capital was merchant capital; for competitive capitalism, the dominant form was industrial capital; and, for imperialism, the dominant form was finance capital. In the mercantilist period, the key use value was woolen goods, produced under the putting-out system. In the liberal era, it was cotton goods, produced by small, entrepreneurial capitalists in atomistic competition. In the imperialist period, it was heavy iron and steel goods, produced on a large scale by oligopolistic joint-stock corporations. Since these were the most important 'manufactured' products in each stage, the accumulation of capital occurred most typically in these industries.

The sequence of wool, cotton and steel in stage theory is not a necessary sequence because it cannot be shown that the transition from one stage to another is necessary; nor can it be shown that the logic of capital must be externalized sequentially in only these three stages. Given the dominance of certain typical forms of production, however, it is possible to demonstrate how the logic of capital must operate in these circumstances, even if the circumstances themselves are not logically deduced from pure theory.

In a purely capitalist society, where use values are idealized (or presumed to be more manageable than they actually are) and the logic of capital operates without help or hindrance from any political agency, the nation state and cross-border trading are absent. The division of the capitalist market into distinct national markets is a contingent matter, which is not part of the logic of capital. While the pure theory can be formulated only when the use-value space is rarefied, idealized or made abstract, real capitalism presupposes a concrete-specific use-value space, which is never completely subsumable under the logic of capital. This implies that, in real capitalism, there are bound to be 'externalities' (factors that exceed the operating principle of the capitalist market). In stage theory, we must begin to confront these externalities and we must accept that historical capitalism must operate within the framework of a nation state, and this, in turn, implies the presence of international trade and payments.

Whereas the dialectical theory of pure capitalism only explains how the economic sub-structure of capitalism would operate in an ideal use-value space existing in thought, where the only use-value resistance which is tolerated is that which capital's logic can autonomously overcome, in stage theory, by contrast, the dominant capital form of a particular historical stage must always receive stage-specific superstructural assistance in the form of the appropriate state economic policies. The most appropriate policy is the one which most effectively manages the dominant use value within that stage. State power and policies must be present to 'internalize' or to reintegrate externalities or to tame intractable use-value and collective human resistance so as to make them subject to the self-regulating mechanism of the capitalist market. If the use-value space is such that its externalities are capable of being internalized by the economic policies of the bourgeois state, capitalism remains viable; if not, capitalism will become moribund.

Although state economic activities establish the conditions under which the inner logic of capitalism works its way out in a particular period, they are not generated by that logic. Capitalism, which produces commodities by means of commodities (including commodified labour power), exists only to the degree that it is a logically self-contained, self-dependent, self-regulating and self-reproducing system. If capitalist activity has largely come to depend on the finance and economic policies of the state, which capital does not generate through its own autonomous motion, then the capitalist mode of production must already have collapsed.

When the dominant nations of the world are capitalist, a world-historic stage of capitalism evolves with stage-specific international economic relations. A world-historic stage of capitalism is best understood by examining the pattern of development in the dominant or leading state. Once the dominant form of capital and its stage-typical mode of accumulation have been correctly identified, it is possible to determine which state's economic policies most effectively support this capital accumulation and, thereby, most adequately serve to guarantee capitalism's survival. Because state economic policy plays a fundamental role in each of the major periods of capitalism's historical development, stage theory derives the names and distinguishing characteristics, which it applies to the three stages of capitalism, from the public finance and trade policies which prevailed in the dominant nation in each of these eras.

Each stage of capitalism is characterized not only by a particular use-value space, economic policy and class structure, but also by the type of energy which fueled economic development within that stage. As the pure theory makes clear, capitalism tends to develop through successive business cycles and, in each, the organic composition of capital is raised such that the rate of profit tends to fall in each successive cycle. In the mercantilist stage, the dominant energy source was wood; in liberalism and imperialism, coal was dominant, although, in the latter stage, capitalism began to rely, as well, on electricity and oil (albeit, to a limited extent, prior to the widespread employment of the internal combustion engine). The stage theory recognizes that each stage has a finite lifespan because, although profit rates never necessarily fall to zero, the introduction of new production technologies, whether wood-based or coal-based, will eventually be unable to raise profit rates enough to provide capitalists with the incentive to continue capital accumulation. Thus, if capitalism is not to be placed in serious jeopardy, a new source of energy must be found that can effectively and dramatically raise the productive powers of labour far more than the technologies relied on previously.

Although our focus in this introductory book will be confined to the study of stage-specific economic policies, this does not constitute the full range of stage-theoretic studies. Particularly important would be the role of public finance as it affects and is affected by economic policy within a stage. Public finance aims to achieve an economic accommodation of diverse sectional interests whereas economic policy, to be successful, must bolster capital's capacity for self-reproduction.

Just as Hegel thought that the empirical sciences, when not mediated by the philosophies of nature and mind, were thoughtless, Unoists contend that empirical studies of historical capitalism are blind, if undertaken without regard for the inner logic of capitalism, even if the logic, because of its abstract nature, cannot directly or fully explain the complexities of the actual historical evolution of capitalism. Thus, dispensing with the intermediary stage theory will either vitiate the integrity of any abstract theory of capitalism or promote an unduly mechanical view of historical capitalism. Once the pure theory and the stage theory have been developed, however, empirical studies, informed by the former, may accommodate any concrete and factual information that is necessary to give as detailed a picture of any aspect of historical capitalism as is required.

THE UNO–SEKINE APPROACH TO NON-CAPITALIST SOCIETIES

The Marxian tradition has always recognized the contradiction, tension or incongruity in the gap between what capital's commodity-economic logic is attempting to achieve and the recalcitrance of use values in real economic life.

Capital is capable of managing material economic life only if society's use-value requirements remain within a very narrow range – something that would not be the case in any historical society for any extended period. Indeed, the logic of capital has never completely subsumed the 'use-value space' of any historical society. There have always been 'externalities' which capital could not overcome by its own autonomous motion. Thus, even if knowledge of that logic does not show the inevitability of the system's collapse, it does make it obvious that any historical capitalism can only be transient. Capitalism is far from being the liberal's ever-present possibility.

I follow Uno and Sekine in believing that it is fruitless to attempt to theorize the post-1945 economy as a new and viable stage of capitalism. Our economic life today entails the production of heavy and complex use values and the provision of technical services by transnational corporate oligopolies, which cannot be regulated by the capitalist market. The present global market is not viably capitalist. It is not capable of overcoming the imposing use-value resistance (to employ Marxian terms) or of 'internalizing intractable externalities' (to employ the language of neoclassical economics) so as to reliably reproduce substantive economic life. When society requires products such as automobiles, jet aircraft, hydro-electric systems, nuclear plants or information and communication technologies, state and supra-state agencies must also participate in the management of economic life.

In the contemporary post-Fordist era, radically labour-saving technologies are being introduced in industry, not just in the developed world but also in the key developing nations. At the same time, capitalist activity is actually retreating to the interstices of economic life as financial speculation, asset accumulation and the redistribution of existing wealth substitute for growth in the real economy, which has become difficult and ecologically unsustainable. Globally, working people have to contend with the spectre of permanent marginalization, underemployment and the enclosure of what remains of the global commons. This means that in the developed, developing and poor nations a significant proportion of the population will not be integrated into the corporate-dominated global economy, but few will have the option of retreating to subsistence agriculture to survive.

Consumers today are massively manipulated by corporate producers prior to their purchase of consumer durables and high-tech gadgetry, in a fashion that would have been unthinkable in the capitalist era, when the available resources, prevailing technologies and market power that relatively small capitalist firms could marshal were insufficient to undermine so thoroughly the autonomous formation of demand. This consumerism, which is a consequence of the sovereignty of producers rather than of consumers, is, nevertheless, becoming difficult to promote, due to ecological considerations, the satiation of the affluent minority and the decline in the standard of living of many in hitherto affluent societies.

If we have the wisdom and the courage to recognize that the contemporary economy is no longer viably capitalist, we can then pose the question as to how Uno's *levels of analysis* approach might be fruitfully employed in this era of ex-capitalist transition. The pure theory not only provides us with a solid reference point from which we can measure just how far we have departed from a viable capitalism (as I endeavour to demonstrate in Chapter 9); it also allows us to clearly isolate or demarcate the *general norms of material (or substantive) economic life*, which must prevail in any viable, sustainable economy, from the commodity-economic logic or laws specific to capitalism, with which they might otherwise be conflated, and then to evaluate how successful our society has been in observing those norms. The knowledge provided by the pure theory also enables us to rethink socialism as the society which definitively transcends capitalism by eliminating impersonal, commodity-economic coercion without, however, reintroducing direct physical coercion into our substantive economic life. Finally, the theory of the imperialist stage allows us to examine what strenuous efforts the bourgeois state had to make to devise a policy which would 'internalize intractable externalities' (or tame intractable use-value resistance) in heavy industry so that the logic of capital might continue to operate. We can then appreciate why such a policy would not be successful today, when heavy and complex use values dominate our economic life to an extent that would have been unthinkable in that earlier era.

Part I

Dialectical Theory of Capitalism: Circulation

1
Commodity, Value, Money and Capital Forms

The dialectical method requires that the capitalist mode of production, as a self-organized subject/object, should first be externally specified as how it presents itself as an immediate whole (as *how it is*). Capitalism introduces itself as a circulation economy – an economy in which products must be circulated or traded before being consumed, either directly or productively. Indeed, capitalism initially presents itself as an immense collection of commodities which have been offered for sale in the marketplace. Although the dialectic of capital does not make it immediately explicit, the theory always presupposes a fully developed capitalist society in which all use values are capitalistically produced as commodities in possession of value and which are, therefore, destined to be sold in a society-wide, competitive market by capitalist firms that employ labour power and material inputs purchased as commodities in that same market.

Capitalist society involves the transformation of social relations between humans into 'social' relations between things or objects outside us. This tendency towards the *reification* or 'impersonalization' of human relations follows from the fact that, in capitalist society, all goods tend to be produced for an impersonal, society-wide market as commodities. Since services are not material goods, and cannot be capitalistically produced as commodities, they cannot be reified or made impersonal. We shall assume, therefore, that in a purely capitalist society personal services are not directly performed by one individual for another; rather, economic agents sell commodities to one another and it is only when these commodities are finally in the hands of consumers that they serve themselves with the assistance of the said commodities. It is by means of this rather drastic theoretical simplification, which we shall remove in the stages theory, that we are able to narrow our focus so as to view only the essential properties of capitalism. Indeed, the Industrial Revolution, which liberal market capitalism made inevitable, did not simultaneously produce a similar revolution in the provision of services. Rather, it tended to undermine the social relations and material foundation which sustained that sector.

A COMMODITY HAS VALUE AND USE VALUE

Prior to any further specification, capital is abstract, commodity-economic, or mercantile (commercial) wealth, possessing *value*, even if the accumulation of that wealth unavoidably entails producing and/or trading goods or *use values*. Therefore, value cannot exist by itself, since a commodity, as a good produced for consumption (either direct or productive), must also be a use value which

21

has natural or physical properties, which will satisfy a human need. As value, a commodity constitutes a fraction of the homogeneous mass of society's abstract-general mercantile wealth, whereas, as a use value, it is a particular, isolated, individual, concrete-specific sample from the heterogeneous aggregate of society's material wealth.

If the value aspect of the commodity accounts for its comparability (or identity) with others rather than its physical and heterogeneous use-value properties, it is the heterogeneous quality of the use-value aspect that negates the apparent indeterminacy of the commodity as value, the form in which 'all the commodity's natural properties are extinguished' (Marx 1973, p.141) or held temporarily in abeyance. Taking either aspect of the commodity in isolation from its opposite leaves the nature of the commodity unspecified, just as taking *being* and *nothing* as self-subsistent in the Hegelian system rather than as moments of a determinate whole, results in their complete indeterminacy. In a commodity, in contrast to a good, there can never be a use value which is not negatively correlated with its value or social being (Dunne 1977, p.18).

Simple use values play no role in the dialectic. Only the use value of a commodity as the negation of its value is germane here. All goods, whether they are commodities or not, possess a use value, in that they are material objects produced as consumption goods or as producer goods, which are consumed in the course of production. No social (or inter-human) relation need inhere in goods, for goods or simple use values may be privately produced and consumed. Goods do not, merely because they each have a use value, automatically develop into commodities.[1] They become commodities only under a definite set of social relations.

Commodities are the social and historic form that goods adopt when their owners are so related as to produce them as values or as instruments of trade, which are mutually exchanged. Thus, even though all wealth, capitalistic or otherwise, possesses a use value, the study of use values as such falls outside the scope of the dialectic of capital. Our focus is on mercantile (or abstract-general) wealth, which can be pursued endlessly, not on the consumption of material or concrete-specific wealth, which eventually leads to satiation.

The *use value of a commodity* refers to its use value from the point of view of a would-be purchaser, while that commodity still belongs to the seller. Although the commodity is a value from the point of view of its seller, it is at the same time a *potential* use value for its would-be purchaser, who would like to consume it. In order to consume that use value, the purchaser must acquire the commodity by paying a price for it. Only when the commodity is purchased by the consumer does it become a non-commodity, as its use value becomes realizable (or consumable). When the commodity is purchased, however, it is also sold. Therefore, by the time its use value becomes realizable, its value too has already been realized. Neither the value nor the use value of the commodity can be realized unless it changes hands or is circulated.

Because of the above considerations, the dialectic of capital, as the economic theory of capitalism, must thus begin with the study of the commodity form instead of mere goods or wealth in general. Capital, the dialectical subject here, can only reveal itself by allowing its value or capitalist–social-relational aspect, its most abstract specification, which is inherent in the commodity form, to prevail over use value, which represents everything other than capital.

The contradiction between value and use value in the dialectic of capital echoes the contradiction between pure, abstract and featureless *being* and *nothing* in Hegel's *Logic*. The triad of 'value, use value and exchange value', which sets the stage for value-form theory in the dialectic of capital, corresponds to the triad of *being, nothing and becoming* in Hegel's work, which prepares the way for the logic of *determinate being (Dasein)*. In each case, the most universal, abstract and seemingly empty category (*being*, value) passes over to its negation (*nothing*, use value) and then to a synthesis (*becoming*, exchange value) in which *being*/value prevails.

At this early stage in the development of the dialectic, the term *value* denotes only an indifference to use values. As value, any representative commodity is indistinguishable from any other. It is the requirement of exchangeability that endows a commodity with its value or its qualitative equality with all other commodities. All commodities relate themselves with one another only quantitatively in prices because they share the property of being socially significant. It is too soon to say, at this very early stage in the development of the dialectical argument, what the objective basis of this social significance is.

Both the logic of capitalism and the logic of Hegel begin with the most abstract, empty, immediate (that is, seemingly unmediated or virtually featureless) category, which represents the subject matter. In each, the first doctrine studies the mode of existence or (operating principles) of the subject/object without reference to its substantive content, inner determinations, specifications or concreteness. Just as *pure being* appears in Hegel as the initial concept or starting point, and only much later is shown to have been the first glimpse of the *absolute idea*, so is the category of value initially introduced as the defining characteristic of the commodity only to be recognized much later as the most abstract or least specified, and, thus, simplest representation or cell form of capitalism. Indeed, a commodity in possession of value implicitly contains or physically embodies all the operating principles of capitalism, but that remains to be revealed. To say that the categories of *being* and *value* appear in their least specified form, as the two parallel dialectical expositions begin, is to say that not only have these concepts not yet been internally differentiated, but also that we are not yet aware of their external relations. Thus, it is initially difficult to distinguish between the categories of *being* and *nothing*, or *value* and *use value*, though we can indicate the primacy of the commodity's 'social' being.

Throughout the doctrine of circulation, the logic of *becoming* or *transition*, the method of external synthesis, which is the same logic that also prevails in Hegel's doctrine of being, plays a dominant role. The socially uniform quality of value, which has to reside in the use value of a specific commodity, gradually releases itself from use-value restrictions as the form of the commodity *passes over* to the form of money and then to the form of capital.[2]

COMMODITIES MUST BE PRICED = VALUE MUST BE EXPRESSED

Consider a particular commodity owner in a trading community. He is in possession of commodities which have no use value for him, but he requires commodities possessed by other members of the trading community. This commodity owner must represent a proto-merchant capitalist and, hence, be viewed as a seller of commodities. The said proto-merchant cannot consume his own commodity, but he can obtain other commodities only if he expresses the value of his commodity through an *exchange proposal*. He selects a determinate quantity of the use value of another commodity which he requires for his personal or productive consumption in order to express the value of his own commodity. By adopting the use value of another commodity, value frees itself from the correlative use value with which it has had to cohabit in the same commodity.

When a commodity suppresses its own use value in order to express its value in the use value of another commodity it takes the form of *exchange value*. The negation or suppression of a particular commodity's use value in that of another commodity characterizes this Hegelian-style determinate value expression (Dunne 1977, p.34). A commodity must be exchanged or sold for another in order to assert its social being. It cannot be a commodity unless it has a determinate social relation with another commodity. The expression of the value of a commodity by its price or exchange value is an unavoidable necessity that must occur prior to the actual exchange of commodities.

This value expression does not envision a direct barter, whereby the owner of linen and the owner of a coat actually confront one another to execute an exchange, in which the values of the two commodities are already reflected in the precise quantity of each other's use value. Barter entails the exchange of simple use values between persons who come face to face with each other, and who are capable of directly negotiating the terms of trade. Instances of simple barter, which are necessarily limited in scope, do not develop necessarily into full-fledged, impersonal commodity exchanges over time. In a mature capitalist market, barter seldom occurs and, in the context of the theory of pure capitalism, not at all. Commodities are sold for money in the open market, and money purchases commodities. All commodity exchanges are, by necessity, mediated by money. The significance (or convertibility into money) of any one commodity cannot be definitively evaluated independently of the social significance of all other commodities. The interdependence of all commodities as value signifies the exchange of all commodities for all commodities. Such general commodity exchanges are always mediated by money, and are never a summation of the moneyless barter exchanges of use values.

All commodities are traded as values because, at least in principle, no commodity seller knows where his potential customers are. Thus, we must recognize that the commodity seller we have been speaking of has not as yet found the person to whom his commodity is a potential use value. Moreover, at this early stage of the dialectic, the two commodities, the one offered for sale and the other that is desired, cannot be exchanged because money has not yet been theoretically developed so that it may play its mediating role. We are here concerned only with an exchange proposal in which the commodity for sale physically exists, but the commodity desired is present only in the mind of the 'proposer' of the exchange. That is why he has to express the value of his commodity by pricing it first so as to test or probe the market. There would be no such need if he were already in direct contact with his customer. The expression of a commodity's value by its owner in terms of the use value of another commodity that he wants is unilateral. His sole concern is the extent to which his commodity turns out to be useful or socially valuable and significant to others. Only to that extent does his commodity demonstrate that it has value or that it constitutes a claim on the mercantile wealth of society, measured in terms of that abstract homogeneous quality we have referred to as value.

Suppose that A is the commodity for sale and B the desired commodity. The seller of A may express its value in the use value of commodity B, which he needs or desires, in the following manner: an amount x of A => an amount y of B, where the symbol =>, or value-projection sign, may be read as 'is yours for'. This is called the elementary, accidental or *simple-value form*. In this exchange proposal, A (the commodity for sale) stands in the position of the *relative-value form*, and B (the desired commodity) stands in the position of the *equivalent-value form*. The relationship between the two commodities is asymmetrical. Their positions cannot be reversed, since no actual barter is taking place and since A's exchange proposal does not imply the existence of B's counter-exchange proposal. To propose the exchange of A for B is to negate A's own use value and to adopt the use value of the other commodity, in this case B, as the reflector of its value.

As a seller, the commodity owner is concerned only with the value of his commodity. The concept of exchange value concretely unifies value and use value, the two mutually incompatible properties of a commodity arising in the mind of the seller, by virtue of the fact that the value of the seller's commodity can only be expressed by the use value of another commodity that is not in his possession. From this context, it is obvious that the quantity of the commodity in the equivalent-value form must be definite, while the quantity of the commodity in the relative-value form may vary. In expressing the value of a commodity offered for sale, its owner can take no further initiative in consummating a proposed trade other than to vary the amount offered. An owner of a commodity, such as a coat, which occupies the position of the equivalent-value form, however, can immediately acquire the commodity offered in the trade proposal. The simple-value expression of one commodity (such as linen) has now given another commodity (the coat) immediate purchasing power or the power of a *little money* within the terms of a particular proposed exchange.

Commodities offered for sale in capitalist society are bound to have price tags, which demand that they be purchased by someone for a definite amount of money.[3] The money price, however, is only a developed form of the expression of the value of a commodity in the use value of another commodity. Value is a property of the genuine commodity produced with indifference to its use value, and thus reflects the degree to which its procurement costs society in real terms. Only later in the dialectic will the unfolding logic be ready to reveal or specify that all capitalistically produced commodities are products of labour. We cannot derive such a conclusion from a mere observation of the exchange of commodities as an empirical fact, or, as Marx erroneously suggested, as a direct deduction from an 'equation' of exchange (Marx 1969, p.45). It is, however, not necessary to know the substance of this qualitative uniformity before demonstrating that it gives rise to prices.

At this stage in the dialectic, it is important to recognize that a commodity is an object for sale, something convertible into money, and, thus, something that must prove itself to be part of the abstract-general, or mercantile, wealth of society. It is this quality of the commodity that constitutes value in the first instance. No commodity can express its value or price except by a given quantity of the use value of another commodity. All capitalistically produced commodities have economically meaningful prices because they are value objects. However, we do not have to know the substance of value to demonstrate that money, the general equivalent, constitutes the external measure of value. Money measures the value of a commodity by establishing its *normal price*. Later, the dialectic will demonstrate that an optimal allocation of society's productive labour lies behind all normal prices. For the present, the value 'equation' shows only that the two commodities in question are equally priced in trade, without any necessary implication that they really are of equal magnitude in value. The 'equation' suggests that two totally distinct use values carry some socially uniform quality, which may be called either value or 'money-ness', and that it is this quality which gives rise to economically meaningful prices for all commodities.

The *theory of value forms*, which we are outlining here, shows the need to price the commodity as a logical consequence of owning it. What the value form theory does, as it develops the simple, the expanded and the general forms of value (in close correspondence to Hegel's triad of *quality*, *limit* and *infinity*) is to remove the qualitative and quantitative restrictions from the little money chosen by the linen owner, and to show that one particular commodity always emerges as the value reflector, general equivalent or full-fledged money in terms of which all other commodities express their values. In expressing the value of a commodity, the owner, in effect, says that it must be useful to someone. This 'someone' becomes increasingly abstract and impersonal as the expression of value perfects itself. First, it is any person who wishes to acquire the commodity offered for sale in exchange and who possesses a use value that the seller is interested in. Later, the potential purchaser becomes more general when we learn that he need not possess a use value that directly interests the seller. Indeed, he need only come forward with money, in which all traders are interested.

In the logic of *determinate being*, the Hegelian dialectic specifies (determines or delimits) the original pure being or *quality* in terms of *others*. Here, too, to say that 'an amount x of A is worth an amount y of B' is to say that 'an amount x of A is not worth an amount z of B', or 'not worth an amount y of C'. It is to specify the value of A by delimiting it with a *finite* (in amount and in kind). In Hegel, however, the *finite limit* is *alterable*. Similarly, a commodity owner does not generally express the value of his commodity through the use value of just one other commodity. He desires, and therefore demands, a free exchange of his commodity for a variety of others. In other words, the value of A can as well be expressed by:

an amount x' of A => an amount z of C,
an amount x'' of A => an amount u of D,
an amount x''' of A => an amount v of E,
... etc.,

We can thus conceive of a very large number of exchange proposals, each of which is an expression of the value of A, but none of which is either final or conclusive. This tabulation is called the *expanded form of value*.[4]

THE SEARCH FOR THE GENERAL EQUIVALENT OR MONEY

How can a commodity, which is a material use value, find a form of expression which will reveal its social worth or its social significance (its value relation) to all other commodities within a community of otherwise anonymous commodity owners? Each commodity owner in the two forms of value we have already looked at only expresses the value or social significance of his commodity subjectively, whether in the use value of another commodity which he may desire in exchange for his own, or in a series of other equivalents, as in the expanded form. However, to privately express the social significance of one's commodity is a contradiction in terms.

This is the reappearance in a more developed form of the contradiction between the value and use-value aspect of the commodity. In the Hegelian system, the contradiction between *being* and *nothing* is overcome and coherence achieved only in an internally related system of *finite beings* which are simultaneously subject and object. In such a system, any particular finite is determined by the totality of all other finites, but simultaneously determines all the others. This is the system (rather than a mere enumeration or string) of finites, or the *true infinite*. We must, therefore, show how capital too develops an internally related trading system in which each commodity owner embodies both the finite and the infinite, both the private and the social, while each commodity is a value as well as a use value.

If a commodity trading system is to be an example of a Hegelian true infinite, rather than a spurious infinite, that which measures the value of any particular commodity cannot be some other commodity or set of commodities subjectively selected by commodity owners themselves, but must, instead, be decided impersonally and objectively by the combined demand of all other traders, who possess a universal equivalent which embodies their combined demand within a socially integrated or interrelated system. The value of each commodity offered for sale would then be determined by the impersonal forces of the market, just as the totality of finites or true infinite determines any particular finite in Hegel's *Logic*. Thus, the true infinite requires that the trading community overcome the limitation and arbitrariness of the subjective expanded-value form, such that commodity owners no longer make private exchange proposals in terms of their subjectively selected equivalents (as finite limits), but instead choose one equivalent that is universally demanded.

The use values a trader selects as equivalents, based on his desire to consume them, would be sufficient to establish the value form of his commodity; but that value form would then be limited by the extent of its owner's desire to consume other commodities. To the extent that the commodity owner reflects the value of his commodity in a use value or use values that he does not urgently require (Sekine 1984, p.115), this limitation begins to be overcome. Because the owners of the equivalent commodities found in the expanded form of value also evaluate their commodities in terms of a similar series of equivalents, there is bound to emerge one or several commodities which is/are most commonly desired in the value expressions of the trading system. At first, one or several commodities are recognized as being commonly desired for its/their substantive and material use-value properties by commodity owners for their personal consumption. Once commodity owners recognize that many are projecting the value of their commodities in the value of the same equivalent(s), they begin to demand the commonly chosen equivalent(s) not primarily for their personal use, but because they know that such (an) equivalent(s) will allow them to obtain any commodity they desire, and not just those commodities whose owners also desire their commodities. Thus, they list in their exchange proposals only those few commodities which have the abstract-social or mercantile property of immediate and universal exchange-ability, and they endeavour to acquire as much of the said equivalent(s) as they can. When a commodity is demanded by all commodity owners as a *general means of purchase* it becomes a Hegelian *infinite* because such a use value, being wanted by all commodity owners, can automatically purchase some quantities of all commodities.

Thus far, we have traced the development of the value expression from the simple, to the expanded, and now finally to the *general form of value* (Sekine 1984, p.115). Only when a single monetary commodity emerges as the *general equivalent* of the trading system can the value of all commodities be adequately expressed. Indeed, the existence of several commodity-exchange systems within a trading community must be a transitory phenomenon. It is inevitable that one commodity will become excluded from the ranks of the commonly desired commodities to become the general equivalent because it will have use-value or physical properties which will make it more attractive for traders (and the monetary authority) to use in that role, and its very popularity will subsequently persuade an even greater number of traders to adopt it, until, finally, its dominance will be conceded by all. Historically, gold has frequently been chosen as the general equivalent; however, the dialectic cannot logically and definitively determine which commodity a specific community will choose.

The development of the general equivalent marks a Hegelian-style *sublation* of the use-value restriction in the expression of value because now commodity owners no longer need to privately express the value of their commodity in terms of the equivalent use values they desire for consumption. The value of gold (or any other metallic money), as the general equivalent, is not expressed in the use value of gold itself. Neither is it necessary for gold to express its value in the use value of any other commodity. Indeed, the use value of monetary gold has become abstract-social. Merchant traders now achieve their desires indirectly by expressing value solely in terms of the commodity which has attained general social recognition and, as such, embodies universal and immediate exchangeability.

Having thus become the general purchasing power, gold can no longer stand in the position of the relative-value form. It is no longer a commodity for sale; it is the *general means of purchase*, which occupies exclusively the position of the equivalent value form. Ordinary commodities, which can no longer stand in the position of the equivalent-value form, are supplied for money. The physical body of gold, as the monetary metal, can express its value directly rather than indirectly by reflecting its value in the use value of another commodity. Gold money, the *value reflector* of all commodities, is no longer anything other than value (value no longer coexists with a material or sensuous use value). Money is that particular commodity in which the *abstract-social use value* of being immediately and universally exchangeable by all commodity owners prevails over its natural use value of being useful for consumption; thus the demand for it will not be subject to satiation.

The necessity of commodities to express their immanent or implicit value has thus led to the development of money as the value-reflecting object or as the external manifestation of value. All commodity owners now express the value or social worth of each other's commodities through this general equivalent. Each commodity is thus socially related to all others in an interconnected trading community. The diversity of the various use values is thus transformed into the homogeneous value system in which each commodity as a value is related to every other commodity as an equivalent bearer of social worth. The Hegelian *being-for-one* of the commodity world, or that to which all commodities are related as values, is the general equivalent.

The *money form (or price form) of value* arises when gold, or some other precious metal, begins to act as the exclusive reflector of value. Monetary gold is a special commodity which overcomes its use-value restrictions as completely as any commodity can. The material use value of gold is remote from day-to-day consumption, and is overshadowed by its social or mercantile use value of being immediately exchangeable for all other commodities. Its material properties can be preserved almost indefinitely so that value can be retained in it more safely than in other metals. The monetary and non-monetary demands for gold do not compete with each other, and this has the effect of stabilizing gold prices. The shortage of gold does not unduly disrupt the real economic life of any community, nor is its surplus particularly burdensome. Since it is generally acquired for symbolic or ornamental purposes, gold is not absolutely necessary for any society's survival. It is this last property that makes gold a particularly dependable commodity in which to reflect values.

In gold money, value has found its own mirror image, its alter ego or Hegelian *being-for-self* of value (Sekine 1984, p.115). The physical attributes of money reveal what value really is like. The three fundamental properties of value are (1) that it is qualitatively one and the same; (2) that it is divisible and can be split into homogeneous parts; and (3) that it is additive and can thus bring together all commodities in a unified social interrelationship. A precious metal lends itself to this task because it can be divided or fused without losing its homogeneous quality.

The *money* or *price form of value*, in which a single monetary commodity is demanded, not for its material or sensuous use value, but for its value or abstract-social virtue of immediate purchasing power or general exchange-ability, may be said to be the *true infinity* of the value expression, because it constitutes an intersubjective, society-wide standard of value. In that role metallic money no longer possess a concrete-material use value.

Hegel's dialectic of *being-for-self*, which proceeds with the triad of *the one*, *the many (repulsion)* and *attraction*, appears to closely parallel the exposition to follow. The power of attraction which resolved the *diversity and externality* of the *ones* into the homogeneous *one* in Hegel's *Logic* corresponds to the socially integrating power of demand which subordinates individual merchant activity to the needs of the trading community. Just as the two Hegelian processes of *repulsion* and *attraction*, though distinct, formed two aspects of a single process of *being-for-self*, the integration and cohesiveness of the merchant-trading system is now concretely unified, in that each commodity is not just abstractly related to the general equivalent, but is instead related to a specific quantity of gold. The theory of the commodity form demonstrates the necessity of money, in terms of which all the diverse commodities are now uniformly priced, such that all values are now expressible uniformly in varying quantities of gold or the general equivalent. All the potential sellers and buyers of commodities come together to form one mercantile market, in which the sellers (commodity owners) represent the forces of supply and the buyers (money owners) represent the forces of demand. Now all commodities can potentially be exchanged for all other commodities. This market must be a proto-capitalist and mercantile one, because a market of consumers could not evolve beyond the expanded-value form.

When each commodity is priced, it becomes possible to aggregate all commodities offered for sale during any time period and talk of their aggregate money value, of which each commodity constitutes a mere fraction. The aggregate supply of a given commodity can then be subjectively evaluated in terms of the aggregate amount of gold desired. The amount of gold so required becomes its *supply price*. Once universal money demands can be aggregated in order to express the impersonal social demand for society's supply of all commodities, the resulting concrete unity of the antagonistic forces of supply and demand allows the system of commodity exchanges to be established in such a way that *negation* falls completely within the self-determining totality of the market. Of course, this does not mean that the determinate, particular beings of commodities and commodity sellers have vanished. Rather, to employ Hegelian terminology, they have lost their character of *self-subsistence*. Only the whole is now self-subsistent and only as a member of the whole is each finite being non-self-contradictorily defined.

The pricing of commodities presupposes money as the *means of purchase*, yet not an ounce of physical gold need be present for commodities to express their value in their supply prices. What money prices express is not a physical relation between gold and other use values; it is *a social relation, which is expressed through the mediation of commodities as values*. Although gold money, as means of purchase, which commodities themselves generate by excluding one of their own as the general value reflector, need not as yet exist physically, it must obviously exist in the minds of commodity owners. For this to occur, it is sufficient that commodities are merely priced in terms of gold money.

If a commodity is merely priced, its *value is expressed but not measured*. To price a commodity is merely to imagine that it is convertible into a certain amount of gold. At this point, we have still not theoretically demonstrated how physical money appears. This pricing is thus still a private rather than a social act, even though the pricing is done in terms of an equivalent that was socially chosen. The act of pricing a commodity does not by itself signify that society has approved of that price. The money price is still a value form which reflects a subjective evaluation on the part of the commodity owner, even if his pricing is made with due consideration as to how other sellers of the same commodity have priced theirs. Now that we have come to the end of the value-form analysis, which theorizes only potential buyer and sellers, we are at last ready to deal with actual exchanges of commodities and money.

MONEY AS THE MEASURE OF VALUE

Just as in Hegel's *Logic*, *quantity*, in the form of money will now begin to subordinate the previously established *qualitative* commercial relations. The three functions of money, as (1) the measure of value, (2) the circulating medium and (3) funds, correspond to the triad of *quantity*, *quantum* (quantity with a determinateness or limit) and the *quantitative relation* (ratio) in Hegel (1969, p.203; see also Sekine 1984, pp.158–9). Because the conception of commodity owners as consumers of particular use values has now been overcome, the impersonal forces of the market, as represented by the pricing of commodities in terms of the monetary commodity, the bearer of impersonal social need, are now beginning to dominate and control the operation of the system. This does indeed parallel the development of the argument in the *Logic*, in which determinate being is revived in *quantitative* form to subordinate the previously developed *qualitative* relations. We shall once again treat the plurality of commodity owners, but, this time, not simply as proto-merchants, who are sometimes difficult to distinguish from simple consumers, but, rather, explicitly as mercantile capitalists, who are primarily interested in the value of their commodity. Thus, merchants are now recognized as being subordinate to the action of the society-wide market, supplying commodities in response to social demand (see Dunne 1977, pp.57–8). In the interaction of supply and demand, values will be measured.

The commodity economy is not a generalized barter system in which consumers and producers directly confront each other and agree on some negotiated terms of trade. Both sellers and buyers are merchant traders who shift their positions from the supply side to the demand side constantly. As suppliers of a commodity, traders can only propose a trade, which they themselves cannot enforce when they price a commodity. All commodities appear in the market with *supply prices* which their sellers (owners) quote tentatively in expressing their values. They respond to the market price, already made observable by previous trading. They revise their prices in response to the market so as to be able to sell their commodities as quickly and as dearly as possible. The *measurement of the value of any commodity* implies an effort, on the part of its sellers, to make it as dear as possible and a counter-effort, on the part of its purchasers, to make it as cheap as possible. The owners of money, representing the forces of demand, buy immediately if the price is low and respond less quickly if the price is high.

The commodity economy is fundamentally a mercantile system. As a money owner, the merchant is universal and impersonal, representing, through the medium of money, an organic unity of the society-wide market's demand for all commodities. He is, in Hegelian terms, *active* and *passive*, *particular* and *universal*, *finite* and *infinite*. Only as the concrete unity of these antagonistic forces is the system of commodity exchanges established.

Money intermediates all commodity exchanges. All commodities are bought, sold and compared with money. Anyone who produces gold is automatically in possession of the purchasing power of any commodity; however, the majority of money owners are not gold-producers and, thus, they have obtained their money by previously selling their own commodities. It follows, then, that, with the exception of the current gold producers, who are a minority, money owners, who alone can freely purchase commodities in quantities as great as their gold will allow, are themselves successful commodity sellers.

Once every merchant has acquired some gold by selling his commodity for it, and all commodities are priced in gold, it is no longer necessary for gold to express its value. Gold, as the general equivalent, has no value form or price. This is so because all commodity owners (not just the original gold producers) can now purchase any commodity desired in quantities as great as their possession of gold permits. Money purchases commodities, but commodities do not purchase money. While commodities are meant to be sold, money is not for sale; it is the means of purchase.

In the abstract context of the doctrine of circulation, capitalist activity is not yet grounded in real economic life and, therefore, the dialectical exposition is not yet prepared to treat the process of production in explicit terms. In this context, value is known only as the 'money-ness' of the commodity. Nevertheless, it must be acknowledged that capitalist society, like any society, must provide for its material needs and wants, and, hence, must have its own organization of production. Money functions to measure the value of a commodity, and, in so doing, establishes its *normal price* prior to its substantive specification as socially necessary labour.[5] Only capitalistically produced commodities have a normal price.[6] Behind the measurement of the value of a commodity lies the determination of its value, which will be dealt with in the doctrine of production. Values stands behind normal prices, but neither the normal price nor the value of a commodity are definitively revealed in a once-and-for-all trade or even in a market-clearing price, which only temporarily equates the demand for and supply of the commodity in the market. Physical money, as means of purchase, must repetitively purchase all commodities without qualitative restriction, indifferently measuring their value as a Hegelian *one*. Only in the doctrine of distribution, however, will the dialectic finally be ready to reveal that normal prices are indeed *equilibrium prices*. We shall learn that the values of capitalistically produced commodities are confirmed only when, in recurrent transactions at prices fluctuating in response to the forces of demand and supply, resources are appropriately reallocated such that the commodities are no longer overproduced or underproduced, and central or *normal prices* emerge, which equate supply prices with demand prices. Commodities are then produced in equilibrium or socially necessary quantities. A general equilibrium implies that society's productive resources are *optimally allocated* to all spheres of production.

Acting as a *measure of value* is only one of the functions of money. It also functions as the medium or means of circulation, as active money, and as a *store of value*, as idle money. *Active money* is money received and spent within a given market period, such as a week, month or year. *Idle money* is held from one market period to another. As *means of circulation*, money stays within the sphere of commodity exchanges, mediating them. A certain quantity of money must always stay in that sphere so as to ensure a smooth circulation of commodities, depending, of course, on their volumes and normal prices.

ACTIVE MONEY OR THE MEDIUM OF CIRCULATION

The exchange of a commodity, C—M—C, is quite unlike the direct exchange of use values, C—C. The former is always mediated by money, and is divided into two parts: the phase C—M of sale and the phase M—C of purchase. It is money in the C—M phase that measures the values of all commodities, while acting as the *means of circulation*. The exchange of commodities cannot be accomplished by an individual person. The network of commodity exchanges is self-extensive, tending to involve more and more traders and an increasing variety of commodities. The money that mediates the individual exchange of commodities, C—M—C, and the money that accomplishes the social exchange of all commodities for all commodities are one and the same. The chain of commodity transactions consists of individual links, but these links are joined or brought together by money.

A communal economy, in which products are transferred directly from one person to another rather than through commodity exchanges, retains its natural size and will not develop as generally and extensively. A commodity economy which is regulated by the market or the sphere of commodity circulation, however, is not constrained by any natural size because commodities can be traded quite impersonally. In such an economy, the social interaction of producers and consumers, which characterizes the real economic life of society, is no longer directly visible. In the sphere of circulation, human relations in society appear as physical relations among commodities. The *sphere of production* and the *sphere of consumption* are separated by the *sphere of circulation*, through which products silently migrate as commodities. In a system of universal commodity exchanges, the hidden economic relations of humans can break all traditional, cultural and geographical barriers and form a truly extensive and integrated whole.

Having been acquired by the sale of a commodity, the means of purchase is *qualitatively* free, in the sense that it possesses the immediate purchasing power of any other commodity, its use value having abandoned a concrete-specific, material character, and having assumed instead an abstract-general, social character, yet it is not *quantitatively* free, because its quantity is restricted by the value of the commodity previously sold. Although the network of exchanges is inherently self-extensive, its scope cannot be unlimited at any given time and place. Only a finite number of commodities can be exchanged in finite quantities among a finite number of persons.

When an excess supply of the monetary metal arises in a purely capitalist society, inflation occurs temporarily. If gold is overproduced and, hence, other commodities are underproduced relative to social demand, commodity prices will be forced above their normal levels. This tends to make gold production unprofitable since, to produce the same amount of gold, capitalists must buy the elements of production above their normal prices. On the other hand, the production of other commodities becomes more profitable and begins to expand. This corrective mechanism works automatically.

Even in the absence of any expansion in the scale of its economic life, a market society must produce monetary gold, which it cannot consume in the same way as other commodities, by using up some of its productive resources to replace what has been abraded or lost. If such a society is to grow, it must devote even more resources to the production of monetary gold. Circulation costs are said to be *unproductive* in a particular sense since, unlike the costs associated with use-value production, they do not directly contribute to the production of surplus value (in Marxian terms) or profit, although such costs are a necessary consequence of capitalism's operation. How can it be that that society's cost of monetary circulation is deemed in some sense unproductive even though the labour that produces the monetary metal is productive? In the dialectic of capital, productive labour, the labour that produces any use value, including the monetary metal, is deemed productive, since it involves the physical transformation of part of nature into a use value. This anomaly arises because productive labour is applied to the creation of an object for a strictly 'unproductive' use. (Another example would be the production of weaponry which was employed in needless acts of destruction.) Monetary gold is required for the strictly commodity-economic purpose of circulating commodities. This is irrelevant to real or material economic life as such. In a natural economy, the scale of economic activities can be expanded directly without requiring the production of additional money to circulate the incremental output.

In opposition to use-value exchanges, commodity exchanges have the advantage of being self-expansive. This advantage, however, can be reduced if the cost of having to produce the monetary metal becomes too heavy. Therefore, the rationality of the commodity economy demands the reduction of such an unproductive circulation cost to a minimum. Provided that they can be converted into the promised quantities of gold when they are withdrawn from circulation, representations of gold or gold symbols can function as the medium of circulation in lieu of genuine gold. However, the capitalist commodity economy cannot develop such a cost-saving mechanism by its own autonomous activity. It cannot generate solutions to all the problems it encounters. *Fiat money* must, therefore, be issued, administered and legitimized by public or state authorities, which are both alien to and prior to the commodity economy.

When capitalism first appeared, it reshaped hitherto existing states to fit its requirements; but capital did not create the state. The same may be said about capital's relation to landed property. Since capital tended to invade existing societies from the outside after flourishing in the spaces between states, it frequently made use of existing institutions, adapting the latter to its ends to the extent that that was possible. The state, however, cannot be made completely subservient to capital. If the state issues fiat money, the latter remains gold equivalent only insofar as its total issue does not exceed the quantity of gold that is required as the medium of circulation. It is, however, a practical impossibility to always issue fiat money in the correct maximum amount, given that the money value of transactions changes all the time. Fiat money, once issued, cannot be automatically withdrawn from circulation or made idle. The issuing of fiat money, which costs virtually nothing to the issuer, but which enables the state to purchase commodities in the same way as gold producers, easily tends to exceed its appropriate, capitalistically compatible limit. Fiat money is only capitalistically warranted by the saving of society's cost of monetary circulation, but the declining purchasing power of fiat money issued to excess only tempts that agency to issue more. If the velocity of circulation of fiat money remains constant, its unrestrained issue will lead to a proportional depreciation of its purchasing power, and the proportional rise of commodity prices in relation to it. Once that happens, it is beyond capital's power to control it.

Since the development of commodity exchanges requires a capitalistically compatible law and order, the presence of institutions that maintain them must be presupposed by the dialectical theory of pure capitalism. In such an abstract, theoretical context, the state cannot be theorized as anything more than an institutionalized arrangement of traders, which oversees the working of the commodity economy from without. We must assume in this strictly economic theory, which aims to reproduce only the logic which capital employs in its attempt to regulate the material economic life of a society, that the issuer of fiat money always endeavours to operate in a manner which is consistent with and supportive of commodity-economic rationality, though in reality, this is frequently not the case.

IDLE MONEY

Unlike fiat money, *credit money* is generated by the commodity economy itself. For example, a trader, who sells a large quantity of a commodity, may not have to spend a significant portion of his proceeds for some time. He is, therefore, in a position to extend credit with money that is temporarily idle. Credit is then an instrument by which traders minimize their individual *circulation costs*. If traders possess plentiful *funds* (reserve money), they give liberal credits to each other and stimulate active commodity exchanges to their mutual advantage; if they are short of funds, they can afford to extend only limited credit; thus, the scope of commodity exchanges is correspondingly restricted. If a trader incurs a debt (liability), he must begin to set aside *means of payment*, which he cannot use actively for transactions. If he fails to liquidate his debt on schedule, he will be declared insolvent. Consequently, the saving of money as the means of payment is compulsory rather than voluntary.

Bank deposits, subject to chequing, are a more developed form of credit money than *trade bills* and are convertible into gold on sight or on demand. In a mature capitalist economy, an overwhelming proportion of the medium of circulation can take the form of central banknotes, drastically economizing the circulation of gold. The banking system can safely issue notes and create demand deposits only up to a certain multiple of its cash reserve in gold. It cannot create these immediately convertible liabilities without limit merely because there is a demand for the circulating medium, because the circulating medium is composed largely of these liabilities.

The central bank must always stand ready to maintain the convertibility of banknotes into gold. If the banking system has plentiful cash reserves, it will provide more means of circulation; but, if its reserve is low, it will not. The system accomplishes this adjustment by easing and tightening bank credit. The gold reserve in the vault of the central bank circulates commodities, measures their values and acts as the means of payment, all by proxy. All functions of money, in other words, presuppose the existence of the physical gold reserve in the vault of the central bank. It is, therefore, not the money value of commodity transactions that determines society's stock of gold reserves as the means of payment, but the reserve.

Funds as *universal money* are the most developed form of idle money. These are the stocks of gold reserves set aside, or saved, not for the purpose of canceling previously incurred debts, but for the eventual purpose of returning to the sphere of circulation to buy commodities for gainful resale rather than for use or consumption. These monetary savings are destined to be transformed into capital. Money as funds regulates or sets the pace of commodity exchanges. No trader can begin or expand his business without first accumulating enough money for that purpose. If, however, the accumulation of this money for expansion is at the expense of the existing scale of society's commodity exchanges, there will be a deflationary effect, which, however, automatically entails an expanded production of monetary gold. For the commodity economy as a whole to grow and expand, *accumulation funds* must be formed. When the whole economy envisions an expanded scale of commodity exchanges, additional banknotes and demand deposits must be created in advance. This, of course, cannot be done unless the gold reserve of the central bank is correspondingly increased. The country's economic expansion, in this case, requires a prior accumulation of gold in the vault of the central bank.[7]

THE FORMS OF CAPITAL

The theory of capital as a circulation form appears to correspond to the dialectic of *measure* in Hegel's *Logic*. The main outline of the dialectic of measure proceeds from *specific quantum* through the *measureless* to the *simple relation-to-self*. Hegel aims to discover the *permanent substratum* or *essence* underneath the fleeting world of *being* or *immediacy*. He thus constructs *measure* as the most synthetic mode or form of being which, despite its variability and transfiguration, remains *self-identical*, and, therefore, is capable of containing within itself the *permanent*. In capital, which endlessly repeats its metamorphosis, value too finds a permanent abode in which it can grow self-identically, as the *simple relation-to-self* (Miller 1969, p.331; Sekine 1984, p.208). Capital is the mode of circulation that has the inner resources necessary to subsume value completely; it is only in the motion of capital that value reveals itself.

Money, as means of purchase, makes the exchange of commodities, C—M—C', possible, and, through this, establishes a market in which exchanges become interconnected in such a way that the sale of any one commodity involves its purchase by another. At this point, the social world of value connections is constrained, however, by the use-value wants of the exchangers, who sell commodities they do not want in order to buy and consume what they do want. Then, exchanges stop. Thus, the motion of value is constrained by the consumption of use values in the C—M—C' circuit. In idle money, unlike in ordinary commodities, however, the material contingency of use value is held in abeyance. Although active money, which mediates commodity exchanges, cannot ignore use values, idle money (or funds), which functions as a *store of value*, is not bound by this use-value limitation. This money may be withheld from the market, not to save up for some article of consumption needed by the saver, but to buy commodities in order to resell them for a profit. When money is so employed, the first form of capital emerges: capital as the *self-augmenting motion of value*. With this development, value expands itself beyond the use-value constraints of C—M—C' and transforms itself into the primitive form of capital.

Since capital is nothing other than the chrematistic use of funds, only the owner of funds can become a capitalist by using them as capital. Here, the word *chrematistic* should be understood to mean the pursuit of mercantile or abstract-general wealth. Capital is, first of all, not a thing, but a form of value augmentation. It is a circulation form, in that it originates in the sphere of commodity exchanges and not in the sphere of the production or the consumption, directly or indirectly, of a use value. The general formula for capital, M—C—M', applies without modification to the form of *merchant capital*.

Capital (M—C—M') is an operation that renders a certain sum of money (M) into a greater sum of money (M'), by taking on and discarding the forms of money and the commodity in the interim. The *metamorphosis of capital* begins and ends with the form of money, which is free from the specific quality of a use value. When funds go into circulation in the act of purchase (M—C), it is for the purpose of gainful resale (C—M'). The value of capital cannot grow from M to M' unless the use value of C permits such growth. Although the latter half of the motion of capital, the act of resale, C—M', involves a 'deadly leap', a commodity which is unlikely to be resold with some profit would not be purchased in the first place. The difference in the value of the endpoint, M', over the value of its starting-point, M, is called *surplus value*, m = M' – M, the monetary expression of which is *profit*. The time required for the transformation of M into M' is called the *turnover time of capital*. The purpose of the operation of capital is to earn the highest *rate of profit*, m / M, within the quickest turnover time of capital. The *efficiency of value augmentation* (chrematistic operation) of capital can, therefore, be measured in a purely quantitative manner. When this turnover becomes the focus of attention, we talk of the *circuit of capital*.

Money can buy a commodity, but a commodity cannot buy money. A commodity merely prices itself and awaits its purchase by money, without any initiative on its part. Therefore, the owner of a commodity cannot set the process C—M—C' into motion by himself transforming his commodity, C, into another commodity, C'. The motion of capital, M—C—M', unlike the process of a commodity exchange, C—M—C', is inherently self-perpetuating. The M in M' will be re-invested as capital to repeat the same operation, unless external conditions so change as to make it impossible. Thus, the form M—C—M' is one of many circuits, beginning and ending with money, which constitute an unending chain, M—C—M'.M—C—M'.M—C—M'.M ... When one circuit follows another in succession, we talk of the *circular motion of capital*.

THE FORM OF MERCHANT CAPITAL

Merchant capital is the most simple and primitive form of capital to appear in history. It is also theoretically prior since it contains only the most basic ingredients of capital. All other forms of capital issue from it. Merchant capital adopts and sheds the forms of commodity (*quality*) and money (*quantity*) in a unified, self-repetitive, unbroken operation of arbitrage. Just as *quality* and *quantity* in 'the process of *measure* ... pass over into each other' in an indifferent manner in Hegel's *Logic* (Hegel 1975, p.111), so also does the underlying operation of capital remain indifferent to the kind of commodity circulated, so long as its chrematistic principle is maintained. Every time capital turns over, it earns surplus value as profit, $m = M' - M$, in the form of money or of immediate purchasing power. Therefore, surplus value too can be invested as additional capital, if a suitable use value is found which may be resold profitably. As much surplus value as circumstances permit will be converted into capital and accumulated, so as to expand the scale of chrematistic operation. The circulation of capital is, thus, not only a self-repeating process, but also a self-expanding one. Capital endlessly pursues profit and is, therefore, not disposed to irrationally hoard as the result of a once-and-for-all chrematistic. Rather, it aims at the maximal self-propelled growth of value in the form of money, at the highest possible speed.

In pre-capitalist societies, two distinct types of trade occurred: long-distance and local. The growth of an urban population and the increased use of money doubtless stimulated both. The latter trade catered to ordinary people and so tended to be situated in and around towns, where it dealt mainly in food and other products of small producers. Local merchants endeavoured to subordinate producers as much as they could by dictating the particular quality and quantity of the use values that they bought and by developing the *putting-out system*, which contributed to the increasing commercialization of local economic life. Yet, even in the case of the putting-out system, in which the merchant maintained unchallenged supremacy over the producers, he could not exploit them to their utter ruin. Local merchants were under more stringent feudal controls than other merchants.[8] Moreover, they were in no position to alter the existing land-holding system. The development of commodity exchange thus originated in inter-communal trade, outside the boundaries of independent communities (rather than within communal economic life), when merchants carried products from one community to another for a profitable resale.

The activity of merchant capital presupposes the existence of price differentials. If a merchant profits from a price differential in space, his operation is *arbitrage*; if he profits form a price differential over time, it is *speculation*. The more developed the capitalist economy, however, the stronger the forces that automatically correct these disturbances and disruptions. Since all commodities tend to be traded at normal prices in mature capitalism, merchant capital cannot remain the dominant form of chrematistic because surplus value can no longer be easily earned in circulation. If all traders tend to buy and sell commodities at normal prices, no one will be permanently in a position to earn profits in circulation. This does not mean that no one profits from buying and selling commodities at prices diverging from normal. It only means that one party's gain is the other party's loss, and that there cannot be a particular class of traders who are always winners in unequal exchanges. Thus, capital must seek profits from sources other than the mere buying and selling of commodities.

By reducing existing price-differentials, by extending the scope of the commodity economy and by uniting hitherto separate markets in Europe, merchant capital undermined traditional modes of production and eroded the self-sufficiency of hitherto largely autonomous economic communities. Thus, by its very success, merchant capital found the scope of its activity increasingly restricted. Although both local and long-distance, inter-communal trade weakened the existing structure of society, neither had the power to alter it fundamentally. The operation of merchant capital did not lead by itself to a complete subversion of the traditional economic order, since the scope of merchant activity was confined mainly to the sphere of circulation and left existing production systems largely intact. The scope of mercantile activities was circumscribed, until the mercantilist policies of seventeenth-century Britain, which were implemented with a view to benefiting internal trade, created a climate in which the conversion of labour power into a commodity would appear as an attractive option to those engaged in the capitalist chrematistic. It was only when labour power was released from the land and converted into a commodity en masse that the prior accumulation of merchant capital, which had profited from expropriation, fraud and violence, could be mobilized for the building of a new social order. When society's labour-and-production process itself became radically commodity-economic with the development of a mature, market-governed industrial capitalism, the formation of a home (or national) market swiftly ensued, thus causing price differentials and merchant capital to tend to disappear.

Capital, in its motion, takes on and sheds both the forms of money and the commodity. Yet the capitalist, whether as the owner of money or a commodity, must buy and sell in the market just like any merchant trader. Not merely in pure capitalism, but also in mature historical capitalism, capitalists continue to be inveterate merchants, willing to profit from arbitrage and speculation whenever an opportunity arises. Even the industrial capitalist can only realize surplus value by the sale of his commodity. Thus, he cannot completely escape this mercantile orientation, which represents the subjective, rather than the objective, side of the motion of capital.

Even though the use value of commodities is not of primary concern to the merchant who sells them, and to whom they are only instruments of chrematistic, he cannot, in practice, make himself sufficiently free of use-value constraints that he can profit from the full range of commodities. He is a 'middleperson' caught between producers and consumers and is typically not capable of handling more than a limited variety of use values. How cheaply the merchant buys a commodity from producers and how dearly he sells it to consumers cannot be determined by any objective standard. Historically, competition among merchants was inherently limited, as was the tendency towards the equalization of profit rates. Moreover, luck, connections and privilege could too often determine a merchant's fate. Thus, merchant capital was not a fully developed form of capitalist chrematistic. It could not be a self-augmenting motion of value, regardless of who operated it, and regardless of which use value it involved. If capital is to approach the complete reification of human relations, it must become impersonal and indifferent to use value; but merchant capital was more severely constrained by use values than any other form of capital.

THE FORM OF MONEYLENDING CAPITAL

The form of merchant capital appears to resemble Hegel's category of *specific quantum* because the chrematistic of a merchant is never free from the specific use values that he handles. At this point, the *determinateness of quality* restricts the *alteration of quantum*. The further development of the forms of capital does not eliminate such use-value restrictions or obstructions altogether, but neutralizes them step by step. Thus, the form of *moneylending capital* circumvents direct involvement in use values by removing itself from merchandise trade. It corresponds to Hegel's *real measure*, because a moneylender deals with a number of self-subsistent merchants, such that his operation is only indirectly restricted by the use values that the indebted merchants trade. Thus, the moneylender can easily exceed his proper limit or measure and become *measureless*, for he can all too easily overlook the fact that his activity only circumvents use values, rather than really overcoming them (Sekine 1984, pp.208–9). The form of moneylending capital does not accomplish what the general formula for capital really requires; nor is it one of the circulation forms that mature capitalism maintains. It is a capitalistically empty and parasitic form of self-enrichment, which remains external to genuine capitalist operations. It consists of intercepting part of merchants' profits, which are earned in the sphere of commodity exchange. In order to earn interest, one need not even have capitalist acumen; one only need be in possession of 'loanable' money.

Moneylending capital is represented by the formula M...M', in which the dots show an interruption of circulation. A moneylending capitalist relinquishes his funds, M, to the borrower, but he retains the contractual right to a given sum of money on a specified date. Once the contract is signed, the lender engages in no capitalist activity, but relies on the enforcement of the law to guarantee that M becomes a greater sum, M'. The monetary expression of the surplus value, $m = M' - M$, which moneylending capital earns, is thus called *interest* rather than profit. Principal and interest, at a certain percentage greater than that principal, are payable at the end of the lending period. Thus, funds available for lending may be regarded as a special commodity and the *rate of interest* as the price of funds made available for a definite period of time.

Moneylending capitals frequently disrupt mercantile activity, but they can also support mercantile operations. Because it is not directly restricted by the intrusion of a specific use value, moneylending capital can regulate mercantile activity from without, and can impose on merchants some order and discipline, thus promoting a more rational allocation of funds and the profitability of trade in general. A merchant who borrows money has to return it with interest, and so cannot as freely or recklessly gamble on borrowed funds as he would on his own.[9] A business must be deemed sound to obtain a loans. Moreover, moneylending capital tends to make more funds available on easier terms to the branches of trade which are relatively more profitable.

The exchange of commodities in even the purest of capitalist societies must presuppose the existence of law and order, including the prevention of fraud and violence, the minting of coins, etc., in order to ensure that the commodity economy is able to operate according to its own internal logic; but the legal process of collecting interest need not always parallel the economic process of generating what is to be paid as interest.[10] If a divergence between the two processes arises, the extra-economic force of the law interferes with the autonomous functioning of the commodity economy by declaring many borrowers insolvent and foreclosing their property, even if that means bringing the commodity economy to a standstill, and depriving moneylending capital itself of profitable opportunities in the process.

As capitalism developed, the class of professional moneylenders, who always lent their money for interest and never invested it in the circulation or production of commodities for a profit, tended to disappear, as merchant capital, upon which it largely depended, lost its profitable sphere of action due to the closing of price differentials and the unification of markets.[11] However, the ultimate failure of moneylending capital suggests how the form of capital must develop if it is really to overcome use-value restrictions. It must stay in the sphere of circulation, where it originates, yet it must not exclude or circumvent use values, but rather internalize and absorb them. Only when the motion of capital can contain and resolve the contradiction between value and use value within itself, by being able to produce any commodity (just as money can buy any commodity), does capital become truly free. The form of industrial capital, which presupposes the conversion of labour power into a commodity, accomplishes this feat.

Although the forms of merchant capital and moneylending capital cannot, by themselves, organize a capitalist society, they both survive as essential ingredients of industrial capital. The form of industrial capital originates in circulation as a synthesis of merchant and moneylending capital. Industrial capital can delegate part of its operation to commercial capital and loan capital, which are reinstatements, respectively, of merchant capital and moneylending capital, as they appear in mature capitalism. If merchant capitalists lose their *profits upon alienation*, industrial and commercial capitalists now earn *average profits*, from which interest can be paid. Industrial capitalists, who endeavour to convert as much idle money as possible into capital, with a view to earning an average profit, find themselves with funds, such as depreciation and accumulation funds, which they must hold for varying periods before they can be converted into capital, in the course of the circulation process of capital. Such idle funds are loaned through the money market to other capitalists, who are capable of using them as additional capital. The form of moneylending capital is thus absorbed as a subsidiary operation of loan capital, or finance, which is spawned by industrial and commercial capitals.

Moneylending capital is capitalistically irrational to the extent that it paralyzes, rather than fosters, the normal functioning of commodity exchanges. This irrationality is preserved by loan capital, even in a fully developed capitalist society. Funds are not capitalistically producible commodities. Having neither physical use value nor genuine value, the *market rate of interest* reflects nothing more than a temporary equality of the demand for and the supply of funds. It possesses no necessary tendency to settle to any normal level when more and more funds are bought and sold over many market periods. For this reason, if funds are temporarily in short supply relative to demand, the rate of interest can easily rise above the rate of profit, such that no further investment of capital in real terms is possible.

THE FORM OF INDUSTRIAL CAPITAL

The activities of both merchant and moneylending capital contributed to the gradual decay and eventual disintegration of feudal societies over several centuries prior to the birth of capitalism, but they did not penetrate and radically alter existing modes of production. Capitalism constituted a historically viable society because the form of industrial capital, unlike the two earlier forms of capital, had the capacity to directly govern the social production process. An absolute indifference to quality and determinateness or the *true infinite of measure*, in Hegelian terms, is only achieved by the form of industrial capital, which can freely produce any use value that best fits its chrematistic purpose (Sekine 1984, p.209). By subsuming the process of production as an intermediate phase of its circulation process, industrial capital overcomes the restrictions of specific use values. Within the context of simple circulation, or commodity exchanges, the social quality of value, immanent in a commodity, cannot be more liberated than in the form of industrial capital, which permits value to grow freely as an unceasing self-propelled motion. The Hegelian logic of *transition*, which operates within the sphere of simple circulation and which abides by the principle of *metamorphosis*, cannot pass over to a more synthetic form than that of industrial capital. Therein, use values are not merely circumvented, but are instead contained and neutralized, as befits the principle of metamorphosis.

The operation of industrial capital may be represented as M—C...P...C'—M', where the segment C...P...C' indicates an interruption of circulation by the *production process of capital*. Industrial capital first advances money to purchase *productive elements*, C, which are available as commodities in the market. These are either capitalistically produced *means of production* (P_m) or *labour power* (L_p). (The role of natural means of production, generically represented by land, will be theorized later.) Without the conversion of labour power into a commodity, industrial capital cannot, in practice, begin its operation. Means of production include all commodities other than labour power purchased by industrial capital. The production process of capital may be written more explicitly as,

$$C < L_p, P_m...P...C',$$

The form of industrial capital holds this production process between two *circulatory phases* (M—C and C'—M') as an intermediate phase. The production process of capital does not lie outside the sphere of circulation, but is enveloped within it. By consuming the commodities purchased in its production process, industrial capital creates a new commodity of its own choice, C', which it subsequently sells for M', an amount of money greater than the capital advanced. A *surplus value* must, in other words, be produced in the production process, C...P...C', if such a circuit is to be viable.

Capital advanced in the means of production is called *constant capital* (c) because it preserves its own value throughout the production process. In this case, the old value that existed prior to production is simply transferred from the means of production (P_m) to the product (C'). The elements of production represented by C in the above formula are as restrictive as the commodities that merchant capital trades. Many of these elements of production are, in fact, produced as commodities by industrial capital, when the latter takes over society's production process. As transactions are repeated in the sphere of circulation, both C and C' tend to be bought and sold at or around normal prices, which excludes the possibility of anyone regularly making a profit or loss in the circulation of commodities. It is, therefore, absolutely necessary that the special commodity of labour power, L_p, be capable of producing more value than it possesses, if capitalism is to be viable.

Labour power is productive in two senses. In one sense, it produces a use value that meets the capitalist's demand. Thus, labour power may be defined as the human capacity for labour that may be used to produce a use value of any description. It is impossible for any production to take place without the intervention of human labour. The labour that produces a use value will be referred to as *productive* and all other forms of labour will be referred to as *unproductive*. In capitalist society, the labour power that produces a use value as a commodity under the direction of capital must also be *value-productive*. Capitalistically produced use values are *intrinsic commodities*, or *value objects*, unlike the use values produced by a small commodity producer. Whether or not the latter sells his output as commodities depends on contingencies outside the production process itself, such as the personal decision to sell. Capital has no such choice because C contains labour power, which was purchased as a commodity. Labour power cannot produce a use value unless it simultaneously produces value. Thus, the capitalist production of use values is necessarily the production of value. (Commodities are produced with indifference to use value.) If properly used by the capitalist, it is the nature of labour power to form and augment value in the new product.

Typically, the capitalist already has value objects, which he may dispose of in the market when he advances capital in the form of wages. The capital paid to labour power is often called *variable capital* (v) because the new value that it produces (v + s) should ideally be greater than its own old value (v), though the risk is that it may be less. Though it is available as a commodity in capitalist society, labour power is not an easy object to consume. It is not inherently a commodity, for it is not a product of capital. No industrial capitalist can sell labour power, since it never constitutes part of C'; but he must always purchase labour power as a commodity, since it necessarily forms part of C. Moreover, labour power must be a *time commodity*, in the sense that it is sold for a definite duration of time, the contractual period of employment. It is purchased at the beginning of that period and paid at its end (Marx 1969, p.165). If the capitalist paid for it at the beginning, he might not be able to keep the worker, the natural owner of that labour power, under his control for the rest of that period. In the production process of capital, labour power loses its value upon being purchased. During the contractual period, labour power cannot be resold by the purchaser–capitalist. Thus, as soon as the contractual period begins, the capitalist does not retain the labour power which he has purchased as a value object; he holds it only as a use value, which yields productive labour capable of producing both new use values and new value in the production process of capital.

The *circulation of industrial capital*, M—C...P...C'—M', is interrupted by a *production process* because it involves labour power, which does not preserve (but loses and then reproduces) its value, while being used. If C contained only means of production, P_m, and not labour power, L_p, this interruption would not occur. If, rather than human labour power, the capitalist purchased an animal, the circulation of his capital would not be interrupted either. The animal, which is a capitalistically produced means of production, is a value object; its 'labour power' cannot be sold separately from the animal itself. As the animal is consumed productively, a new product emerges. The value of the animal is preserved in the production process and is merely transferred from the animal, as means of production, to the new product. The capitalist can, at any time, sell either the undepreciated portion of the animal or the newly produced commodity, and retrieve the original value that he advanced.

The same condition would hold, if, instead of an animal, a slave were purchased as a means of production. If labour power were sold, once and for all, its owner would become a slave, a dependent person, and no longer capable of selling and reselling her commodity for a limited period. The capitalist who purchases cattle-power can resell it with the cattle if he no longer needs it. The same applies to slave-power. The capitalist does not conclude an employment contract with either cattle or slaves for a definite period of time. A slave-owning capitalist is a contradiction in terms. A slave owner appropriates surplus labour directly by the application of extra-commodity-economic coercion, whereas a capitalist typically appropriates surplus labour only in the form of surplus value, without resorting to direct, physical coercion. The point here is that only the human labour power of a worker, free in the double sense (as in, free to sell his/her labour power but not free not to do so) can be sold and purchased as a commodity, separately from its natural owner. Only the purchase of *labour power*, the human capacity to perform productive labour, involves an employment contract. Therefore, this special commodity must be treated differently from the means of production.

If a small commodity producer were to purchase only the means of production as commodities in order to produce a commodity, C', with the assistance of the labour power of others, acquired by other than commodity-economic means, this production process could not be characterized as genuinely capitalist, even if C' were to be sold for a higher price than that for which C was purchased. Such a production process would depend on non-commodified labour power, exogenous to the capitalist economy, and, therefore, would not be fully adaptable to capitalist laws of motion.

In capitalist society, the natural owner of labour power cannot decide on his/her own how to use it, because, having sold it, [s]he no longer owns its use value. Labour power is a peculiar commodity in that the purchaser cannot independently consume it either. Although, after its purchase, labour power belongs to the capitalist as a use value, its consumption requires the physical exertion of the worker, its natural owner. It is up to the purchaser–capitalist to determine how productively it should be used. During the contractual period, the industrial capitalist has the right to use the labour power that he has purchased for the period as he sees fit – provided that he does not apply any extra-economic coercion to its natural owners. Since the worker who sells his/her labour power, unlike an independent craftsperson, is totally indifferent to the use values that [s]he produces, [s]he must receive the appropriate instructions in order to know how [s]he should apply that labour power.

Because labour power cannot be resold during the contract period, it is a categorical imperative that the purchaser–capitalist use it productively. The capitalist incurs significant risk in purchasing labour power. The skill of an industrial capitalist can be measured by his ability to ensure that a commodity, C', is produced and then sold for a price that is as much above the cost of the means of production and labour power, previously purchased in the market as commodities, C, at the lowest possible price and consumed in the subsequent production period. If he fails to supervise or instruct the workers properly, they can exercise their labour power inappropriately, and the purchaser–capitalist will have to absorb the cost. For, although it can produce more value than it itself possesses, labour power can also produce less value than it itself possesses if it is improperly used to produce a commodity which is not in demand or which cannot be sold at a competitive price.

When a capitalist can produce any use value that best fits his chrematistic purpose, within the scope of the socially available technology, capital is no longer constrained by a particular use value, but only by *use values in general*. In this way, capital achieves absolute indifference to the specificity of the use value that it sells. It can choose to sell any commodity, C', which yields the greatest surplus value, just as money can purchase any commodity in the market. It is labour power that frees the chrematistic of capital from entanglements with particular use values. Labour power has the ability to produce any use value demanded, provided the technologies exist to permit its production as a commodity by the capitalist method. This capacity is increasingly secured, together with labour power's commodification and the *simplification* of production processes at the margin in all industries, as capitalism matures. In this fashion, industrial capital subsumes the entire production process of a society, converting it into a capitalist society, in which all use values are, in principle, capitalistically produced as commodities by means of commodities alone.

Even as a commodity, labour power is inseparable from the person of the worker and cannot be reproduced except in his individual consumption process. His *means of subsistence* must, therefore, be sufficient to maintain him in his normal state as a labouring individual. His natural wants, such as food, clothing, fuel and housing, vary according to the climatic and other physical conditions of his country. On the other hand, the number and extent of his so-called necessary wants, together with the modes of satisfying them, are themselves the product of historical development and unique cultural requirements. The workers must, therefore, be paid a *subsistence wage* sufficient to purchase the specific basket of wage goods necessary to ensure the resupply of their labour power in the next period within a specific social and historical context. Thus, this subsistence cannot be exhaustively and precisely determined by what is biologically required to reproduce that labour power. A subsistence wage must permit the purchase of enough means of livelihood that workers may raise and educate the children who will take their places when they retire from active working life. In other words, the subsistence standard of living of a worker must be such as to perpetuate the typical living conditions of working-class family life in a particular socio-historical context, for it is in that family life that labour power is reproduced, not only day by day, but also from one generation to another. It will be demonstrated later that capitalism not only maintains such a family life but permits a natural growth of the working population, as Marx maintained (1969, p.164).

It is the value of the means of subsistence, so defined, that is equal to the value of labour power. Indeed, when the free worker prices his/her labour power by way of its value expression, the normal price of that labour power tends to settle to the normal price of the prevailing means of subsistence. For if the normal price of labour power exceeds that of the means of subsistence today, the worker can buy more means of livelihood than is sufficient to reproduce his/her labour power, and may fail to market it tomorrow. If the normal price of labour power falls short of that of the means of subsistence, the worker will be unable to resupply his/her labour power tomorrow in the condition required for a normal day's work. Therefore, society's existing labour power can be maintained if, and only if, the normal price of labour power tends to equal that of the worker's means of subsistence. Since labour power is not a capitalistically produced commodity, it does not possess a value other than that imputed to it by the value of the worker's means of subsistence.

Labour power can be used to generate both productive and unproductive labour. It can also be consumed in recreational activities. For such a human capacity to become a commodity, the worker must be doubly free in the Marxian sense, which means that a worker can freely dispose of his/her labour power as a commodity, but, given that the worker has no other commodity to offer for sale, [s]he cannot choose not to dispose of it. In order for the worker to be free from the possession of any other commodity but labour power, [s]he should be deprived of the means of production with which to produce a commodity for sale, and the means of subsistence on which to live, until [s]he finishes a contractual period of work. For, if [s]he has sufficient means for the production of a commodity from the sale of which [s]he may earn a livelihood, [s]he has the choice of not selling her/his labour power as a commodity.

If the worker were not a free person, her/his appearance in the market as the seller of her labour power could be legally forbidden or otherwise restricted. The conversion of labour power into a commodity is indeed a historical institution peculiar only to the capitalist mode of production. A very special social relation is needed to maintain the formal separation of this work capacity from its natural owner. We examine the capitalist social relation in the pure theory; but the conversion of labour power into a commodity, which constitutes the necessary and sufficient condition for the form of industrial capital to commence operating, cannot be deduced from the logical development of the commodity economy. It should not be assumed that a capitalist society automatically evolves as soon as commodity exchanges reach a certain state of development or sophistication. Nor does it follow logically or theoretically from the preceding argument in the doctrine of simple circulation. Rather, some very peculiar historical conditions must be satisfied before a class of modern, property-less workers, who freely sell their labour power because they must do so to survive, makes its appearance. It follows that the dialectic of capital's commodity-economic logic cannot, and does not, explain the historical cause of the primitive accumulation necessary for the formation of capitalist society.

Primitive accumulation in the sense not only of the accumulation of mercantile wealth, on the one hand, but also of the creation en masse of property-less wage workers, on the other, must be presupposed as an initial condition of mature capitalism and the theory that attempts to understand it. Primitive accumulation entails the divorce of the direct producers from the land. In traditional societies, the direct producers were tied to the land as peasants, and were subject, in one form or another, to the master–servant relation, based on pre-capitalist landownership. The *enclosure movement*, which began in Britain in the sixteenth century, initiated the primitive accumulation that eventually led to the conversion of labour power into a commodity. When the peasants were evicted from the land, whether by the enclosure movement or otherwise, and were, thus, denied access to the natural means of production represented by land, they found themselves free, not only from feudal bondage, but also from their means of production and of livelihood. They were, in other words, left with nothing else to sell but their own labour power. Only when the worker was detached from the land could capital purchase labour power as a commodity and then appropriate the product of the worker's labour. At the same time, the traditional landowner, whose land was now largely free of peasants, could hardly provide the labour necessary to exploit the natural means of production that he possessed. He was, therefore, obliged to rent his land to capital for productive exploitation. In this way, capital obtained access to labour power and land, the two original sources of productivity.[12] Since capital could, by itself, produce all intermediate products once the original elements of production were available, nothing limited the unfolding of its productive activity. The mercantile wealth that had been accumulated in the sphere of circulation could now be poured into the sphere of production, thus establishing the unchallenged supremacy of industrial capital.

As in Hegel's realm of being, in pure thought, the trading system in the doctrine of circulation is a self-determining system only implicitly, or *formally*, since its material substratum lies outside its own motion. In the realm of the forms of circulation, no mention is made of labour as the substance of value. Yet, the mode of operation of the trading system provides the basis for the reification of economic relations, which permits capital to manage the labour-and-production process that constitutes the material foundation of all societies. This is the point of transition form the doctrine of circulation to the doctrine of production in the dialectic of capital. If, according to Marx, 'value is here the active factor in a process' which invests money and commodities with 'the occult quality' of self-expansion, of being able to lay 'golden eggs' (1969, pp.153–4), it is only in the context of the doctrine of production that the substance of value can be explicated. (There we find out how capital manages to produce 'golden eggs', or commodities.) The real and logical premises of the capitalist trading system are necessarily presupposed in the doctrine of circulation, but are not made explicit.

Part II

Dialectical Theory of Capitalism: Production

2
Capitalist Production

The development of the argument which makes possible the transition from the doctrine of circulation to the doctrine of production in the Uno–Sekine dialectic of capital parallels the transition from the doctrine of being to the doctrine of essence in Hegel's *Logic*, in which the dialectic of *quality, quantity* and *measure* ends with an *absolute indifference* to *quality* or *determinateness* (Sekine 1984, pp.206–9). In each case, a diversity of *forms of being* is demonstrated to be the *outward show* or *appearance* of '*an underlying essence, which must appear*' (Hegel 1969, p.479). Thus, in the doctrine of production, the dialectical subject no longer delimits itself by excluding, circumventing or *passing over* what is other than itself. Rather, it makes the necessary changes within itself to allow it to cunningly internalize obstacles in its path and, thereby, to adapt to its surrounding condition or *appearance*, albeit without sacrificing its basic orientation or *ground*. Indeed, it provides the ground with a more solid foundation as *actuality* by allowing it to contain that foundation within itself and so becomes *self-determined*.

Translated into the language of the dialectic of capital, the parallel development of the logic in the doctrine of production might read as follows: The M—C—M' of capital was not self-determined and self-dependent in the doctrine of circulation, because it was not possible for all members of the merchant community to profit by buying cheap and selling dear. In Hegelian terms, 'the ground was not yet determined by objective principles of its own' (Hegel 1975, p.179). In order to provide a more solid foundation for its chrematistic activity, capital, having taken control of the labour-and-production process, must begin to produce, as commodities with value, the use values it sells for profit, while at the same time satisfying the general norms of economic life that any viable society must observe. In this way, capital in the doctrine of production provides a secure foundation for its chrematistic activity in the form of a self-dependent commodity economy. Only with the transformation of M—C—M' into M—C(P_m, L_p)...P...C'—M' can it be made explicit that the commodities purchased by capital consist not only of means of production but also of labour power, which are then appropriately combined to produce commodities for sale at a profit.

Thus, the doctrine of production demonstrates that the forms of circulation must arise from the production process of capital as the forms of appearance which the productions of capital take on. For example, commodities and money can no longer be external givens, with which capital performs its chrematistic operation, but must be products of the capitalist production of commodities as value. Moreover, it is now made explicit that capitalists must be more than mere merchants; they must be industrialists and purchasers or users of labour power.

THE CAPITALIST PRODUCTION OF COMMODITIES AS VALUE

A purely capitalist society may be said to be only externally represented by the circulation forms of commodity, money and capital which can exist independently of the capitalist production process. These forms are both historically and logically prior to the capitalist mode of production. Commodity trade, typically intermediated by money as well as capital, mobilized idle money to buy cheap and sell dear, so as to profit through arbitrage in pre-capitalist societies, and was obviously operated independently of a capitalist production process in these societies. Capital would still be subject to the restrictions of use values if its operation always consisted of the buying-cheap-and-selling-dear of specific commodities. Only when capital can produce *any* commodity that fits its chrematistic purpose does it become truly indifferent to use value.

To acquire self-determination in this Hegelian sense, the commodity economy must demonstrate its capacity to produce any use value whatsoever as a commodity with value, thus achieving a status equivalent to that of *quality* in Hegel's system, and, hence, achieving full or absolute 'indifference' as to what use value it is required to produce. To accomplish this objective, merchant capital must necessarily be superseded by industrial capital, which has the capacity to subsume the labour-and-production process, which is common to all societies.

Once the form of industrial capital is firmly established, the recurring contradiction between value and use value, which parallels the contradiction between *being* and *nothing* in Hegel's *Logic*, returns in the form of a contradiction between capitalism's value augmentation and the use-value production which prevails in any viable economy. The dialectic of capital must demonstrate how a commodity-economic form of value augmentation, indifferent to use values, can contain – at least in principle – the production of any use value which capitalist society requires. The Hegelian triad of the *ground, appearance*, and *actuality* is translated into the following propositions of the dialectic of capital: (1) capitalist production secures itself on the basis of the workers-versus-capitalist production relation; (2) industrial capital must circulate without interruption, while avoiding all unnecessary waste of resources; and (3) capitalist society reproduces itself on an expanding scale, supplying means of production and articles of consumption in an appropriate proportion, while alternating between the *widening* and *deepening* phases of capital accumulation. In so doing, capital simultaneously reproduces commodities and capitalist production relations. The *essence*, or inner constitution, of capitalism is, thus, only laid bare when the compatibility of use-value production in general and the specifically capitalist production of value, including surplus value, is demonstrated in (1) the production of value inside the factory; (2) the circulation of commodities outside the factory;

and (3) the reproduction process of capital, as the continuing activity of the aggregate social capital.

From the viewpoint of the commodity economy, the labour-and-production process that is common to all societies is initially a Hegelian *other*. Yet it is not an other which the commodity economy can simply *pass over*. The production process of capital corresponds to Hegel's *intro-reflection* (or *essence as reflection within itself*) which unfolds through the triad of the *ground*, the *existence*, and the *thing*. The ground (or *bare essence divested of being*) must be explained by the category of *reflection* or *internalization*, which in turn consists of a triad of the thrice repeated categories of *identity*, *difference* and the *ground*. *Reflection* consists of specifying a concept, not by an 'other' that lies outside of it, but by one that is posited inside of it. Such a reflected concept is *dual*, in the Hegelian sense. Thus, in the dialectic of capital, every concept in the doctrine of production that, at first, appears self-same or *identical* (such as productive labour) contains differences within itself. These differences must be so posited as to form two contrasting aspects of the whole (such as the concrete-useful and the abstract-human aspects of productive labour). Only when the relation between these *dual* aspects is specifically established does the original concept become non-empty or well grounded, as it reveals itself to be something real.[13]

In the dialectic of capital, the triad of *identity*, *difference* and the *ground* is repeated three times in the exposition of the labour-and-production process, and *difference* itself goes through the stages of *distinction*, *duality* and *opposition*. The production of use values in general is an identity composed of the two elements, the labour process and the production process. The unity of these two elements, the labour-and-production process, is dependent upon productive labour, an identity consisting of the dual of concrete-useful and human labour.

In the case of the commodity, the co-existence of value with a use value immediately led to the suppression of the original use value in the synthetic concept of exchange value, in which value expressed itself in the use value of another commodity. In the case of productive labour, however, the abstract-human aspect does not attempt to suppress the concrete-useful aspect. Abstract-human labour cannot be released, or become free, from concrete-useful labour by becoming something else; productive labour is abstract-human only because it is also concrete-useful. The concept of productive labour is enriched by this *duality*, which accounts for its significance in the labour-and-production process.

Dual productive labour also entails the notion of the expenditure of labour or labour time, an identity which is necessarily composed of the dual of necessary and surplus labour. The concept of productive labour is valid for all epochs, but productive labour only becomes deskilled, simplified, homogeneous and abstract so as to be capable of being easily shifted from one branch to another with the maturing of capitalism. Since we are looking at the universal labour-and-production process from capital's limited point of view, all dual categories have both implicit value (or specifically capitalistic) and universal material-economic (or use-value) aspects.

THE LABOUR-AND-PRODUCTION PROCESS

The economic process of use-value production forms the material foundation of trans-historic economic life, regardless of its social form. No society can exist without *material production*, which entails the human being's purposive activity on nature, so as to transform part of it into readily (that is, directly or productively) consumable use values. This process normally occurs under various extra-economic socio-cultural restrictions. Only the capitalist production of use values as commodities in possession of value can be free from such restrictions. To the extent that labour power is transformed into a commodity, its consumption by the purchaser–capitalist does not involve extra-(commodity-)economic and, therefore, direct physical coercion.

Because of its radically commodity-economic nature, the production process of capital, which is a value-formation-and-augmentation process, allows the production of use values in general, which is common to all societies, to stand alone as the substrate of its operation, no longer entangled within the web of other non-economic human pursuits. Thus, the *labour-and-production process*, as viewed by capital, and, therefore, as a legitimate part of the dialectic, is that process as it appears in capitalist society, but with its commodity-economic integument set aside or bracketed. It is not only free of extra-economic human relations, which frequently interfered with production in pre-modern societies, but also from thermodynamic restrictions on production, because, for capital, all material economic activity is akin to factory-style industrial production. The growing of agricultural goods in harmony with natural cycles and the hunting and gathering of wild plants and animals are not contemplated by capital. Clearly, this concept of the labour-and-production process, which is restricted to the dialectical theory of capitalism, is a far narrower concept than the concept of *use value production in general*, as understood from the point of view of historical materialism.

The production of use values is a *labour process*, in which humans work with the definite purpose of transforming natural objects into readily consumable use values. Although people create consciously and not by instinct, the ultimate purpose of this labour is to make it possible for humans to survive as natural beings in harmony with their environment. Productive labour is an activity of self-preservation, because it is through the consumption of the products of their labour that humans reproduce their labour power. *Labour power* may thus be defined as the aggregate of the mental and physical capabilities people exercise when they produce use values.

The objects to which humankind apply their labour may be called *objects of labour*. Such an object might be the wood, which is converted into lumber, and other building materials, or the raw produce of the land, but in most cases these objects have already been transformed by previous labour. Labour is made more effective by *means of labour*, such as tools and machinery. *Accessory*, *supplementary or auxiliary materials*, such as oil products, employed to fuel or lubricate machines, are also used. These categories classify means of production in terms of their proximity to nature.

Though the labour process could and should also be viewed as a process of human–nature interface, we take the point of view here that the human being is the subject, who confronts nature as an object in this process. [S]he purposively works on nature so as to transform part of it for human use. Here, nature is 'objectified' and remains completely passive, ready to be 'conquered' or 'dominated' by the human being, the only active agent. Thus, although no society would survive if it failed to produce, that is, if it ceased to transform part of nature into the directly or indirectly consumable use values necessary for human existence, the need for a productive technology to be embedded in the ecology of nature is deliberately de-emphasized by this capitalistically and industrially bound or limited concept.

The production of use values always involves a techno-social organization and a social division of labour. This aspect is emphasized by the *production process*. Once the labour process is finished, the produced use values become products which are, of course, the concrete results of the labour process. Produced objects are external to humankind. From the point of view of these products, the labour process may be regarded as a production process of things by things. In this context, objects of labour, means of labour and supplementary materials may all be categorized merely as means of production, which, when combined with labour power, constitute the *elements or factors of production*. When use-value production is viewed in this light, it is reduced to a purely technical *input–output process*, rather than being seen as the conscious, purposive activity of humans, as they transform nature. The advantage of viewing production as a purely technical process is that we can see that the output of one labour process can also be the input of another labour process. This implies, in turn, that labour processes do not occur in isolation, but, rather, are organized and integrated to ensure the continuity of these processes.

The use-value production in any society may be viewed as either a technically organized arrangement of things or as the conscious, purposive transformation of nature, which is carried on by humankind to ensure the survival of society. Both points of view are valid for particular purposes, but bourgeois economists and capitalists tend to view production in a purely technical way, while ignoring the human-creative and social-relational dimension. Moreover, both approaches share the limitation that they assume that production is intrinsically industrial and need not concern itself with the fact that industry is no longer subordinate to agriculture and is, therefore, no longer comfortably 'embedded' within a sustainable local or regional ecosystem.

THE NATURE AND SIGNIFICANCE OF PRODUCTIVE LABOUR

In the production process, it is labour power which is active and means of production which are passive. Labour power can be adapted to the production of any use value, while means of production are developed to produce specific use values. The *duality of productive labour* derives from the fact that all human labour has a concrete-useful aspect and an abstract-human aspect. To speak of *concrete-useful labour* is to speak of the specific labour tasks direct producers perform. At the same time, these specific labour tasks may be viewed as part of the total social labour which a society must perform to produce all use values, or, in other words, as *abstract-human labour*. The chief use value of labour power is that, as abstract-human labour, it can be adapted to produce any good that society requires, and not merely a specific one. From this angle, labour power is the basis for the development of labour of all kinds, and is, thus, the basis for the development of the scope of human productive achievements and the range of human societies as well.

Although productive labour is the material foundation of any society, planning and decision making are also indispensable. The uncoordinated production of use values carried out at random by isolated labourers does not secure the material basis for a society's survival. Indeed, even a Robinson Crusoe must plan how to allocate his labour so as to complete the tasks necessary to provide him with use values. Use-value production is always organized and integrated to some degree. Society's productive labour must, therefore, always have both abstract-human and concrete-useful aspects in any society and not merely in capitalist ones.

The fact that, in all societies, productive labour has an abstract-human aspect makes labour power, in principle, a *non-specific factor of production*. This means that, at some finite cost, human labour can always be shifted from one branch of use-value production to another. Labour can be described as *simple* if direct producers can switch from one form of concrete-useful labour to another relatively easily or without great social cost. It is through the *simplification of labour* that the potential of abstract-human labour is fully realized. Labour power always has the capacity to adapt to the production of whatever use value is required, but technical, institutional and educational barriers may prevent its potential for abstract-human labour from being adequately realized. The concept of a labour which produces all forms of wealth may be validly applied to all epochs, but it took the development of industrial capitalism to make labour quickly and easily adaptable to the production of whatever form of material wealth society required. Thus, although some labour always had to be able to switch from one task to another in order to guarantee the production of goods, this capability was developed to an unparalleled degree in capitalism.

The simplification of the labour process occurs in proportion to its importance to society's economic life. For example, in an agriculturally dominated society, a peasant's labour ought to be simplified, but manufacturing labour need not be. Such a society could survive if manufacturing were carried on by skilled craftspeople, whose skills could not be easily duplicated, but it would have perished if a peasant could not easily shift from the production of one crop to another. In fact, in all societies, direct producers must shift from one form of essential labour to another if society is to survive. This may be difficult to see in feudalism, for example, where the relatively simple labour of agricultural production is subject to a wide range of natural irregularities, and is conducted under extra-(commodity-)economic master–servant relations such that, even under identical, natural and technical conditions, agricultural production may be carried on differently from place to place. By contrast, in capitalism, all labour tends to be simplified, although manufacturing labour is simplified to an even greater degree than agricultural labour. This is due to the fact that, whereas the material basis of feudal society rested on agricultural production, in capitalism, it rests on manufacturing. Thus, in capitalist society, it will be demonstrated that the production of the same commodity, under identical natural and technical conditions, must produce the same results. This makes capitalist society a very productive one.

In order that labour power, which is the capacity to perform productive labour, may be sold on the open market in capitalist society, workers must first be dispossessed of any means of production or livelihood. Capital can then purchase this labour power as a commodity and use it to produce to satisfy society's demands. To produce any commodity which capitalist society requires means to produce with indifference to use value or, in other words, with indifference to the concrete-useful forms of labour required to produce them. Thus, the labour power purchased as a commodity by the capitalist must be able, within the scope of the socially available technology, to produce any use value which capitalist society requires, without being bound by vocational or occupational restrictions. Industrial capital becomes a true form of chrematistics only when it develops the ability to produce any use value which is technically feasible. If a capitalist wanted to produce steel ingots, but the labour power which he purchased could only produce cotton goods, the chrematistic of industrial capital would be as constrained by use value as that of merchant capital. In that case, the development of the form of industrial capital would not represent an advance over that of merchant capital, or of the small commodity producer. If a 'capitalist' had to depend on irreplaceable and highly experienced craftspeople, then he would not be a true personification of industrial capital. The skills and craftsmanship of craft producers would determine the quality of the capitalist's product, and the business would survive only so long as the public continued to appreciate that product. However, a fully developed and representative industrial capital is capable of producing anything that promises the maximum profit.

After capitalism developed *modern mechanized industry*, it gained the capacity increasingly to simplify and standardize all forms of productive labour, so that the abstract aspect of human labour was made apparent, not only theoretically, but also historically. In such a context, abstract-human labour specifically appears as value-producing labour and concrete-useful labour as use-value-producing labour. Capital can expand or contract its production of a use value and migrate from branch to branch of use-value production in response to social demand and profit rates. Moreover, the development of the capitalist method of production and the attendant simplification of labour tend to reduce the production costs of commodities, which otherwise would remained prohibitive. Unfortunately, in the process, labour becomes an abstract disutility to the worker. Regardless of which concrete-useful form of simplified or deskilled labour one performs, it can only be approached with indifference.

The labour which produces a use value (a material object which we intend to use or consume) is called *productive labour* in order to distinguish it from the labour by which one renders a service to another, which will be termed *unproductive*, since it does not involve, either directly or indirectly, humankind's purposive action on nature to produce use values and, therefore, is not part of the labour-and-production process underlying the motion of industrial capital. Although some unproductive labour is essential to society's survival, services are neither use values nor objects outside us. Services do not embody, materialize or augment value; thus, capital finds it difficult to subject them fully to commodity-economic management. Services cannot be 'factory-produced' as genuine, full-fledged commodities, even though they may ostensibly assume a commodity form. The *reification* or 'impersonalization' of human relations follows from the fact that capitalist society transforms social relations between humans, engaged in commodity production, into social relations between things; but services cannot be reified in a similar fashion.

Services may be personal, governmental administrative or business administrative. In the dialectic of capital only the third category of service is theoretically significant. The capitalist's unproductive managerial labour, while indispensable to capitalism, is not productive of value and will be treated in detail later. The second category is extra-economic and ought properly to be ignored at the level of pure theory, because the state must remain implicit if capital's laws of motion are to operate without either impediment or extra-market assistance. The first category, personal services, does not play a prominent role in capitalist society, because of capitalism's tendency to replace or materialize interpersonal services with an increasing variety and abundance of material commodities which we can consume without assistance. Because capitalism tends in this direction, it is possible to arrive at a definition of production which clearly refers to the creation of use values and, just as clearly, excludes as unproductive all interpersonal services. In theorizing pure capitalism, it is assumed that this tendency for the material-ization of personal services has been completed.

As abstract-human labour, productive labour is either necessary labour or surplus labour. *Necessary labour* is productive labour performed for the purpose of reproducing the labour power currently consumed in the production process. A society is said to be viable if its direct producers have a guaranteed access to the product of their necessary labour. Labour performed beyond what is necessary to reproduce the labour power of the direct producers is *surplus labour*. Necessary labour includes the stockpiling of use values, such as foodstuffs, so that they might be available when fresh goods are not (due to predictable seasonal changes or unpredictable natural events), or to provide goods either for workers who are temporarily incapacitated due to illness or for children, who constitute the next generation of workers. The productive labour performed for the old, the infirm, the terminally ill or otherwise permanently incapacitated can only be surplus labour since it does not contribute to the maintenance of society's labour power.

A Robinson Crusoe cannot perform surplus labour, since all the use values he produces are for his own consumption, either now or in the future. Surplus labour can only arise in a social context, since the use values produced during surplus labour time are consumed by members of society who are not themselves producers. These non-producers may be divided into natural and social dependents. *Natural dependents* are family and society members who are provided with use values by a compassionate society, because they cannot support themselves, due to the fact that they are too old or too sick or otherwise incapacitated to do so. *Social dependents*, such as administrators, spiritual leaders and military personnel, are supported because society believes that their presence will enhance the quality of social life. Indeed, social dependents can play important (and even indispensable) social roles generally and, with respect to externally supporting the labour-and-production process, in particular. The number of natural and social dependents which a society can support is limited by the number of productive workers available to support them and by the current development of the productive forces within that society.

Merely because they have performed enough surplus labour to adequately maintain the class of social dependents does not mean that the direct producers will be permitted to cease their labours. Historically, it is undeniable that groups of social dependents, relieved from productive labour, have been able to employ extra-economic and direct, physical coercion to appropriate an excessive quantity of products from productive workers, and to expand their numbers beyond what would be consistent with the efficient management of the labour-and-production process, such that many social dependents do not even perform the unproductive labour of assisting in the supervision of the labour-and-production process. They are, thus, entirely parasitic, dedicating their lives to idleness and leisure. The differing types of class societies which first emerge at an early stage in human society are rooted in this phenomenon.

The specific kind of class structure which prevails in a historical society depends upon the exploitability of surplus labour and upon the mode of appropriation of surplus products resulting from that labour. The extent to which surplus labour is actually carried out depends on the class relation prevailing between productive workers and the class or classes of social dependents which dominate them. In slavery, the labour power and person of productive workers was owned by individual slave-masters. In serfdom, productive workers, tied to the land, were contractually obligated to perform surplus labour for their feudal lords. Historically, the number of parasitic dependents was limited in pre-capitalist societies because, once the social dependents who constituted the dominant classes in pre-capitalist societies achieved a certain level of affluence, they had little incentive to exploit the direct producers any further. In capitalism, however, capital is driven to exploit to the fullest the labour power it has purchased as a commodity, in its quest for value augmentation. The operation of the logic of capital stretches surplus labour to its physical limit. This explains why capitalism is more productive than all previous societies.

The *labour-and-production process*, which materially underpins the notion of industrial capital, exists in some form in non-capitalist societies, but it is a socio-technical organization without a motive force of its own. It must be subsumed by an operative principle, specific to a given social formation, before it can be activated or set in motion. More specifically, the direct producers in all societies must expend productive labour on nature to obtain use values. In pre-capitalist societies, however, the direct producers had to be subjected to various forms of coercion if specific ruling classes were to compel their surplus labour in order to obtain surplus products from them. In capitalist society, the labour-and-production process, together with the social division of labour, is uniquely organized according to commodity-economic principles, which permit the capitalist class to expropriate surplus goods produced during the surplus labour of the direct producers without resorting to direct, physical coercion, merely by allowing the capitalist market to operate without impediment.

TOWARDS THE VALUE-FORMATION-AND-AUGMENTATION PROCESS

Capitalism requires that production be carried out according to its own objective, chrematistic or commodity-economic principles. The labour-and-production process must, therefore, be activated or *grounded*, in the Hegelian sense, by being organized not merely as the production of use values but also as the formation and augmentation of value. For Hegel, the unity of the *ground* and the *grounded* is *existence* and existence is, in turn, one of an *indefinite multitude of existents* (Hegel 1975, p.175). Each capitalist operation too is one of a multitude of existents, producing a particular use value independently, but also interacting with other firms in a network of firms unified in their pursuit of value by the operation of commodity-economic principles (or the law of value).

The dialectic of *reflection* must show (1) that the capitalist formation and augmentation of value can wholly absorb the labour-and-production process, or the production of use values in general, which is common to all societies; (2) that the capitalist production process, so constituted, ensures its continuity in the circulation process of capital; and (3) that capital, which both produces and circulates commodities, has the power to make its reproduction process a self-dependent totality. If use-value production in general can be fully contained and subordinated by the value-augmenting motion of capital, capitalist society will constitute itself as such a totality.[14] In order for the autonomous forms of circulation to subsume the production process, they must, therefore, be able to subject that most essential ingredient of production, labour, to the capitalist principle. In other words, only when labour power, which is the source of productive labour, becomes a commodity, and, therefore, adopts the mode of behaviour peculiar to this commodity-economic form, can the labour-and-production process be integrated into the chrematistic system of capital. Labour power, purchased as a commodity, must now become the source of the augmentation of value.

Capitalism presupposes commercial activity, but the reverse is not necessarily true. The simple exchange of 'commodities', in contrast to capitalism, does not, of necessity, entail the conversion of labour power into a commodity. However, the development of the form of industrial capital, together with the production of value and surplus value, requires, in addition to the accumulation of monetary wealth, a period of primitive accumulation, during which is formed a class of property-less workers who are free, not merely from feudal bondage, but also from the means of production necessary for their reproduction. Only then can capital ensure that no productive labour is expended on nature without its mediation. For, indeed, workers would be unwilling to offer their labour power to capitalists in exchange for wage goods unless this initial condition was met. Labour power becomes a commodity only because the direct producers, stripped of their means of production in a commodity economy, cannot survive without selling their labour power as a commodity.

The conversion of labour power into a commodity is a necessary condition for the capitalist subsumption of the labour-and-production process, but it cannot be explained logically or theoretically. The conversion of labour power into a commodity, which translates the *ground* into *existence* or the *thing* (Hegel 1975, p.181), does not follow from the *logic of transition* (or *passing over from one form to another*). Only the historically contingent fact of this conversion, which is a recollection of something from the past that has been internalized (*erinnert*) by capital, introduces the *essence* of capitalist production. We shall not discuss this topic in any detail here in pure theory; nor shall we discuss in any detail how capitalists gained access to land and, in so doing, undermined the power of the pre-existing ruling class (the landed aristocracy) to compel the surplus labour of the direct producers. These topics are, of course, of crucial importance in a stage theory of capitalism's historical development (which we shall delve into in Chapter 8) and in historical studies of capitalism, but at present we are investigating how a capitalist economy reproduces itself once labour power has already been converted into a commodity that capitalists, in their capacity as agents of capital and as managers of the labour-and-production process, can purchase (together with material commodities) and employ in such a fashion that the products of labour also become commodities and, therefore, the products of capital. Pure theory can assist us with historical research, however, because it shows us what conditions must prevail if a capitalist society is to establish and to reproduce itself as a viable entity.

After capital commodifies labour power and subsumes the labour-and-production process, it carries on all use-value production as the production and augmentation of value under the chrematistic form of capital. Thus, capital becomes fully grounded and establishes its essence, in the sense that it contains the source of its value augmentation within itself.[15] The doctrine of production can and must show how capital successfully manages this production, such that the social relation between the purchasers and sellers of labour power is materially supported rather than undermined. Indeed, a scientific theory is needed to explain how it is that industrial capital can purchase and employ the single, homogeneous commodity of labour-power in such a way that productive labour, through its capacity for abstract-human labour, can be applied indifferently to the production of any use value, as a commodity or value, which capitalist society requires (just as money buys any commodity), while at the same time guaranteeing both that the direct producers obtain only the product of their necessary labour and that capitalists receive the products of the workers' surplus labour. In short, we need to show how capitalism can reproduce itself and material economic life by producing commodities to sell in a society-wide market by means of commodities, whether labour power or means of production, purchased in that same market.

The *capital–labour social relation*, which may also be referred to as the *value relation*, is independent of, and prior to, the general pricing of goods in the market; thus, this relation is invariant to the pricing of goods. Indeed, in the doctrine of production, the dialectic is not yet ready to deal with the constraints presented by specific types of use value in circulation. It must first demonstrate its ability to ensure the provision of use values in general, since this constitutes the material foundation of economic life in all societies. Hence, the focus here is not on the *private cost calculus of the capitalist*, but on the *real cost of capitalist production to society*. This is distinguishable in principle. For example, capital must pay for the use of land, but land is a gift of nature to society and, in principle, costs nothing. On the other hand, capitalists can, by their operations, severely damage the natural world and treat this as an *externality*, even though such devastation is costly to society.

Since the point of view or focus of this doctrine is on the social costs of capitalist production, and not on the private costs of capitalists, capitalists are here viewed primarily as purchasers and users of the single homogeneous commodity: labour power. They are not yet distinguished according to the specific use values which they produce with differing industrial techniques. (Indeed, at this stage in the development of the theory, the organic composition of capital, in Marxian terms, must be assumed to be the same for all capitalists, because only in this abstract context can the law of value determine the real social cost of every commodity. Thus, production prices cannot even be defined here.) To reiterate, the focus here is on the value (capitalist-versus-worker) relation, not on use-value relations prevailing among competing capitalists who have specialized in the production of one of a multitude of use values.

Once we have a scientific explanation of how capitalism is able to accomplish the material-economic reproduction of society by commodity-economic means in the absence of political coercion we shall also be in a position to see clearly something which was not hitherto immediately obvious about the nature of non-capitalist societies. Even in societies where the material-economic reproduction of society was accomplished by other than commodity-economic means and where, consequently, the economic and political relations were not clearly separated, productive workers had to perform surplus labour to provide use values for those who were not engaged in production, but who, nevertheless, often provided essential managerial or other services in order that society remain economically viable.

Capitalist production is managed by industrial capital, which follows the formula $M—C(P_m, L_p)...P...C'—M'$, where M is the money advanced, C is the commodities of labour power and means of production purchased to carry on production, P is the production period, C' is the newly produced commodities of greater value than those purchased to carry on production and M' is an amount of money greater than that advanced or invested to carry on production. The form of industrial capital contains the production process, $C...P...C'$, within the circulation phases of capital, M—C and C'—M', as an intermediate phase. The production process of capital does not lie outside the sphere of circulation, but is enveloped within it. That is to say, industrial capitalists prepare for production by advancing money to buy the commodities of labour power and means of production. Production then interrupts this circulation process. When an industrial capitalist purchases means of production (P_m) and labour power (L_p) in the M—C phase, the value of the former is called *constant capital* (c) and that of the latter *variable capital* (v). The purpose of the production process (...P...) is to produce a commodity which can be sold for a greater value than the capital advanced. The circulation process begins again at the end of the production period, when the commodities produced by those workers who have sold their labour power to capital are put on the market for sale. Since capitalists have paid only for the value of the labour power and means of production consumed in the production period, and since workers can produce greater value than this (referred to as *surplus value*, or s) during that period, the capitalists are able to sell commodities of greater value than those which they purchased, pocketing the difference as their profit.

Capitalists must obtain a value (c + v + s) which is greater than the value they invest in (c + v) to begin the process. The production process, insofar as it newly produces v + s, is the *value-formation process*. This process transfers the pre-existing value from the means of production to the new product. When a surplus value greater than zero is produced, it is also a *value-augmentation process*. Although the value of labour power or variable capital (v) advanced to begin the production process is quantitatively equal to the variable-capital (v) component appearing in the product, the variable-capital component of the product is newly created during the production process, together with surplus value. Indeed, the variable capital used to purchase labour power at the beginning of the process disappears as soon as labour power is purchased.

Labour power is neither an intrinsic commodity nor even a product which capital can produce. Not only is it inseparable from the person of the worker, it ceases to be a commodity as soon as it is sold to capital and, thus, cannot be exchanged or resold as a commodity. The exchange of labour power for wage goods is, therefore, not an ordinary exchange of commodities. It occurs, rather, through the mediation of the capitalist production process. When two ordinary commodities are exchanged, they both already exist when the exchange takes place, but when labour power is purchased, wage goods or their equivalent do not exist. They are produced only when the labour power purchased is productively consumed in the capitalist production process as productive labour. Moreover, labour power may be consumed or used only during a given period of time. It is up to the capitalists to see that they do not purchase more labour power than is necessary, and that use-value production is carried on in the time allotted, such that the value of the new product produced at the end of that period is greater than the value of labour power and means of production advanced as capital and consumed during the same period. (In other words, labour power must form a value greater than its own during the production process of capital in which it is consumed.)

The term *variable capital* suggests that, although labour power is capable of producing surplus value, it can also fail to do so if it is allowed to remain idle or if it is employed to produce a use value which is not in demand and cannot be sold as a commodity. While workers are in no position to refuse the instructions of capitalists as to the use of their labour power, they cannot be held responsible if particular capitalists either fail to manage and instruct them properly or fail to equip them with means of production that are competitive, such that they squander their energies. Thus, while *constant capital* preserves its value in the production process by transferring the old value of means of production consumed to the newly created product, variable capital not only loses its value, but must be managed properly to ensure that it reproduces itself in the production process.

THE LABOUR THEORY OF VALUE AND THE LAW OF VALUE

A *capitalistically produced or genuine commodity* acquires value while being produced. Indeed, it is produced as a value object; it is not a use value which has been produced for contingent reasons and subsequently acquires a value when the opportunity arises to offer it for sale. Such a use value has become a commodity by chance, whereas a genuine commodity is destined to be offered as a value object from the beginning.

Capital cannot form the new value, v + s, by producing any arbitrary use value. It has to produce use values which are socially demanded in the order of their social priority. Capitalists who perform unproductive managerial labour must operate under and respond to the discipline of the market. Even the industrial capitalist is a commodity seller in that he produces C', a commodity of his choice, first and tests (or probes) the market later. As a commodity seller, he can make a trade proposal, but he cannot dictate his terms of trade. He must wait and see how the market responds to his offer and then passively adjust to the social demand which the impersonal market reveals to him by this method of trial and error. Capital can, however, shift from one branch of production to another, seeking greater profit; and, in doing so, capitalists do produce the use values capitalist society requires and demands. They are guided by the fact that use values which are in short supply relative to demand command high prices and yield relatively greater profits than other commodities. If capital produces a use value in excess of demand, its price will eventually fall, eliminating profit and even falling short of its production cost, so that a loss is incurred. In this fashion, a permanent overproduction is avoided. If capital produces a use value which society does not demand, no amount of exploitation will yield a surplus value greater than zero. Capitalists thus abide by the commodity-economic principle of 'buying cheap and selling dear'. They endeavour to maximize the profit earned in any given period. When all industrial capitalists follow this principle in capitalist society, the competitive market sees to it that the anarchic production of use values as commodities will tend to conform to an autonomously shaped pattern of social demand. Commodities will thus be produced in the socially necessary (or equilibrium) quantities.

When commodities are produced in socially necessary (equilibrium) quantities and are, therefore, neither overproduced nor underproduced, it may be said that only *socially necessary labour* has been spent for their production. If all use values tend to be produced in the socially desired quantities and if society's productive labour tends to be allocated by capital accordingly, then this allocation of productive labour tends toward *optimality*, because, given the existing technology – about which we shall say more later – each use value tends to be produced with no more labour than is socially necessary. Thus, every capitalistically produced commodity tends to embody or represent a definite fraction of the aggregate social expenditure of society's productive (abstract-human) labour, and every commodity tends to embody only the *real social cost* required to produce it. The magnitude of the value of a commodity is defined (determined) by the quantity of socially necessary labour embodied in it. It is this quantity which constitutes the substance of value. The *labour theory of value* states, therefore, that socially necessary labour forms the substance of commodity values. Indeed, the capitalist production of commodities as value means nothing other than the production of commodities as embodiments of socially necessary labour. The qualitative uniformity of all commodities produced with a capitalistic indifference to use value derives from the fact that they are embodiments of socially necessary labour.

Since commodities are produced by individual capitalists, according to the method of trial and error, without the knowledge of what other capitalists are doing, it is not possible to calculate the value of (or the socially necessary labour required to produce) a commodity in advance. Its normal (or equilibrium) price can only be found out after the fact, when large quantities have been purchased in the society-wide market by a great many buyers. (Because capitalists cannot understand, predict or plan what values and prices will be established in the market, they can come to believe that commodities themselves, animated by some supernatural power, establish those values and prices autonomously. This delusion is referred to as the *fetishism of commodities*.) This is in striking contrast to the expenditure of concrete-useful labour. The capitalist or worker can easily calculate how much time is devoted to the production of a particular use value.

The specifically capitalistic manner in which productive labour is expended in capitalist society is defined by the *law of value*. This law refers to the automatic tendency in historically viable capitalist societies for the labour theory of value to hold true. If the law of value (the labour theory of value as it necessarily operates in capitalism) holds, so that all use values are produced as commodities with socially necessary labour, then capitalism can exist as a viable historical society. The *necessity of the law of value* is the proposition that the viability of capitalism ensures, and is ensured by, the validity of the labour theory of value. (All commodities produced with a capitalist indifference to use value must tend to embody no more and no less than socially necessary labour.) When the labour-and-production process is operated in a consistently capitalist fashion as a value-formation-and-augmentation process, the law of value necessarily enforces itself.

All societies practice some *division of labour*. When the division of labour becomes truly extensive, as in modern industrial societies, it is difficult to see how each portion contributes to the whole. At one extreme, the management of that whole can be centrally coordinated by state planning; at the other, it can be market regulated, as in capitalist society. In both cases, however, the organization of productive labour is required for the provision of use values that society requires. Even the commodity that is regularly traded in the capitalist market for a profit is a material use value, and, as such, is a product of the division of labour. What is specific to capitalism is that this trans-historic requirement of human society is satisfied by capital and its society-wide market.

Value cannot be wholly absorbed into the sphere of circulation, nor can it remain exclusively in the sphere of production. Thus, it cannot be one-sidedly identified either with price or with abstract labour. *Value* is the concept that relates or mediates what takes place inside the market (in the commodity-economic or specifically capitalist sphere) with what occurs outside it (in the real or material economic realm, which transcends specific societies, such as capitalism). It links the capitalistically specific and historically transient exchanges of capitalistically produced commodities with the production of use values in general, which is common to all societies. In the value-formation-and-augmentation process, the duality of productive labour appears specifically as value-forming labour, which is 'abstract', and use-value-producing labour, which is 'concrete'.

Commodity prices represent capitalistically specific value forms, while *socially necessary labour* constitutes the substance of value, because, under other circumstances, the same labour could have produced any other commodity. Labour that could have produced any commodity has been allocated to the production of this particular commodity so as to satisfy capitalist society's demand for it. The condition for productive labour to be value-forming is also the condition for all commodities to be produced by socially necessary labour. It is this capacity which enables capital to form a historical society. To understand value is to understand the *differentia specifica* of capitalism.

Value presupposes an initial distinction between the *circulation of a commodity* and the *production of a use value*. The former belongs to the commodity economy, which is historically transient, and the latter is suprahistoric in the sense that all viable societies must engage in the production (or hunting, gathering or growing) of use values. If there were no distinction between the *formal (market-based)* and the *substantive (real economic)* aspects of economic life, the question of relating them would not arise. If all or no societies were capitalist, the distinction could not be made. Liberal and neoclassical economists fail to distinguish between the formal and the substantive senses of the word 'economic'. They recognize, in other words, no tension or cleavage between the real economic and that which pertains only to the market. For bourgeois economics, there is no economic life that is not market-oriented or capitalistic. Since we are then assumed to be totally integrated into the market, all our relations appear as reified 'thing-to-thing' price relations or trade-offs.

The *law of value* should be viewed as a system of accounting in terms of the social real cost of capitalist production and not as a theory which claims that, in historical or pure capitalism, commodities produced with an equal amount of labour were/are either necessarily exchanged for one another, or that their equilibrium prices were/are proportional to the quantities of labour spent for their production. In the doctrine of production, we do not know enough about the technology of commodity production to be able to determine all prices and a general rate of profit simultaneously. We are not yet ready to make explicit the differentiation of capital into specific spheres of use-value production. The focus of the doctrine of production is on how capital relates to wage labour. This relation is invariant, whether individual capitalist firms produce cotton goods or machinery. Thus, it makes no sense to distinguish one capitalist firm from another according to the specific use value they each produce. It is, thus, legitimately assumed that the same value composition of capital prevails in all spheres of production. In this abstract context, prices can be assumed to be proportional to values, even if surplus value is produced. At a more synthetic level, in the doctrine of distribution, this simplifying assumption must and will be removed.

For a more fully determined or more concrete and, therefore, more synthetic theory of values and prices, we must know more about the nature of productive techniques. The value of labour power is relative to the existing complex of productive technology, and this, in turn, can only be identified as the labour cost of reproducing labour power in the period of average activity in a given business cycle. This subject will be pursued later, but we can now make the observation that, if commodities are capitalistically produced as value so that the law of value tends to hold, there will also be a set of equilibrium prices and a uniform rate of profit consistent with this *viability condition of capitalist society*. It must be recognized, however, that, in order for productive labour to create value in the value-formation-and-augmentation process of capital, it is necessary that commodities should normally be exchanged at prices which are *not* proportional to the amounts of socially necessary labour required for their production. This does not, in any way, discredit the labour theory of value as distinct from a *labour theory of prices*, with which it has often been confused. For even though the capitalist market determines prices as though such things as values never existed, *production prices* (or *equilibrium prices*) in a capitalist society are, in any case, *tethered to values*, and, as we shall learn, only diverge from proportionality to values (or from value-proportional prices) in a strictly determined and predictable fashion. Moreover, production prices will be shown to be positive if and only if values are positive. That is hardly surprising, since only commodities that are capitalistically produced as value can have normal prices or production prices. These prices ensure that commodities tend to be supplied in only the socially necessary (or equilibrium) quantities. The pricing of capitalistic, or genuine, full-fledged, commodities must guarantee that society's productive labour is properly allocated for the production of all use values in the socially necessary quantities. The prevailing technical conditions then determine how much labour must be embodied per unit of each of these commodities.

The labour theory of value does not attempt to explain the relative prices of commodities, since that is the role of the theory of production prices, which will be introduced in the theory of profit. The *labour theory of value* simply reaffirms the fact that capital produces all commodities as value with indifference to use values by tending to allocate only socially necessary labour for their production. It is this fundamental fact that enables capitalism to form a historical society.

The validity of the labour theory of value cannot be demonstrated unless labour power has already been converted into a commodity. The theory cannot be demonstrated to hold in an imaginary regime of simple commodity production. A society in which all use values are supplied by small commodity producers is never viable. Nor did it ever exist in history. A simple commodity producer is someone, like a craftsman master, who possesses some means of production and employs it, together with his labour power and, if necessary, the labour power of others in producing a 'commodity'. His production process is not that of industrial capital. It does not constitute a value-formation-and-augmentation process; it does not even form an integral part of the labour-and-production process. Such a producer has a stake in a particular use value. His skill, experience and tools belong to a particular trade, and are not easily transferable from one to another. Thus, if a sudden change occurs in the pattern of social demand, small commodity production cannot flexibly adapt to it. A regime of simple commodity production would not necessarily tend to produce commodities in the order of social priorities, nor would it allocate society's productive labour optionally. Value is a specifically capitalist concept. Only a capital-istically produced commodity can have its value rigorously determined by socially necessary labour. A good produced otherwise may, however, supply a small portion of the socially necessary quantity of a commodity, if it sells at the normal or equilibrium price.

FURTHER COMMENTS ON THE VIABILITY OF CAPITALIST SOCIETY

Every viable society, including capitalist society, must have a working community of direct producers at its core. A historical society is said to be *viable* if the direct producers have a guaranteed access to the product of their necessary labour. The fact that human beings work on nature to acquire the wherewithal to live does not appear in a straightforward manner in capitalist society, but rather in a form adapted to the operation of capital. Capital does not obtain surplus products from the direct producers by applying extra-economic coercion to them from the outside. Instead, capital turns the whole system of use-value production into its instrument of value augmentation. The *validity of the labour theory of value* or the proposition that, in capitalist society, all use values tend to be produced with socially necessary labour, implies the *viability of capitalist society*, which further implies the prior conversion and perpetuation of labour power as a commodity. In capitalism, all use values that society needs are produced as value objects, because even labour power is converted into a commodity. In the exchange of labour power for wage goods the law of value appears in its purest form.

The ultimate test of a society's historical existence may be accomplished by a procedure that transforms specialization and trade back into the individual allocation of labour over time. If everyone in society can produce what he or she must consume to survive, then that society cannot fail to be viable. Specialization and trade only make life easier in such a society. In principle, this test must be applied to any society to see if it is really viable. Let us examine several hypothetical cases to illustrate this point.

Imagine a *Robinson Crusoe* who in each hour of a six-hour day produces one of the six use values adequate for the reproduction of his labour power. If he manages to do this, then six 'Crusoes' on adjoining islands, who are equally fit, could form a working community in which each person specializes in the production of one of these six use values throughout a six-hour work day. Let us suppose that they come to an agreement to exchange their products subsequently according to the hours of labour spent to produce them. They are in effect sharing their necessary labour by engaging in a voluntary, non-market exchange of products according to the amount of labour spent on them, because they have collectively agreed that that option makes good sense under the circumstances.

In their working community, the Crusoes spend nothing but productive labour in order to acquire products as use values. The so-called 'capital goods' they have are what they themselves have produced by expending productive labour. We may assume that cost-free services are provided by self-renewing, natural means of production. If we also assume that the pattern of consumption remains unchanged and the efficiency of production makes little material gain in the process, the situation prevailing before and after their agreement will be, for all intents and purposes, identical. Since each man could have survived in isolation as a Robinson Crusoe, it is only reasonable to expect that each worker will be capable of producing at least as much, as part of this working community. Therefore, when trading takes place, each of the community members can obtain at least the six use values required for their reproduction, just as did the isolated Robinson Crusoe. In other words, equivalence is here established between *diversified production in isolation* and *specialized production with mutual trade*. This minimum condition must be met for a society to be viable. Since commodities are exchanged for one another at value-proportional prices in this imaginary or hypothetical association of Crusoes, it can provide a reference point when we are evaluating the capitalist exchange of commodities, which must take place at prices that diverge from values.

Next, imagine that a pirate ship arrives on the scene and demands tributary goods from the Crusoes. The pirates are not direct producers; they obtain use values by coercion. While the community of Crusoes is individually and collectively productive, the pirates, who live off the avails of extortion, are unproductive and parasitic. If the Crusoes, as direct producers, produced only for themselves and paid themselves a money wage just adequate to permit an exchange of all commodities produced, prices would be proportional to values. Since they must now work to feed the pirates, value–price proportionality cannot be maintained.

Although it is accomplished without direct physical coercion, the appropriation of surplus value from the direct producers in capitalist society accounts for a similar divergence of prices from values in that society. This does not change the fact that the *real social cost of capitalistically produced commodities* is the expenditure of socially necessary labour, just as in any society. This cost must be recognized as distinct from the *private* (pirate or capitalist) *cost of the appropriation of products* (from the Crusoes or industrial workers respectively).

The pirates of our fable have no reason to value tributary goods in proportion to the labour spent by others for their production. This non-proportionality does not matter so long as the relation between them and the Crusoes is strictly extra-economic. The economic life of the exploiting class and that of the exploited class can be effectively segregated here, as it can in any pre-capitalist society, because the economy is not governed by commodity-economic principles. Let us now examine some of the complexities of capitalism, where commodity-economic principles do prevail and the segregation referred to is not maintained.

In capitalist society, the supply of material commodities is regulated by the price mechanism of the society-wide market, such that if a commodity is overproduced, a fall in its price checks overexpansion and, if it is underproduced, a rise in its price encourages further expansion. During the period of balanced growth, in the prosperity phase of the regularly recurring capitalist business cycle, market prices tend to reflect, however indirectly, the values of commodities. The same thing, however, cannot be expected in the case of labour power. The rise and fall of its price cannot bring about a swift adjustment of its supply. Because labour power is not a capitalistically produced commodity, its value cannot be determined in the same way as the value of other commodities. The labour market does not determine an equilibrium wage rate, but rather a *feasible wage range*. Although labour power is not 'factory produced', it has a value equal to the value of 'subsistence' (or of the basket of wage goods a productive worker employed by capital must buy and consume to reproduce his or her labour power).

The exchange of labour power for wage goods is not an ordinary exchange of commodities. It is an exchange of commodities through the production process. In an exchange of material commodities, both commodities exist at the moment of exchange. When labour power is purchased at the start of the production process, however, wage goods, their equivalents and surplus value, symbolically represented as v + s, do not exist. They only emerge as a result of the capitalist's investment in c + v, or in constant and variable capital, to begin that process. They are produced when labour power is productively consumed in the production process of capital. Thus, by purchasing labour power as a commodity in exchange for wage goods, capital converts all products of labour into products of capital. The 'distribution' or division of the *value product* (v + s) into that which is needed for the reproduction of labour power (v), together with surplus value (s), is a foregone conclusion in the very process of forming the value product (v + s). The latter is not a pre-existing pie to be freely shared between labour and capital. It is rather akin to buying a hen's ability to lay ten eggs with five that it will only later lay. It is through such an irregular trade that capitalism hangs together.

Capitalistically produced commodities, exchanged at normal prices, ensure that productive labour is optimally allocated in the socially necessary quantities, while the wages paid to wage workers enable them to buy back the entire product of their necessary labour (or the wage goods necessary to reproduce their labour power). Capitalists will not only recover the value of their capital, they will also appropriate the entire product of the workers' surplus labour as surplus value.

Capitalism synthesizes the pirates' method of pricing with a viability condition that must be satisfied in any society, which is that all direct producers are guaranteed access only to the product of their necessary labour. Just as the pirates had to ensure that the Crusoes were able to continue reproducing their labour power, even as they began to produce tributary goods as well, so also does capitalism see to it that the pricing of goods as commodities ensures both the ongoing reproduction of labour power and the appropriation of surplus value by capitalists.[16]

The labour theory of value stems from the fact that only productive labour, because of its abstract-human property, can be applied *indifferently* to the production of all use values as commodities in a capitalistically managed production process. Though we employ the term 'value' to refer to this economic principle, which is specific to capitalism, there is nothing ethical or subjective about this use of the term. Productive elements are often broadly classified into three categories: natural means of production (N_m), the 'produced' means of production (P_m) and labour power (L_p). Of these factors, the 'produced' means of production are intermediate goods, and the others are original factors of production. All these factors are, without question, productive of use values. That is to say, they all yield services which contribute to the production of a use value. That, however, does not guarantee that they are also *value productive*.

The factor of production that forms value must be capable of performing not only concrete-useful labour but abstract-general labour as well. In other words, it must be a factor that is not bound to the production of a particular use value. Non-natural, reproducible means of production, or 'capital goods', are capitalistically produced commodities (C') and are, as such, in possession of value from the outset. When they are productively consumed, their old value, as constant capital, c, in c + v is preserved and transferred to the value of the new product (c + v + s), but adds no new value to that product. Being non-malleable, means of production are specific to the production of a particular use value and are arranged in a manner that is specific to its production; thus, they cannot achieve an indifference to use values. The service that a 'produced' means of production yields is, in other words, always 'concrete-useful'. There is no such thing as abstract-general or abstract-physical capital which is capable of producing any and all use values indifferently. Not only can heterogeneous means of production not form the socially uniform quality of value, they must depend on the concrete-useful aspect of productive labour, simultaneously engaged by industrial capital, if their value is to be transferred to the product. If they are not employed together with labour power, they cannot even preserve for long the value already embodied in them.

It might be hypothesized that the natural means of production, generically represented by land, is responsible for the formation of value. Actually, the means of production provided by the earth do not participate in the production of value at all. Since land and other natural resources are 'free gifts' of nature they possess neither value nor any social cost, provided they are used wisely rather then squandered. As it happened, landlords in nineteenth-century capitalist Britain tended to take the stewardship of land very seriously and, therefore, made certain that capital did not destroy the productivity of land. Because the responsibility of maintaining the productivity of nature fell on the class of non-capitalist landlords and not on the capitalist class, capitalists and their apologists could view the land they rented or leased from responsible landlords as having an unlimited capacity for self-renewal.

A purely capitalist society (on which the definition of capitalism must be based) assumes the presence of a class of landlords as a 'presupposition', or an initial condition, which must be present if capital is to begin its autonomous operation. Just as the state's presence is implicit in purely capitalist society, so also is an adequate conservation of the natural environment. Over the past century, however, corporate and state-dominated societies have destroyed topsoil, wildlife, water resources and many other fragile and non-renewable resources, so we cannot simply appropriate the naive, early-nineteenth-century capitalist view that land and regional ecosystems will necessarily possess adequate resilience to resist the devastation humans visit upon them.

Natural means of production play an essential role in the production of material wealth, but their services are unfit to create value because they are employed quite specifically for the production of a particular use value. They cannot be applied indifferently to the production of any use value. Land comes only in various concrete-useful forms. Pieces of land are acquired for their location, fertility, etc. Thus, unlike labour power, means of production, whether natural or produced, cannot yield the abstract-general service of producing any commodity required.

PRODUCTION OF ABSOLUTE AND RELATIVE SURPLUS VALUE

When the labour-and-production process common to all societies is capitalistically operated as a value-formation-and-augmentation process, the prevailing workers-versus-capitalist relation, which is perfected as labour power, becomes increasingly commodified, enabling capital continuously to raise the productive powers of labour, in order to maximize the product of the workers' surplus labour in the form of surplus value. Since the value of the means of production, which were produced earlier, is transferred to the new product during current production as these means of production are consumed, they clearly do not form or augment new value. Although it is undeniable that productive labour cannot be performed without the assistance of means of production, they are really only an instrument which enables variable capital to produce surplus value. *Surplus value* thus refers to the difference between the newly produced value, created by workers during the production process, and the value paid for their labour power. Hence, when a capitalist advances $c + v$ to produce $c + v + s$, the relation between labour and capital is expressed by the *rate of surplus value* (s / v) rather than by the *rate of profit* ($s / [c + v]$). The rate of surplus value shows how socially necessary labour time is divided into necessary and surplus labour time.

The rate of surplus value (s / v) can be interpreted as being determined either by the length of the working day ($t = s + v$), given the length of the necessary labour time (v), or by the length of the necessary labour time (v), given the length of the working day (t). In the former case, we are fixing our attention on *absolute surplus value*; in the latter case, we focus our attention on *relative surplus value*. Any production of surplus value is both absolute and relative depending on how one looks at it, Marx's view notwithstanding (1969, p.299). If it is viewed simply as an excess of newly produced value over the reproduced value of labour power, surplus value is absolute. In other words, if the production of surplus value is increased while the necessary labour time is held constant, then absolute surplus value is said to have been produced. Absolute surplus value can be increased by extending the length of the working day or by intensifying the labour, assuming a given technology and value of labour power. If it is viewed as relative to the technical conditions determining the value of labour power, then surplus value is relative. If surplus value is increased by a technical advance which lowers the value of labour power, while the working day is assumed to remain constant, then relative surplus value is said to have been raised.

The point of view of absolute surplus value enables one to study surplus value production with a given technology for the production of wage goods. Capital strives for as *extensive* and *intensive* a working day as possible. Given the quantity of necessary labour, the production of absolute surplus value is possible up to the point where the worker no longer is capable of reproducing his labour power through consumption and rest. In other words, capital strives (1) to extend the working day; (2) to intensify labour; and (3) to reduce real wages to the limit. What the limit will be depends on physical and historical conditions. Capital's ability to pursue greater absolute surplus value by lengthening the working day has been limited by state legislation and union contract in historical capitalism, but, even in the absence of such legislation, capital cannot continuously overextend the length of the working day without threatening the reproduction of labour power. Thus, it is correct even at the level of pure theory to assume a limit to this practice.

Even if the length of the working day is fixed and the intensity of labour unchanged, it is still possible to extend the surplus labour time by shortening the necessary labour time. The necessary labour time is shortened if less time is taken to produce the basket of wage goods required by workers, thus permitting an increase in the rate of surplus value. The production of relative surplus value, as this is called, best suits capital because there is no limit, in principle, to the advancement of capitalist society's powers of production.

The production of relative surplus value involves a technical change that lowers the length of the necessary labour time. While technical progress in the production of luxury goods (consumer goods for capitalists) does not entail a higher productivity in wage goods, a technical improvement in the production of capital goods does have an indirect effect on the production of wage goods and, consequently, does lower the necessary labour time and the value of labour power while raising relative surplus value.

Individual capitalists do not set out to improve the technical method of production generally in society when they strive to lower the reproduction cost and value of labour power. They do so inadvertently in their quest for *extra surplus value*. Individual capitalists gain extra surplus value when they are among the first to adopt new productive methods. They are able to produce their commodity with less labour time than their competitors and so derive extra surplus value. However, this only encourages competing capitalists also to adopt the new method, so that the value of the commodity falls as the labour time required for its production decreases and the extra surplus value which went to the innovator disappears. With the diffusion of the innovative technique, the social value of the commodity is soon determined by that technique, because labour generally has become more productive, while the total outlay of both capital and output have, in most cases, increased. The diffusion of the new technique usually extends over some duration, allowing a few progressive capitalists to earn extra surplus value during that period. The reason for this is that the new technique is, in most cases, embodied in fixed capital equipment (such as machinery) which will not be introduced by the majority of capitalists in an industry until their old machinery is sufficiently depreciated.

Even though a class of property-less workers is created during the process of primitive accumulation, this does not guarantee that capitalists will be able to employ them to produce surplus value. The factory must be adapted to make the best use of available labour power. The production of absolute and relative surplus value presupposes an industrial process in which capital can consume the labour power of wage-earning workers, without vocational or occupational restrictions. Such a condition is satisfied only with the establishment of the modern factory system, a form in which craftsmanship and specialized skills are, by and large, eliminated.

THE MODERN FACTORY SYSTEM

Capitalism exploits the productive powers of *collective labour* by (1) *cooperation*, which entails the gathering together of a group of labourers in a single location to permit capitalist supervision; (2) dividing up shop labour so that, increasingly, unskilled labourers may be employed in a process referred to as *manufacture*; and (3) mechanizing productive instruments in modern *mechanized industry*, such that the work is simplified and deskilled, at the same time that control over the means of production passes from workers to capitalists. The latter are, thus, in a position to see that the speed and intensity of labour are increased to the greatest degree possible, thus raising productivity. Once these three conditions are met, workers generally can no longer maintain their lives without labouring in a capitalist factory equipped with machinery. The use of an assembly of machines entails the increasing perfection of labour power as a commodity.

The maturation of the capitalist method of production simplifies the labour process and renders the mobility of labour virtually costless. Labour power is *standardized* and is reduced to the single Hegelian *matter* of an unskilled working capacity, which is indifferent to the specific character of that labour. To this matter, however, the *form* of cost becomes attached, because the capitalist, whose production no longer depends on the specific labour power of particular workers, but rather on standardized labour power, purchased in a vast, impersonal market from anonymous workers for a money value, does not recognize the *difference* of this particular *thing* from the other elements of production he has purchased. Thus, we have just described, in the appropriate Hegelian terms, how *matter* is submerged in *form* as the capitalist method of production matures (Hegel 1975, pp.184–8).

Cooperation socializes the labour-and-production process. Craftsmanship becomes less important as labour power becomes more uniform. Productivity rises, not because of the increased skills of individual workers, but because of the discipline and specialization made possible by collective labour. In the process, workers become indifferent to the alienated labour they perform, but capitalists are better able to exercise their authority in order to ensure that waste and inefficiency are minimized and means of production costs are reduced. Since it is the capitalists who organize the workers' labour, the increasing productive powers of that labour appear as the productive powers of capital.

In *manufacture*, no single worker goes through the whole process of production, but only a narrowly subdivided part of it. Workers lose touch with the integrated whole of productive activity. Because they are no longer capable of functioning as independent craftspersons, the speed and intensity of organized labour is more easily raised, thus increasing the productivity of the capitalist enterprise. The organized division of labour promotes the skill and efficiency of the workers in each specialized section of the capitalist factory and differentiates tools and machines accordingly, whereas the simplification of labour allows some completely unskilled workers to be employed, even if they are still subordinate to their more highly trained colleagues whose technical skills cannot yet be eliminated.

Whereas cooperation makes the capitalist the workers' supervisor, thus ensuring their punctuality and regular performance, manufacture makes him their organizer. However, it is only the development of *modern mechanized industry*, with its centrally coordinated machinery, which enables him to organize and supervise the direct producers by means of the machinery they set in motion – whether these are *machines to generate power, transmission machines*, or *working machines*. The first two types of machine magnify the productivity of the last, which may be viewed as derivative of the traditional hand tools which were taken out of the hands of workers and incorporated into mechanical systems. Working machines are thus no longer the servile instruments which handicraft workers operated at their own initiative, but mechanisms by which capitalists reduce workers to appendages of machines that are intended to control their every movement. The mechanized labour-and-production process is an engineering process into which labour power is fed like raw materials. The cooperation and division of labour, combined with mechanization, so reduce the need for handicraft skills that unskilled labour becomes almost universal in the working process.

The increase in the productivity of the mechanized capitalist factory during the liberal era was unprecedented and made possible dramatic industrial progress. Machines were not adopted by the capitalist because they lessened the quantity of labour required for the production of use values, however, but because they raised the rate of surplus value. In other words, a more productive machine is introduced in a capitalist society because an extra surplus value accrues to the innovating capitalist. It is, therefore, quite consistent that the mechanization of industry does not reduce the expenditure of productive labour. Indeed, the immediate effect of the Industrial Revolution was the intensification of labour and the extension of the working day.

More important to the social position of the working class, however, is the fact that the simplification of labour accomplished by mechanization confirms or completes the conversion of labour power into a commodity. Machines render the skills or extra physical strength of most workers useless, and allow women and even child labourers to compete for employment on equal footing with male workers, whose skills have been rendered obsolete. This extends the working population employed by capital, while depressing wages. This simplification of labour, which standardizes labour power, makes it possible to fire workers as easily as they can be hired, in response to changing market conditions. It presupposes an advanced division of labour, which, in turn, presupposes collective labour. Hence, a modern worker is characterized by (1) lack of individuality; (2) loss of skill; and (3) indifference to labour.

Mechanized methods of production tend to displace traditional methods swiftly because of their incomparably greater productivity, while leading to greater concentrations of capital and the formation en masse of available labour power. The groundwork of capitalist production is thereby laid as the workers become subservient to the machinery, which represents the power of capital.

WAGES, OR THE PRICE OF LABOUR POWER

With the establishment of the modern factory, *labour power* becomes available to capital as the source of completely indifferent productive labour. Yet labour power is not a capitalistically producible commodity. It remains the only simple commodity involved in capitalist production. Labour power cannot be exchanged for existing products. It can only be exchanged for that which it itself produces, since the capitalist does not have the wage goods to pay for labour power at the beginning of the contractual period. Labour power is thus paid only at the end of that period, when wage goods have already been produced. Although the exchange of labour power for wage goods is no ordinary exchange of commodities, the capitalist–production relation cannot be maintained unless this exchange is endlessly repeated.

Even though the capitalist pays money corresponding to his variable capital in order to buy labour power, labour power is a commodity only at the moment of purchase. As soon as it is purchased, it can no longer be resold and, hence, ceases to be a commodity. This makes it easier for the capitalist to avoid seeing that he has bought it as a commodity. He prefers to believe that labour services are purchased rather than commodified labour power. This impression is, of course, fallacious, because waged workers in capitalist society cannot perform useful services on their own initiative and responsibility.

Labour is the service yielded by the consumption of labour power; it is not a material object that can become a commodity. Since the capitalist has purchased this labour power for a definite period, he has the right to decide how to consume it during the same period. This may not be acknowledged, however, because labour power is a special commodity, inseparable from the person who owns it and offers it on the market. The worker must work in order to generate labour; hence, it appears as if the worker were consuming his/her own labour power rather than the capitalist who purchased that labour power. However, once labour power is simplified and standardized, it is the capitalist purchaser who decides how it is to be used. The worker is not permitted to consume his/her own labour power or to exercise his capacity to produce use values without instructions from the purchaser as to what use value is to be produced and how his labour power is to be exercised during its production.

The *wage form* predates capitalism and will doubtless survive its demise. It originally arose as compensation for a definite piece of work performed by a craftsperson, such as a carpenter. However, the wage-payment system is an appropriate form in which to contain the unnatural trade of labour power for wage goods, because it allows the capitalist to avoid paying the value of labour power until after it has produced value for him. Still, it must be emphasized that labour power is a commodity, not because of the form of the wage-payment, but in spite of it.

The value of labour power is always paid after the expenditure of productive labour. The abstract and the concrete aspects of this labour are performed concurrently, producing value and use value simultaneously. Moreover, no bell rings in a capitalist factory to indicate when workers have completed their necessary labour and have begun their surplus labour. This creates the illusion that the payment received by the wage-earner, whether as a *time wage* (the value of a day's labour power divided by the number of hours worked) or as a *piece wage* (the value of a day's labour power divided by the units produced therein) is for the labour they have performed. In reality, workers' wages are determined by the *value of labour power* (v) and not by the *value product* (v + s) that is produced, as their labour power is exercised or consumed.

The delivery of the use value of an ordinary commodity is assumed to take place at the moment of purchase or payment, whereas labour power surrenders its use value slowly as it is productively consumed in the production of value objects for the capitalist. The capitalist cannot pay for the value of labour power until the worker has produced commodities that embody value. A purchaser of a normal commodity would demand a refund if it proved to be defective; however, in the case of the special commodity of labour power, it is sold with the concession that payment need not be made until its use value is consumed, because the worker who has sold his labour power may not always be able to exercise it (for example, due to illness).

Despite fundamental differences in substance, the wage form is the same, whether paid to a traditional service worker or to a capitalist productive worker. Hence arises the confusion between the value of labour power, v, and the value product, v + s, it produces, which the capitalist rationalizes as a mercantilist operation of buying v + s cheap and selling it dear. Knowledge of the law of value, which demonstrates that the existence of capitalism is identical with the validity of the labour theory of value, allows one to overcome the confusion of v and v + s. It reveals that if wage-earners received more than the product of their necessary labour, labour power would not be reproduced as a commodity and capitalism would not exist as a historical society.

The value of labour power is determined by the reproduction cost of that labour power; that is, the cost of a typical worker's wage-basket of commodities. Capitalists regard the wages they pay as their labour cost of production. However, if a direct producer works for twelve hours a day and reproduces his/her labour power in the first six hours, the real cost to society is twelve hours of productive labour, even if the capitalist employer only pays the equivalent of the first six hours. By regarding money wages as the price of labour rather than that of labour power, the capitalist fails to see how he acquires the surplus value representing six hours of surplus labour in the production process of capital. Since the money value of the investment, c + v, represents the cost of production to the capitalist, the output C' of C...P...C' cannot contain any more than the money value of c + v. Thus, from the viewpoint of the capitalist, the production of surplus value is itself the realization of surplus value in the process, C' – M'. The *capitalist's conception of cost*, therefore, makes it impossible to isolate the production process of capital C...P...C' from the sphere of circulation.

Industrial capital, like merchant capital but unlike moneylending capital, constitutes a *metamorphosis of value*. That is to say, the value of capital assumes and alternately discards the forms of money, productive elements, and a commodity for sale. *Productive elements* consist of the means of production, which retain their value in the production process, and labour power, which does not. The concept of metamorphosis does not apply to the labour process, because labour power is not a capitalistically produced commodity which necessarily embodies value. Labour power acquires value only contingently in the act of sale, due to the operation of factors external to itself. Wage earners reproduce their labour power as a use value in their individual consumption process. Unlike capitalists, they have not chosen this particular use value from many other use values because it is the best way to form and augment value, but because they cannot offer anything else. In reproducing their labour power, therefore, wage earners do not produce value, but a use value that acquires value indirectly through the operation of the commodity economy that converts labour power into a commodity.

Since wages are paid after the labour is performed, capital need not conceive of wages as the direct expression of the value of labour power. Moreover, with the adoption of the form of wages, capital no longer need view its production process as interrupting its circulation process. Rather, it can subjectively dissolve its production process in an uninterrupted flow of its circulation process – a process in which managerial and productive labour appear to cooperate in order to generate the capitalist's revenue and the workers' wages, and only the means of production are viewed as 'capital'. Indeed, because wages are paid out of the income from the sale of the product, it does not appear that variable capital is advanced at all, and, thus, the wage bill can be viewed as the workers' legitimate share of the value of the new product. This capitalist rationalization not only mystifies the true source of surplus value, while reasserting the original concept of capital as the circulation form in which nothing but the metamorphosis of value can take place; it also suppresses the distinction between the production and formal transformation of value. Capital in the form of industrial capital is now ready to rediscover itself as a circulation form.

3
The Circulation and Reproduction of Capital

Following Sekine (1984, p.366), the circulation process of capital parallels Hegel's doctrine of *appearance*. If the operation of capital is looked at from the side of production, 'it is matter or subsistence'; if it is looked at from the side of circulation, it 'is also form'. But it is always capital, which produces and circulates commodities. If capital only produced or only circulated, it would not be capitalism at all. According to Hegel (1975, p.186), 'essence must appear or shine forth. Its shining or reflection-in-it is the suspension and translation of it to immediacy ... As reflection-on-self it is [not only] matter or subsistence [but] ... also form, reflection-on-something-else, a subsistence which sets itself aside'. Similarly, in the dialectic of capital, the *appearance*, or circulation process, of capital holds in combination the two elements of 'reflection-into-self' and 'reflection-into-another'. *Reflection-into-self* may be interpreted to apply to what capital does inside the factory, and *reflection-into-another* applies to what capital does in the open market.

Capital does not merely transform productive elements into use values inside the factory. It also simultaneously forms and augments value. Capital must not only produce but also circulate commodities. No value or surplus value is created in the *circulation of commodities*, but some capital must be invested in circulation if a costly interruption of production is to be avoided. It is imperative that capitalists minimize *circulation costs* to maximize the production of surplus value. From the point of view of the *circulation process of capital*, no value is produced unless realized and no value is realized unless produced. Thus, the motion of industrial capital cannot be fully comprehended in isolation from its circulatory phases of buying and selling commodities (M—C, C'—M') outside factories. The production process of capital (C...P...C') is enclosed within these circulatory processes that together constitute the circulation process of capital (M—C...P...C'—M'). Thus, in this context, the term 'circulation process' does not refer to the simple circulation of capital, which can only buy and sell commodities already made, but to the circulatory motion of industrial capital as a whole, which can also organize the material process of production that constitutes its foundation. From the vantage point of the circulation process of capital as a whole, the capitalist is a merchant–producer, not merely a merchant or even just a producer. Being a merchant–producer, the capitalist cannot just produce a commodity; he must also trade or circulate commodities.

THE CIRCULAR MOTION OF CAPITAL

As a genuine form of capital, industrial capital must repeat its chrematistic operation ad infinitum. In order to establish the self-repeating necessity of industrial capital, and to determine it as a never-ending circular motion, we must now investigate the three circuits of capital: the *circuit of money capital* (M—C...P...C'—M'); the *circuit of productive capital* (P...C'—M'.M—C...P); and the *circuit of commodity capital* (C'—M'.M—C...P...C'). The *circular motion of capital* can only be fully accounted for or adequately represented by the unity of these three circuits.

The circuit of money capital represents the purely commodity-economic or mercantilist view that capital is a chrematistic operation motivated by the individual desire for self-enrichment. The circuit of productive capital enables the continuing motion of capital to accommodate itself to the nature-imposed necessity of reproducing use values. This circuit, which views the circulation of commodities (C'—M'.M—C) as an interruption of its capitalist activity, represents the classical view of capital. For it, the primary function of capital is the individual capitalist accumulation of wealth in real terms. Thus, this circuit emphasizes the periodic renewal of real capital (means of production) necessary for the reproduction of wealth as use values. The factory, at any moment of time, consists of productive elements and semi-finished products of various kinds and at various stages of completion in definite proportions. Depending on whether P at the beginning of the circuit is equal to or smaller than P at its end, reproduction is defined as *simple* or *expanding*.

The circuit of commodity capital differs from the other two in beginning and ending, not with the advance of capital in money or in material form, but with the result of capitalist production. This circuit views the motion of capital as the unceasing supplier of use values in the form of commodities. Thus, it begins with C', which already contains surplus value. The formation and augmentation of value is, therefore, a fait accompli. There is a fundamental difference between C, which contains labour power, and, therefore, cannot remain in the circulation sphere, and C', which does not contain labour power and must immediately enter that sphere. Its output, C', has, therefore, been produced indifferently to use values.

In the circuit of money capital (M—M'), the sequence of sale and purchase (C'—M'.M—C), which involves the exchange of C' for C, depends on the capitalist's will to enrich himself. One capitalist can complete his process of self-enrichment with C'—M' only if another capitalist starts a similar process with M—C. The dependence of the one on the other, however, is accidental, not necessary. The circuit of money capital, in other words, is dependent on a universal desire for self-enrichment, which, by itself is subjective and *contingent*. In the circuit of productive capital (P—P), the same sequence is viewed as imposed by the *natural necessity* of reproduction.

In contrast with the above circuits, the circuit of commodity capital (C'—C') must ensure a further supply of C'. It is inherent in the operation of this circuit that the proceeds of its commodity products should be ploughed back into C, which is required for further commodity production (C'). Indeed, the circulatory phase, C'—M'.M—C, of this circuit ensures that the process of commodity exchanges, C'—M—C, is an on-going one. The conversion of C' into C, which guarantees the continuing motion of industrial capital, takes place only in a *social* context. When a capitalist society sells its commodity products in C'—M', that same society must already have bought elements of production in the M—C of another capital. Thus, only this circuit, which highlights the cross-sectoral interconnection and exchange of all commodities for all other commodities, reveals the commodity-economic necessity to maintain the *circular flow of capital*. All *circular-flow models* of the capitalist economy are, therefore, based on the circuit of commodity capital. The exact structure of this inter-sectoral exchange will be elaborated upon later, in the theory of the reproduction schemes, which is based on this circuit.

The *continuing motion of industrial capital* consists of a triplex of all these circuits. Every capitalist enterprise holds part of its capital in the form of money, commodities and functioning productive elements. Indeed, viewed spatially, a capitalist firm is typically divided into its factory, sales office (warehouse) and purchasing department (cashier's office). The factory supervisor typically views capital as consisting of productive elements; the sales manager views capital as primarily consisting of the stock of saleable commodities; and the purchasing department typically views it as the money available to buy productive elements. These different conceptions of capital are all one-sided: capital is indeed all of them!

Money capital and commodity capital may be viewed collectively as *circulation capital*, as opposed to *productive capital*. The magnitude of capital tied up in each depends on the lengths of time required for the circulation (purchase and sale) and the production of a particular commodity. The *turnover time of capital* consists of the durations of the circulation and production periods. Capital incurs *circulation costs* by having to take time in the unproductive process of circulation and, hence, by having to hold circulation capital unproductively. Capital saves this cost by going through the circulation period as quickly as possible, thus progressively reducing its length. The *ordinary circulation cost* is the amount of additional surplus value that could have been earned if it were possible to reduce the circulation period to zero.

Commercial labour, which may be viewed as an extension of the capitalist's own managerial labour, includes all forms of labour relating to the adminis-tration of the business. Managers and technocrats assist capitalists, because capitalists alone cannot oversee all aspects of the administration of the business. The capitalist's unproductive labour, unlike the productive labour of wage-earners, does not tend to be simplified with the development of the capitalist mode of production. Rather, it becomes increasingly complex and diverse, thus requiring more and more specialized expertise and personnel. Just because no productive labour can be exercised without the capitalist's or his agents' management and direction does not mean that either may be deemed productive workers or direct producers.

Capitalists must also invest capital and firms must commit resources to the purely circulatory, and, therefore, unproductive activity of buying and selling products as commodities. Sales shops must be maintained and books must be kept. Such activities give rise to *pure circulation costs*, sometimes referred to as the capitalist's *unproductive costs*, since purely commercial labour not only does not form or augment value, as does productive labour; it does not even transfer the value of the material resources that it consumes to a new product that it produces. The distinction between *productive* and *unproductive labour* is absolutely crucial to the understanding of the law of value. Any labour which does not directly or indirectly involve the physical transformation of a natural object is unproductive by definition. Thus, the labour that is specifically required for the functioning of the commodity economy, such as the buying and selling of commodities, is neither trans-historic nor productive.

The production of use values, unlike the circulation of commodities, is supra- or trans-historic. So is productive labour, unlike commercial labour. No society can exist without its members purposively organizing themselves to work with nature to derive use values. Productive labour also produces value and surplus value in capitalism, because no use value can be produced therein except as value which, in turn, includes a surplus-value component. Only productive labour produces value and surplus value because only it produces use values. Therefore, labour which does not form value or produce surplus value is unproductive, and vice versa.

Pure circulation costs represent a deduction from surplus value already realized. Capital strives for the shortest possible circulation period. While unproductive workers are not exploited in the Marxian sense that they produce commodities and surplus value, the capitalists do endeavour to pay commercial labourers as little as possible and strive to have them work as long and intensely as possible. In this fashion, capitalists significantly decrease the deduction of pure circulation costs from surplus value. The unfair treatment of these workers does not affect the production relation between capitalists and workers, established in the production process of capital. The extent to which the capitalist 'exploits' his sales personnel and other unproductive workers determines only how much of the surplus value, which the capitalist has already appropriated from productive workers, must now be shared with unproductive workers. To reiterate, the pressures that capitalists impose on unproductive workers do not affect the rate of exploitation, which entails the appropriation of surplus value from productive workers.

Only the unproductive, business administrative labour of the capitalist and his agents can legitimately be dealt with in pure theory. Unproductive, personal-service labour and public-administrative labour play no part in the theory of pure capitalism. The provision of services involves direct personal relations which cannot be reified by the commodity economy. However, since the commodity economy tends to materialize economic life, pure theory is justified in assuming an economy in which all social relations are commodity economic and, thus, susceptible of objective explanation. Stage theory and empirical history will treat the provision of such services, which also contribute to the survival of societies – including capitalist ones – in the light of the theoretical distinction between productive and unproductive labour developed in pure theory.

The storing and transporting of productive materials and products, although closely allied to the circulatory operation of buying and selling, also materially affect the 'consumability' of use values in capitalism. To the extent that the storage and transportation of use values cannot be avoided in any society (or inside particular production facilities), they must be considered part of the production process. In capitalist societies, however, goods are moved or stored not merely to deliver use values at the right place and time, but also to profit from speculation. This activity, together with the labour entailed in it, is not common to all societies, nor is it derivative of use-value production; thus, it must be judged unproductive.

The case of storage and transportation illustrates an important aspect of the labour theory of value, namely, that the *substance of value* is supra-historical, though its form is commodity economic. Without a commodity there is no value; hence, productive labour does not form value in all societies. Yet in capitalist society, which organizes its economic life according to commodity-economic logic, the labour which forms value is itself not uniquely commodity economic. Value is the commodity-economic expression of the universal social norm that, in any society, the provision of a use value costs or entails productive labour. An objective analysis of the capitalist mode of production would be impossible if this concept of *social real cost* could not be distinguished from the capitalist concept of *private, individual cost*.

THE TURNOVER OF CAPITAL

Capital maximizes the *efficiency* (or minimizes the costs) *of value augmentation*. The *production of value* (rather than of use value) cannot be completed in the production process of capital. A use value that is meant to embody value is created therein, but it is in circulation that value is measured and the commodity is confirmed as a value object. Thus, not until the commodity is sold for money is its value either realized or produced. For capital, therefore, circulation is just as important and essential as production. Capital cannot waste time or money either in circulation or in production. If too much must be deducted from surplus value as circulation costs, the production of commodities may not be profitable.

If the purchase cost of productive elements is reduced as far as is technically feasible, the efficiency of value augmentation can be further improved only by a shortening of the *turnover time of capital*. The capitalist rationality of a quick turnover compels not only the shortening of the circulation period as much as possible, but also the shortening of the production period (by the intensification of labour, for example) so as to accelerate the production of surplus value. By making sure that no capital value stands idle within a given turnover time, the capitalist ensures that the efficiency of value formation and augmentation is as great as is technically possible.

Means of production, as part of productive capital, are classified into *circulating constant capital* or *fixed constant capital*, depending on whether all their value is transferred to the product during one or a number of production periods. For example, raw materials are entirely consumed in one production period, but tools and machines are used over many production periods. Supplementary or auxiliary materials such as fuels, which are only indirectly conducive to the production of use values and which are unlikely to be used over many production periods, may be categorized as circulating. The distinction arises strictly because of the mode of transfer of value; thus, this classification does not apply to items of unproductive circulation capital or pure circulation costs.

The distinction between fixed and circulating constant capital does not depend on how heavy, complex or durable the capital good is. Moreover, the same physical object can be classified either as fixed or as circulating depending on how it is used in the production process. For example, if cattle are used over many circuits to produce milk for the market, they are categorized as fixed, but, if they are raised and then slaughtered to produce meat for the market, they are considered as circulating capital. When cattle are sold as commodities, however, they are commodity capital, and, hence, are neither fixed nor circulating. Incidentally, routine plant maintenance costs are circulating, if regularly incurred, whereas unpredictable breakdowns must be covered by insurance, which is a circulation cost.

The *turnover time of circulating capital* is determined by the sum of the production period and the circulation period, because together they constitute the time which elapses between the initial purchase of circulating capital as the means of production and the moment at which its value, having been recovered in the form of money, is capable of repurchasing the same items. The magnitude of circulating capital which must be advanced and tied up is directly proportional to the length of its turnover time.

Although the turnover time of capital is fundamentally determined by the turnover time of variable capital, which produces surplus value, variable capital does not really turn over, as does constant capital. Constant capital literally turns over because the same value is preserved throughout many periods of production and of circulation and undergoes only a formal metamorphosis. First, constant capital in the form of money purchases means of production that then transfer their value to the product, which is sold for money. Finally, the pre-existing value comes back again in the same form and is ready to begin another cycle. By contrast, variable capital loses its value as soon as it purchases labour power and, therefore, does not transfer its value to the product. The value of the original variable capital is paid out as wages, which are spent by the workers, not as capital but as revenue that is entirely devoted to consumption. Workers must reproduce the value of their labour power and embody it in the commodity product if capital is to be successful. The reproduced value of labour power first appears in the newly produced commodity, together with surplus value. It is this newly reproduced value of labour power, not the original value advanced as variable capital, which flows back to the capitalist in the form of money, when the commodity is sold and the capitalist is capable of investing it once again as variable capital. Thus, the *turnover time of variable capital* is not the duration of time required for the reappearance in monetary form of the old value advanced, but rather the duration of time required for the reproduction (or renewal) and realization of the value of labour power consumed in the production process.

The *turnover of fixed capital* cannot be ascertained easily, because it takes place over a number of production processes and thus requires a lengthy period of time to complete itself. The value of fixed capital is thus transferred to the new product piecemeal as it wears out such that every sale of the product must recover part of that advanced value in the form of money. The money recovered at the end of each turnover period of circulating capital must be accumulated as *depreciation funds*; it cannot be used to repurchase the depreciated part of the fixed capital until the renewal time arrives. Thus, the capital value invested in a machine with a five-year lifespan cannot turn over in less than five years. We may conclude that the *turnover time of fixed capital* is determined by the durability of the particular machinery purchased and employed.

The dependence of capitalist production on fixed capital becomes decisive as a result of the mechanization of the production process that completes the conversion of labour power into a commodity. An increasing reliance on fixed capital becomes typical. The presence of ever-increasing amounts of fixed capital adds to the magnitude of total capital which must be advanced for an industrial operation and leads to the *concentration of capital and production*. As will be demonstrated later, investments in heavy machinery and plants tend to occur towards the end of the depression phase of a business cycle. Therefore, the *turnover cycle of durable equipment* tends to shape the periodicity of economic crises.

The capitalist always behaves as if he is consciously pursuing the highest rate of surplus value, because his efforts to raise both the *annual frequency of turnover* and the *efficiency of value augmentation* (or what will later be identified as the rate of profit) in any given turnover also raise the *annual rate of surplus value*.

In order for the capitalist to be able to exchange his commodity, C', for the necessary elements of production, C, the capitalist class as a whole must produce, as commodities, all the use values needed for the reproduction of capitalist society. This means that the aggregate social supply of commodities must include means of production, wage goods necessary for the reproduction of labour power, and consumption goods for capitalists. Of this aggregate supply of commodities, the means of production are purchased by individual capitalists in the C'—M'.M—C process, and wage goods are purchased by workers who receive wages in return for the labour power they have already made available to capitalists. These goods are purchased with money that is originally advanced as capital; however, goods that are produced for the consumption of capitalists and their associates can only be purchased with money, m, which is not originally advanced as capital, but is drawn rather from the *consumption funds of capitalists*. Capitalists can, of course, only advance a sum of money, M, which will be recovered in M' after the turnover period has elapsed, if they also purchase goods to provide for their consumption during that period. Thus, an advance of money M, as capital, is always accompanied by the simultaneous expenditure of money, m, by capitalists out of their consumption funds. The quantity of money required for the circulation of all capitalistically produced commodities is, therefore, greater than the quantity of money advanced as capital by the amount of the aggregate consumption fund of the capitalists.

THE CIRCULATION OF SURPLUS VALUE

Capitalist production cannot continue unless capitalists earn enough surplus value in each turnover of capital at least to maintain an adequate standard of living in the following turnover. The capitalist is not recovering capital he earlier advanced; rather, he is appropriating a portion of the current production of surplus value for his consumption. To say that the whole of surplus value earned in any turnover of capital is used as a consumption fund is to speak of a *simple reproduction*. A simple reproduction occurs when the extent of value augmentation corresponds with the magnitude of the capitalist's consumption fund. Simple reproduction thus constitutes the minimal condition necessary to sustain the circulation process of capital.

The assumption of a simple reproduction is unrealistic. Capitalists are not content to consume excessively. The part of their income that is not strictly necessary for the maintenance of a given standard of living will be saved. In a purely capitalist society, *hoarding* does not mean a miserly accumulation of precious metals, but the temporary holding of surplus value in the form of idle money or funds as part of the turnover of capital. Capital is a form of value augmentation. It pursues value augmentation for its own sake. Capitalists are always attempting to raise their rate of surplus value by turning over their capital faster, by intensifying labour, by extending the working day, and by introducing technical innovations when appropriate. It is the accumulation of capital, not the hoarding of money, which motivates the capitalist pursuit of surplus value that may be converted into additional capital.

The intended accumulation of capital induces a prior pooling of the monetary commodity outside the circulation process. The holding of these accumulation funds is the means rather than the end of the capitalist accumulation of wealth. It is potential capital, or universal money, which is ready to purchase productive elements as soon as the first opportunity arises. This, in consequence, generally leads to a greater mass and value of commodities in circulation, which oversteps the bounds of a simple reproduction, thus allowing capitalists to earn greater surplus value than is required for their consumption funds. By the conversion of freely disposable surplus value into accumulation funds, which eventually yield additional capital, the scale of reproduction becomes *expanded*, which allows a greater scope for the value augmentation of capital.

The circulation of capital generates funds or idle money in a variety of ways. There is, respectively, the consumption fund of the capitalist, a wage fund which need not all be spent immediately, a *depreciation fund* which remains idle until fixed capital must be renewed, and an *accumulation fund*, which must be held over many turnovers until it is large enough to convert into additional capital. The shortening of the circulation period also releases idle money. There are *reserve funds*, which are held by capitalists to guard against unpredictable price fluctuations in the market. When more and more money is held as funds and less is available to be spent on goods, a shortage of monetary gold is the result, but capital has the flexibility to deal with this, as will become clear.

Capitalism, as a rational economic system, strives to minimize the waste of resources. Thus, even money must be economized in capitalist society to the maximum degree compatible with its necessary functions. That is why a *credit system* develops to activate the idle money generated by the circulation process of capital. All kinds of funds currently held by the capitalist, whether for accumulation, consumption, depreciation, or wage payments, but not immediately needed as means of circulation, are deposited with the banking system, which loans them out to other capitalists who are in need of active money for specified periods of time. The credit system makes possible the efficient use of the existing stock of money, thus minimizing the need for an additional production of monetary gold.

Assume that society's productive labour is so allocated that all use values, including gold, are capitalistically produced in the socially desired or necessary quantities. No use value is either overproduced or underproduced relative to demand, because the law of value has already worked its way through the economy. A just adequate production of the monetary metal is guaranteed by the gold-producing industry, which is distinguished by virtue of the fact that its product, C', is already in the form of money, M', and requires no selling operation. Hence, the producers of the monetary metal, who advance money capital, M, and spend a consumption fund, m, throw the sum of M + m into the circulation market. When they produce new gold, C' = M', however, they absorb no money from the market. Thus, the gold-producing sector unilaterally injects money into the circulation sphere by purchasing commodities without selling any.

Even in simple reproduction, the abrasion and loss of some of the circulating monetary gold are unavoidable. Therefore, the production of gold must include a supply of new monetary gold corresponding to the physical depletion of the existing stock of money.

In an agricultural society, the surplus product that is not currently consumed may immediately take the form of productive elements. Grain that is not currently consumed can be used as seed. To expand the scale of its reproduction, more labour may be immediately applied to cultivate more land by planting more seedlings. It is not necessary for gold production first to expand to mediate an expanding reproduction as in capitalist society, where surplus value must always be realized in the form of money. Part of this monetized surplus value feeds into accumulation funds, which will eventually be spent on commodities that are suitable for accumulation, such as additional elements of production. Therefore, an expanded reproduction in capitalist society always presupposes the *formation of accumulation funds*.

The process of accumulating 'investible' funds is by itself sufficient to stimulate the production of monetary gold.

The production of the monetary metal in capitalist society is a *productive* activity, since it transforms part of nature into a use value. In another sense, however, it is also *unproductive*, since this particular use value is strictly commodity economic. In order to accumulate wealth, capitalist society must produce money which cannot be consumed as an ordinary use value, by allocating a portion of society's productive resources for that purpose. To the extent that this occurs, the production of ordinary use values must be sacrificed.

In principle, money in capitalist society is originally a commodity. Only a commodity that can be supplied in the socially desired amount can function as money in capitalist society. There cannot be either a permanent shortage or an excess of the monetary metal in capitalist society. The circulation process of capital, whether in simple or expanded reproduction, is not restricted by the production of gold, which automatically supplies whatever quantity of gold is socially necessary. If more gold is produced than is necessary to meet society's monetary or non-monetary demand for it, the socially necessary labour for its production, or its value, must fall below the quantity of labour actually spent for its production. Thus, gold is overproduced when more than socially necessary labour is spent for its production. This misallocation of resources will cause the market prices of all commodities other than gold to rise above their normal prices. The gold-producing sector, which must buy its productive elements from other sectors, will become relatively less profitable, and its expansion will be slower than in other sectors. If gold is underproduced, the reverse situation will occur. A shortage of the monetary metal sooner or later brings about a rise in the value of money, thus stimulating the allocation of more social labour, current and stored-up, to the gold-producing industry. Hence, the operation of the law of value guarantees that an appropriate quantity of gold or the monetary commodity will tend to be capitalistically produced just as any other commodity.

The actual conversion of surplus value into capital also requires the prior presence of both labour power and means of production, which can be purchased with accumulation funds. However, at this point the circulation of capital or value can no longer be discussed apart from the circulation of product-values. We must now turn to the *reproduction process of capital* in order to explain how accumulation funds are able to convert themselves into additional capital on the basis of available elements of production, which are somehow already present in the market.

THE REPRODUCTION PROCESS OF CAPITAL

According to Sekine (1984, pp.454–5), the reproduction process of capital parallels Hegel's doctrine of *actuality*. The circulation process of one capital presupposes that of other capitals, such that the motions of all the separate units of capital make up the interconnected and integrated motion or actuality of the *aggregate social capital*, which systematically produces and circulates all commodities. This unity of production and circulation recalls the Hegelian 'unity become immediate, of essence with appearance, or of inward with outward' (Hegel 1975, p.200). Similarly, the dialectic of capital demonstrates how production inside factories is controlled and regulated by commodity-economic logic as it operates in the sphere of circulation outside these factories.

For capitalism to be *actual*, it must first be shown to be *possible*. If capitalism is *actual* because it is one of many possibilities, its presence is only *formally necessary* or *contingent*. This *formal stage of actuality* presupposes the reproduction of the value relation, which ensures the reproduction of labour power as a commodity, and proceeds to show that, under this constraint, variable and constant capital, together with surplus value, and the capitalist–production relation, can also be reproduced by capital. If capitalism is *actual*, in the sense that it can satisfy all the material conditions that make it a possibility, capitalism may be said to be a *real possibility* or a *relative necessity*. In the *real stage of actuality*, it is shown that the reproduction of goods by capital in the form of commodities satisfies all the conditions for capitalism to actualize itself. In other words, capitalist society must, like any viable society, produce all goods that are required for its existence. If capitalism is shown to be *self-determined*, such that its *actuality* and *possibility* are no longer separable and it thus only depends on those conditions of existence that it produces for itself, then it has become an *absolute necessity* or *unconditioned actuality*. When the *necessary* becomes *a self-conditioned, self-dependent and self-determined totality*, it attains the status of *absolute actuality* or *absolute necessity* in the Hegelian dialectic (Hegel 1975, p.212). The actual process of capital accumulation is unconditioned in this sense. Capital no longer depends on a contingency after it develops the law of relative surplus population, because capital itself can now make available to itself as a commodity the labour power that it requires to survive. The law of value is thus no longer subject to any external restriction, even though it cannot manufacture or directly produce that labour power.

Since society cannot cease to consume, it cannot cease to produce things. However, since production is socially organized, it must be a continuous or self-repeating process. Since all societies reproduce themselves by reproducing things, the process of production in any society must be a process of reproduction as well. The specific form of organization by which a society arranges itself to ensure that goods are reproduced is called the *mode of production*. The functioning of a mode of production sustains a corresponding *production relation*, but is also dependent upon it. Hence, the reproduction of goods by humankind is never exclusively a natural activity; it is one that is constrained by a social organization of production that envelops it. Every society reproduces not only goods or use values necessary for its survival, but, as well, the specific production relation or social organization of people which sustains the production process in that society.

With respect to labour power, for example, society must guarantee not only the reproduction of goods by which labour power is reproduced through the individual consumption of workers, but also the reproduction of the social relation which ensures that labour power will continue to be available for the reproduction of goods. In feudal society, where goods were produced under a master–servant relation, the reproduction of goods reconfirmed and perpetuated this relation. In capitalist society, where goods are produced as commodities, the reproduction of goods implies the reproduction of the capitalists-versus-workers production relation, just as the reproduction of capital by capital implies the reproduction of material goods or use values as commodities.

The theory of the reproduction process of capital cannot be adequately developed until after the production and circulation processes of capital are fully understood. First, the production process of capital, which produces commodities, is established as the inner core of capitalist society. It then becomes apparent that the continuity of the capitalist process of production also depends on the circulation of capital. Unless a definite part of the total capital advanced takes the unproductive form of circulation capital, the production process of capital will not be able to avoid interruptions. We now must examine the *reproduction process* as the total process that, by synthesizing the production and circulation processes of capitalism, enables capitalist society as a whole to reproduce itself. In this context, the activity of capital is studied, not solely from the viewpoint of production, which constitutes the material foundation of capitalism, nor exclusively from the viewpoint of circulation, which constitutes the chrematistic principle by which this foundation comes to be organized, but rather from the viewpoint of production and circulation, considered as a unified whole. It is this unified process that constitutes the *reproduction of capital by capital* itself.

In our earlier examinations of the production process and the circulation process, we adopted the view of the representative individual capital. However, no aspect of the reproduction process of capital can be understood solely from this point of view. In this view, capital maintains its own value over time through the preservation of the value of constant capital, the transfer of the pre-existing value to new products and the transformation of one type of constant capital into another. Thus, the expenditure of productive labour appears irrelevant. It must be recognized, however, that the circulation process of one capital presupposes that of other capitals. When the motions of all separate units of capital are unified, organized and integrated into an interconnected totality, which systematically produces and circulates all commodities, the *reproduction process of the aggregate social capital* stands revealed. Capitalism forms a historical society only because this process of production and circulation can be organized to allow old means of production to be transformed into new ones on a society-wide basis through the application of productive labour.

The necessity of shifting the focus of attention from the individual to the social first arises in the treatment of the circulation of surplus value. The analysis of the circulation of surplus value requires the point of view of the circuit of commodity capital. From the viewpoint of the circuit of commodity capital we can see that a capitalistically produced commodity (C') has to be exchanged via money for elements of production (C) and for whatever purchases are made from surplus value (c). For an individual capital to successfully complete C'—M—(C, c), however, the aggregate social output must have the appropriate composition of use values. If this point is taken into consideration, the production process of capital can no longer be adequately represented by P in C...P...C' of the production process of the individual capital, but by P in C...P...C' of the production process of the aggregate social capital in which productive capital, variable and constant, is reproduced together with surplus value. Indeed, the reproduction of constant capital at the macro-level depends on the reproduction of variable capital. So long as the presently employed labour power can be reproduced as a commodity, both the variable and the constant component of the aggregate social capital can be maintained and 'reproduced'. On the basis of this P, the circulation process of capital becomes the exchange of the aggregate commodity capital for the aggregate commodity capital.

The aggregate social capital must continually supply the market with means of production and articles of consumption, whether wage goods or capitalists' consumption goods (also called luxury goods). The total output of the aggregate social capital may, in this context, be supposed to have the value composition $c^* + v^* + s^*$. If the constant-capital component, c^*, of the total output physically consists of means of production only, and, if the value-added component, $v^* + s^*$, is entirely in the form of articles of consumption, reproduction repeats itself on the same scale, so that a *simple reproduction* will occur. Indeed, the value-added component may be entirely consumed if reproduction is to continue at the same scale as previously. If the scale of reproduction is to expand, additional investment must originate in s^* or surplus value. If part of the surplus value component, s^*, of the total output contains some means of production, an *expanded reproduction* is about to take place. The case of simple reproduction will be considered first because the fundamental mechanism of the reproduction of the capitalist production relation is best established in this context.

SIMPLE REPRODUCTION

The reproduction process of capital does not just reproduce means of production and livelihood as material things, but also the peculiar capitalists-versus-productive-workers commodity-economic social relation. The continuity of the reproduction process of capital requires that an appropriate quantity of commodified labour power also be reproduced and made available for purchase by variable capital. Since capitalists do not perform productive labour, they cannot maintain themselves without appropriating the surplus labour of their productive employees in the form of surplus value. Labour power can neither be reproduced as a commodity in the production process of material things, nor can it be consumed as an ordinary commodity in the consumption process, properly speaking. Unlike other commodities, labour power remains with its owners though it is sold repeatedly. Labour power must be reproduced by workers in their individual and private consumption of material use values, purchased as commodities, if capitalism is to reproduce itself over time. These use values are created when labour power is exercised or consumed to produce wage goods as part of the reproduction process of capital.

Productive workers, who must repeatedly sell their labour power as a commodity to capital, produce commodities which belong to it as well; consequently, they will be forced to spend the wages they receive from capital for their current labour to buy back from it a portion of the goods they have previously produced as their means of livelihood, which they currently require for the reproduction of their labour power. Thus, when capital pays wages to the working class, it is indirectly ensuring the reproduction of the labour power it requires, because that money invariably returns to capital through the workers' purchase of wage goods. Moreover, while producing the consumption goods that they will have to buy back in the future, workers must also produce the consumption goods of the capitalists, which are the fruit of their surplus labour.

The division of the annual product of consumer goods into wage goods and non-wage goods is essential for the preservation of existing capital. The owners of labour power and the owners of capital remain segregated so long as the owners of labour power have no access to the means of production. The value of labour power depends on both economic and non-economic factors. However, it does not matter what assortment of use values is purchased by the real wage, provided, first, that the aggregate social capital produces only that value of wage goods which can be purchased by the workers' wages, and, second, that the total wage bill paid to the working class, as their freely disposable income or consumption fund, detachable from the circulation process, purchases these goods and only these goods. If workers received less or more than what was required to reproduce their labour power, then the reproduction of labour power and that of capital itself would be in jeopardy. It is the social condition under which workers without income-producing property reproduce their labour power that ensures the constant reconversion of labour power into a commodity. By producing value and surplus value in the new product, the wage-earners' labour today reproduces their social position tomorrow.

The reproduction of capital divides the new value product, $v + s$, into a variable-capital component and a surplus-value component. Capitalists derive a regular income, as surplus value, year after year only because they invest given magnitudes of constant and variable capital in a continuing production process. The maintenance of the aggregate capital value, $c^* + v^*$, ensures the regular formation of capitalists' income. Since capitalist reproduction is carried on as the reproduction of commodities by commodified labour power, both the v and c components of the product value ($c + v + s$) are 'capitalized' and must be recaptured through the sale of the product. When capital realizes the value of its product (C') in the form of money (M'), it invariably repurchases both the means of production, corresponding to those which have been consumed in the production process, and labour power, which is reacquired by again paying the workers' wages, thus enabling workers once more to purchase their means of livelihood as commodities in the market.

Since the surplus-value and variable-capital components from the preceding reproduction period have already been entirely consumed in the form of consumption goods by the capitalists and workers respectively during that same period, the v-component of the value product cannot just be purchased in the market, as is the c-component. Labour power must instead be allocated to the various spheres of production, where, under the direction of capital and employing means of production previously acquired, it reproduces not only the value paid for itself (v), but also surplus value (s), through the exercising of its capacity for productive labour. The *value of labour power* is determined by the labour time required to produce the daily livelihood of the worker. In material terms, workers must produce not only the consumption goods they will later buy back as their means of livelihood, but also consumption goods for capitalists, together with whatever means of production have been used up in this same period and need to be replaced. Labour power functions as productive labour, transferring old value to the new product, while simultaneously augmenting value. The *value product*, v + s, may be entirely consumed, while maintaining the existing capital intact, because it is newly produced during the same period in which it is consumed.

The continuity of the labour-and-production process requires that an appropriate quantity of labour power be reproduced. When labour power is purchased as a commodity, however, it cannot, through the consumption of its use value, materialize labour in a commodity belonging to the worker. The consumption of labour power in the production process of capital forms value in the form of commodities, including wage goods, which belong to capital, because capital advanced variable capital to begin this process. In turn, the *reproduction of labour power* simultaneously restores the variable capital, which is the instrument of its exploitation (in the Marxian sense), to capital.

If the direct producers' articles of consumption were not produced as commodities, as was the case of peasants under the obligation of corvée, labour power could not be reproduced without extra-economic coercion. During their necessary labour time, corvée peasants produced their own means of livelihood, which they did not have to buy back with wages. Since the lord could not control the reproduction of the peasants' labour power, peasants would not have offered their surplus labour in the absence of coercion. By contrast, wage-earners under capital do not own the fruit of their own necessary labour. They can reproduce their labour power only by purchasing wage goods, which they themselves have produced, returning to the aggregate social capital all the money they received from it in wage form.

From the point of view of an individual capitalist, who has advanced wages before the completion of his product, the value of variable capital paid to acquire labour power may not immediately return as the value of the finished commodity. However, from the point of view of the aggregate social capital, if capital parts with value, which it initially possessed in the form of money as variable capital, it will immediately regain the same value of variable capital in commodity form as wage goods. The reproduction of labour power automatically restores or reproduces variable capital in monetary form to the aggregate social capital. Capitalist society, governed by the law of value, reproduces labour power, while ensuring that the workers' consumption of material things is, at the same time, the reproduction of labour power as a commodity. The working class, the capitalist class, and the social relation that binds them together, are reproduced by means of this commodity-economic mechanism.

Constant capital has no power of its own either to maintain or to reproduce itself. If means of production are left outside the labour process, they decay rapidly and lose both their value and their use value. However, the maintenance of constant capital is automatically accomplished by productive labour, which capital consumes in its process of value formation and augmentation. Since c^* consists solely of means of production, the reproduction of constant capital is reduced to the transformation of old into new means of production. As old capital goods are used up, new capital goods are produced. Though it does not involve the formation of any new value, this transformation is accomplished by the concrete-useful aspect of productive labour. Individual capital appears to recover the value of constant capital in the form of money automatically. It then is able to reconvert it into necessary means of production, thus maintaining its own value through time. Even the v-component of the value of the new product is viewed as part of the initially advanced capital, which is now recovered, while s, or the surplus-value component, though it has been newly created by labour, together with the v-component, appears to be self-generated by capital and is, therefore, viewed as legitimately and freely disposable capitalist income. From the point of view of the aggregate social capital, however, the possibility of selling commodities for prices that will recover the value of c^*, which has been used up or consumed, and the market availability of new means of production to replace the said value of c^* are both consequences of the reproduction of c^*, which is made possible by the concrete-useful character of productive labour. The supply of the latter in an appropriate quantity is, in turn, guaranteed by the reproduction of variable capital. The reproduction of constant capital, c^*, in other words, presupposes the reproduction of variable capital, v^*.

THE CASE OF EXPANDED REPRODUCTION

In the case of simple reproduction the aggregate surplus value, s^*, which the aggregate social capital appropriates consists solely of articles of consumption for capitalists. The capitalist class maintains or reproduces itself by consuming these articles while keeping the value of the aggregate social capital intact. If the capitalist production relation always reproduced itself at the same scale, the capitalist mode of production would never have become dominant in modern society. In order for capitalism to form a historical society, the scale of reproduction must not be rigidly fixed.

Even in simple reproduction, however, the capitalist production relation already contains the possibility of its own expansion. The capitalist production relation always generates surplus value, which capital can dispose of freely without detracting from the existing capital value. The fact that surplus value forms a freely disposable income for capitalists implies that it need not be used entirely for consumption goods, but rather that it may be saved and added to the existing value of capital.

Before surplus value can be set aside as accumulation funds, a portion of it must be given over to the capitalists' consumption, ensuring them a certain standard of living, which varies historically, but which must, of course, be higher than that of the working class. This income is dependent on historical conditions, and cannot be completely determined in theory. It has already been remarked that the individual consumption of the capitalist is, from the point of view of capital as the personification of the capitalist chrematistic, a necessary evil, which constrains the conversion of surplus value into the accumulation of capital. As an automatically expanding form of value augmentation, capital enforces a ceaseless expansion of the scope of such augmentation, which compels the capitalist to moderate his luxury consumption, even in the absence of such contingent factors as, for example, the presence of the Protestant ethic. In other societies, in which the production process is not governed by capital, surplus products are typically squandered in ostentatious consumption.

The *rate of accumulation* or the *capitalist's propensity to save* is the ratio of accumulation funds to surplus value, from which capital is generated. It takes a while before an individual capitalist's accumulation funds reach a magnitude suitable for investment in additional means of production and an expanded scale of operation, but, for the aggregate of social capital, even the smallest saving of the capitalist class is adequate to stimulate additional investment. For expanded reproduction to be possible, however, additional means of production and of livelihood must be made socially available by the production of capital generally. There is no inherent difficulty in securing the investment of additional constant capital in the means of production, since the aggregate social capital can directly produce it and supply it to the market. The fact that the capitalist class has saved accumulation funds implies that it does not need to use all of its income to satisfy its demand for consumption goods. Instead, it demands some additional means of production for increased accumulation. The price mechanism, implicitly assumed here, will ensure that both means of production and workers' consumption goods will be produced.

Capital does not produce with direct knowledge of the structure of social demand, but each individual capital satisfies part of that social need, while aiming merely to augment value, because it is, nevertheless guided by the movement of prices. *Social demand* is itself shaped in the reproduction process of capital. Means of production are demanded in order to produce further means of production as well as articles of consumption. Articles of consumption are demanded by workers and capitalists for their consumption. Within the limits of the prevailing technical capacity, capital will produce whatever goods are socially demanded, because this enables capital to accomplish its chrematistic purpose while satisfying the general social norm of rational economic management in its own unique fashion, provided, of course, it can acquire the required labour power, which it does not directly produce.

It is only sometimes possible to extend the working day or intensify labour to generate further capital accumulation. It is also true that, even if full employment prevails, a natural growth of the labouring population will make further growth possible. Ultimately, however, the accumulation of capital cannot become real unless capital itself can somehow devise a method to acquire the additional labour power it requires.

The prevailing wage rate must be adequate not only to reproduce the labour power of productive workers, but also to reproduce the normal conditions of their family life. Indeed, if capital paid wages that were sufficient only to support childless workers, the working population could not be maintained beyond one generation, and capitalism would not survive. It is therefore necessary that the wage rate paid to productive workers should be adequate to provide for the sustenance and education of their children. Only with this provision can a supply of new labour power be made available as a part of the existing labour power disappears with the retirement of older productive workers.

Capital is also flexible enough to allow for a 'natural' growth of the working population. If capitalist reproduction rigidly maintained a stationary scale and was unable to absorb the incremental growth of the working population, capitalism would fail to organize a society according to its own commodity-economic principle. The aggregate social capital, however, is always ready to accumulate, as long as additional labour power can be found. (Historically, it has been observed that a rapid population growth under capitalism often led to accelerated economic growth.) Thus, the conversion of surplus value into capital will necessarily occur, to the extent that the natural growth of the working population permits it. Given a level of productivity at which not all of surplus value need be consumed by capitalists, a *formal possibility* of accumulation on the part of capital necessarily develops into an *actual* accumulation in correspondence with the natural growth of the working population. Thus, out of surplus value springs capital. This is due to the fact that the money which realizes surplus value forms a freely disposable fund. In order to set capital into motion, it is necessary, first, to accumulate freely disposable universal money of a certain magnitude. Part of this money may be converted into capital if the remainder guarantees the capitalist's consumption during the turnover time of that capital.

THE REPRODUCTION SCHEMES: THE REPRODUCTION OF COMMODITIES

In order to examine the material aspect of the unceasing process of reproduction carried on by the aggregate social capital, it is helpful to observe the circular flow of the whole economy by means of *reproduction schemes*, which are a type of Quesnay-inspired *tableau économique*. The reproduction schemes ascertain the *real possibility* of the capitalist mode of production, assuming the availability of labour power (Sekine 1984, p.456). The schemes offer a framework within which the reproducibility of capitalist society may be studied from the point of view of commodities, while deliberately holding the presence of commodified labour power and the viability of the capitalist production relation implicit. In this way, the schemes are able to demonstrate that capitalist society, like any society, can reproduce all the goods required for its reproduction, so long as the supply of labour power is guaranteed. Instead of treating labour power explicitly as a commodity, the schemes focus on the production of the wage goods workers must consume and the luxury goods consumed by capitalists.

At this stage, capitalist society is assumed to consist solely of a capitalist class and a working class in the absence of a class of landowners. Although the reproduction schemes show the manner in which capital organizes production at an aggregate level, the necessary division of the total production into means of production and means of consumption do not, at this stage in the development of the dialectic, imply a concomitant division of the economy into industries of one kind or another, given that any production here considered must be either of means of production or of articles of consumption. Since no specialization of capitalists has yet been made explicit, all capitalists ought to be viewed as producers and sellers of the same mix of use values. The dialectic must make this assumption in order to show that capital can satisfy the *condition of self-replacement*, regardless of what pattern of capitalist specialization in the production of use values later emerges. In other words, to remain a viable economy, capitalism must ensure that its value relation remains consistent with the self-replacement condition that each means of production must be produced in a quantity which is at least equal to what has been used up in a given period, so as to allow production to continue under capitalist management. Of course, any viable economy must ensure that this self-replacement condition is somehow met.

A demonstration of capitalism's capacity to approach market equilibrium is not an issue in the reproduction schemes or *tableaux économiques*, nor is the behaviour of individual capitalists and workers. Such considerations are premature in the doctrine of production, where capital has not yet explicitly developed the capitalist market; rather, attention here is to be focused on the essential value relation between capitalist and workers, while the market remains very much in the background.

The reproduction of capitalists and workers is contingent upon the appropriate conversion of the aggregate social product (C') into the necessary elements of production (C), to replace the means of production and wage goods consumed in the previous circuit, together with the consumption goods (c) of the capitalist class. Thus, the reproduction schemes divide the economy into two sectors, one producing *basic goods* or means of production, which are inputs into the reproduction process, and the other, *non-basic goods*, or *articles of consumption*; and then they proceed to show how the annual flow of goods and the counter-flow of money in this network of classes and sectors accomplishes the required conversion of C' into C and c on a society-wide basis.

Capitalism, like any historical society, must reproduce basic goods and non-basic goods in an appropriate proportion in order to reproduce itself. In all societies, the *continuity of annual reproduction* depends on the allocation of both labour power and the means of production to the two sectors of production, according to the degree of intensity to which each sector's products are socially required. Capitalism satisfies this norm through the operation of the law of value, which asserts itself through the movement of prices. Guided by the motion of prices, capital allocates the means of production and labour power necessary to meet the annual society-wide demand for commodity products, whether means of production or articles of consumption. If a commodity is overproduced, a fall in its price enforces a reduction in the scale of its production; if a commodity is underproduced, a price rise induces an expansion in the scale of its production. Hence, the labour time required for the production of each commodity never diverges very far from that which is socially normal. The *law of value*, which governs the commodity economy, sees to it that not only is no more than the necessary labour time devoted to the production of each specific commodity, but also that only the necessary, proportional quantity of the total social labour time is devoted to the production of the various groups of products required. Individual capitalists and labourers may not perceive how this general economic norm of social reproduction asserts itself, but their anarchistic productive activities, regulated by the law of value, bring order to the individual pursuit of private interests.

We shall assume, during our discussion of the reproduction schemes, that the operation of the law of value, which regulates capitalist commodity production, has already worked its way through the economy and has thereby eliminated the overproduction and underproduction of use values in relation to the existing pattern of demand, and that, consequently, outputs will tend to be produced in the socially necessary quantities, employing only socially necessary labour.

It is implicit in this context that the *socially necessary labour* is the labour that produces an *equilibrium* quantity of the commodity. Since this equilibrium is still only hypothetical, commodities are represented by values rather than by prices. The schemes must presuppose equilibrium, even though they cannot show how it is attained, because a circular-flow model could hardly exhibit the reproduction of an economy if a 'disproportion', an 'underconsumption', a 'realization' crisis or any other disequilibrium state were annually reproduced. The inter-sectoral relation prevailing in the reproduction schemes indicates what the appropriate quantities of means of production and articles of consumption would be in a given period (such as a year) if an equilibrium is assumed. The schemes present the capitalist reproduction process as a system in which the outputs, C', of the aggregate social capital in the preceding period are mutually exchanged as commodities so as to permit an aggregate production in the current period, which, in turn, will prepare for reproduction in the following period. Even though the schemes do not explain how a capitalist economy reaches and maintains equilibrium, they do show that the capitalist economy would be technically viable if it always tended to maintain it.

The exercise of the workers' labour power is necessary for production to be carried out. The schemes assume that the reproduction of labour power as a commodity is ensured by the articles of consumption that capital produces. In equilibrium, the direct producers are paid just enough wages to buy back the product of their necessary labour.

If we look at this process of reproduction as it occurs within the repetitive motion of industrial capital (M—C...P...C'—M'.M—C...P...C'—M', etc.), the link, M'.M, which involves the re-conversion of money into capital, does not threaten the circulatory phase, C'—M'.M—C, of the continuing motion of industrial capital and, thus, can be viewed simply as an exchange process, C'—M—C, in which money acts only as a medium of circulation and C' consists of some means of production (P_m), some wage goods (W_g) and some luxury or capitalist consumption goods (L_x). These are to be exchanged for C which, in turn, consists of some means of production (P_m) and labour power (L_p).

To study this process, a reproduction scheme divides the economy into several sectors and shows the flows of goods and services (and the counter-flows of money) among them. The scheme consists of two accounting identities and a constraint, but no behaviour equations to determine equilibrium. The first sector or department produces means of production (or capital goods), and the second produces articles of consumption (wage goods and luxury goods). In each case, the total output (u) is made up of the constant-capital component (c), variable-capital component (v), and surplus-value component (s), which may be written in general form as follows:

$$\text{I} \quad u_1 = c_1 + v_1 + s_1$$
$$\text{II} \quad u_2 = c_2 + v_2 + s_2$$
$$c_2 \le v_1 + s_1$$

The last (weak) inequality represents a general constraint on capitalist reproduction in the sense that, if it is not satisfied, the economy will fail to reproduce itself. In Marxian terms, this is the *condition of reproduction*. If equality is maintained, the economy is in simple reproduction; if a strong inequality holds, it is in a state of expanded reproduction. In the case of simple reproduction, the condition becomes $u_1 = c_1 + c_2$, which means that means of production currently produced are used up entirely for the replacement of means of production currently consumed. If any capital good fails to meet the condition of self-replacement, it is bound to become a bottleneck in the capitalist system of reproduction. If, for instance, the system uses more coal than it produces currently, the stock of coal in society will soon be depleted, and the production of commodities for which coal is a necessary input will cease. No system of reproduction can afford to let that happen. A condition of self-replacement for capital goods must be satisfied if the law of value and, therefore, capitalism itself is to continue to operate. In the Uno tradition, this condition is referred to as the *absolute foundation of the law of value*.

Under expanded reproduction, $u_1 > c_1 + c_2$ prevails, which means that more means of production are produced than are currently consumed (used up), and the increment can also be applied to accumulation. It is also the case that $u_2 < (v_1 + v_2) + (s_1 + s_2)$, where the expression inside the first set of parentheses represents wage goods, just as it would in simple reproduction, whereas that inside the second represents not only luxury goods for capitalists, as in simple reproduction, but additional means of production which may be used for further accumulation. Thus, if the surplus-value component of the product of the aggregate social capital consists solely of luxury goods, a simple reproduction prevails; if it also contains additional means of production, an expanded reproduction prevails.

The reproduction schemes illustrate how capitalist society satisfies the *fundamental conditions of simple and expanded reproduction*, which all societies must satisfy, in its uniquely commodity-economic way. For now, we may ignore variations in capital compositions and rates of accumulation since such complications do not prevent capital from satisfying the fundamental condition of reproduction. The above theory specifies only the material constraint under which capital accumulation must take place. It does not tell us which of the many possible growth paths constitutes the preferred capitalist choice. Only in the context of actual capital accumulation, and not in the reproduction schemes, does such a problem arise. Nor does the above theory contradict the theory of the equalization of profit rates, which we shall examine later. Along any feasible balanced-growth path, there exists a set of prices that makes all sectors of the economy equally profitable. If that were not the case, a theory of the circular flows (reproduction schemes) which assumes (as the present one does) the full working of the law of value would not be possible.

Since a reproduction scheme is a *circular-flow model*, the flow of commodities from one sector to another always presupposes a counter-flow of money as means of circulation. It is, therefore, necessary for us to find out how money mediates the circulation of commodities in the reproduction schemes. Articles of consumption, purchased by workers' wage incomes, can drop out of the reproduction process of capital only on the condition that they are consumed in the reproduction of labour power, which subsequently returns to the reproduction process of capital. The surplus-value component of the new product, which forms the capitalists' income, on the other hand, can be disengaged from the reproduction process of capital and freely disposed of.

Thus, the capitalists' income is net revenue (net product) and can initiate the accumulation of new capital, since it can either be consumed or saved.

As capitalism develops and the productivity of labour rises, the capitalist class will begin to save some of its income in the form of money held outside the system of reproduction, thereby draining a corresponding amount of the means of circulation. The capitalist propensity to hoard gold as accumulation funds makes an expanded reproduction possible. Any ensuing shortage of the means of circulation thereby created is temporary, because such saving stimulates the capitalist production of new monetary gold. The reproduction schemes assume an equilibrium state in which all goods including gold are produced in the socially necessary quantities. This does not mean that disequilibrium can never occur. Gold, like any commodity, can be temporarily overproduced or underproduced by capital. The reproduction schemes assume only that no disequilibrium situation permanently reproduces itself because the law of value sees to it that such a tendency is eventually corrected.

If the first condition of the accumulation of capital and the expansion of the scale of reproduction is the formation by capitalists of potential accumulation funds outside of the reproduction process, the second condition is that these accumulation funds should return to that process and be converted into productive elements. In other words, there must be additional labour power and means of production available. If, by the formation of a relative surplus population, the existing stock of labour power, which capital cannot directly produce, is ensured, then capital can meet the increasing demand for labour power which arises as part of the accumulation of capital. The process of expanded reproduction can then proceed without depending on anything but the products of capital.

In the reproduction schemes, where the reproducibility of capitalist society must be studied from the point of view of the circuit of commodity capital, fixed capital can only be treated insofar as the commodity form can subsume it; that is to say, only insofar as it renders no free service. It must be strictly distinguished from permanent assets, such as the forces of nature, which cannot be produced as commodities, and which cost society nothing if conserved properly. It resembles these forces only to the degree that its life expectancy increases. In other words, *fixed capital* is both a means of production which must be regularly reproduced, and a means of production which need not be reproduced every year, since it only gradually wears out. For example, machinery typically loses its value piecemeal, as it transfers that value to the products bit by bit. There is, therefore, no need for the capital-goods sector to reproduce the worn-out portion of heavy capital equipment annually. To the degree that these instruments of labour create new products without adding value to the product (that is, they are fully utilized but only partly consumed), they perform free services like such natural forces as water, steam and air. From the point of view of annual reproduction, machines and plants may be treated as if they were natural gifts of free productive capacity, except that *depreciation funds* must continually drop out of the reproduction process. A plant or machine which lasts for ten years cannot be replaced when it wears out unless depreciation funds are accumulated for its renewal over that entire period.

In the schemes of simple reproduction, the replacement of worn-out fixed capital can be easily dealt with; but simple reproduction is a drastic abstraction from capitalist society, because that society never reproduces itself simply. Expanded reproduction is less schematic than simple reproduction in that it allows for capital accumulation; but the conversion of surplus value into fixed capital involves a problem which can only be satisfactorily treated later, in the more concrete context of the actual process of capitalist accumulation.

As capital accumulates through time, the difference between the capital employed and the capital consumed increases. In other words, there is an increase in the value and the material mass of the instruments of labour, such as buildings and machinery, which function for varying lengths of time, in processes of production which are constantly repeated. These items of fixed capital are commodities and must be treated as such in the sphere of circulation, but they refuse to be consumed in the same manner as ordinary goods are consumed, either directly or productively. The prevailing technology and the organic composition are, therefore, assumed to remain constant in the schemes of expanded reproduction, because the schemes are not equipped to cope with the accumulation of fixed capital. The fact that as capital accumulates the lack of proportionality or correspondence between value and use values is increased, together with the life expectancy of machines and plants, is but another example of the form of value not being fully capable of subsuming real economic life.

The reproduction schemes do exhibit certain aspects of capital accumulation. Even in this abstract context, the scale of reproduction will expand when circulating constant capital is generated from surplus value. If an improvement in the method of production has to do only with circulating capital, such as raw materials and fuel, and involves no change of fixed capital, the improved method will immediately be adopted by all capitalists, since in a purely capitalist society the adoption cannot be obstructed by such non-economic restrictions as patents.

THE LAW OF RELATIVE SURPLUS POPULATION

A mode of production which was characterized by the chronic underemployment of the direct producers or working population could form neither a self-sufficient mode of production nor a viable historical society. It is also a general norm of economic life, common to all societies, that, unless there is technical progress, the scale of social reproduction cannot be expanded faster than the given current growth of the working population. If productively employed, however, labour power will not only maintain itself with the product of its necessary labour, but will also, in most cases, grow at a rate determined by biological and socio-cultural factors. It follows that if it is to grow faster than the rate at which its population naturally grows, a society must have a method of introducing labour-saving technical devices.

According to Marx, '[e]very special historic mode of production has its own special law of population, historically valid within its limits alone. An abstract law of population exists solely for plants and animals, and only insofar as man has not interfered with them' (Marx 1977, p.592). An economic theory of population, as opposed to a biological or Malthusian theory of population, takes a positive growth rate of the working population as a given and examines the relationship between that rate and the growth rate of productive capacity, output and employment. In many societies, the scale of reproduction cannot be expanded faster than the rate at which the population grows naturally, because technical progress occurs only by chance. The expansion of the capitalist production relation has so far been studied as depending on the natural growth of the working population. In capitalist society, the rate of growth of society's reproduction process regularly exceeds the natural growth rate of population.

Capital cannot continue its accumulation process unless additional productive elements, including labour power, are readily available as commodities in the market. Since productive elements other than labour power are exclusively capitalistically producible commodities (with the exception of natural means of production, which will be dealt with later), it is crucially important that the commodification of labour power should be sufficient to ensure the production of all the material commodities capitalist society requires. Following Marx, the most important factor relating the accumulation of capital with the working class is the organic composition of capital (1977, p.574).

The advancement of the productive powers of labour, which results from technological progress in the area of production methods, ensures that a quantitatively greater proportion of the material means of production will be employed relative to labour power. Since the means of production, as a whole, is a medley of various items, it is not possible to say how much labour is needed to operate a particular item of the means of production, taken separately. It is not a directly measurable ratio. The closest approximation would, however, be the ratio of living labour $(v + s)$ to dead, or stored-up, labour (c), which is the measure of *roundaboutness* in the methods of production, or what Marxian economists term the *technical composition of capital*. Thus, provided that the rate of surplus value has not changed in the interim, an increase in the technical composition of capital is proportional to an increase in society's *value composition of capital*, c / v, since $c / (v + s)$ is equal to $(c / v) / (1 + [s / v])$. Society's value composition of capital, insofar as it reflects the technical composition of aggregate social capital (or round-aboutness of technology), is that which Marxian economists call the *organic composition of capital*. In other words, the value composition of capital, c / v, insofar as it reflects the technical composition of capital, is the organic composition of capital.

The operation of the law of value ensures that additional means of production, wage goods, and monetary gold will all be produced whenever capital prepares for accumulation; but a supply of additional labour power, over and above that which the natural growth of the working population allows, must also be assured if the accumulation of capital is to become *actual* (*wirklich*). With the exception of funds, labour power is the only commodity that capital cannot directly produce. Nor is it a product of labour. Thus, the supply of labour power cannot be easily adjusted to the social demand for it by the ordinary functioning of the commodity economy. As the theory of cyclical accumulation will later show, there exists a unique, commodity-economic mechanism which regularly compels capital to introduce new methods of production, and, thereby, to generate a *relative surplus population*. The *capitalist law of population*, which supplements the law of value by defining the value of labour power, establishes the ability of the capitalist mode of production to contain labour power permanently in the form of a commodity.

Since labour power is not a product of capital, the standard of living cannot be determined by the price mechanism of the market, given that the market cannot determine a 'natural' or equilibrium wage rate for labour power. However, although the real wage which reflects the value of labour power is determined outside of the market, that does not mean that its determination is exogenous to the inner structure or commodity-economic logic of the capitalist system, which contains that market, but is not limited to it. Nor does that mean that the living standard of the worker is rigidly fixed at some biological or physiological subsistence level. Subsistence also allows for historical, cultural and sociological factors. In the development of capitalism, the accumulation of capital in any period generates a standard of living suitable to that level of accumulation. The determination of the real wage together with the living standard of workers entails identifying a *normal rate of surplus value*, consistent with the reproduction of labour power in any particular period of capitalist history.

Indeed, the prevailing value of labour power is established in correspondence with the particular level of technology, which capital is under the commodity-economic compulsion to adopt at a given moment in history. In the course of accumulation, given the technological base upon which the capitalist production relation is founded, there is a lower limit below which the rate of surplus value cannot fall without rendering further accumulation of capital meaningless. There is also an upper limit beyond which the rate of surplus value cannot rise without rendering the reproduction of labour power impossible. A *feasible wage range* must then fall between a minimum wage, which would provide a biological subsistence, just adequate to reproduce the worker's labour power, and a maximum wage which would fall just short of one which would bring about an absolute *excess of capital*, as large numbers of workers cease selling their labour power. If a feasible wage rate cannot be maintained, capital must somehow generate the structural changes to re-establish that rate or capitalism will collapse. (Workers must not be able to save enough to leave the working class and capitalist employment.) We shall return to this topic in the next chapter.

Although the assortment of wage goods deemed necessary for the reproduction of labour power cannot be specified, the value of the wage goods necessary for the workers' consumption and reproduction can be determined in the market. The amount of labour socially necessary to produce that value can be regarded as constituting the *value of labour power*. Given the length of the working-day and the intensity of labour, the rate of surplus value determines the length of labour time necessary for the reproduction of labour power. Since the prevailing technology is already a given, the output of wage goods producible during the necessary labour time is also determined. Thus, the value of labour power is not exogenously determined at a subsistence level; it is determined endogenously in the actual process of capital accumulation and depends on the extent to which the aggregate social capital incorporates the available technology of production.

CYCLICAL ACCUMULATION OF CAPITAL

Even if the natural growth rate and size of the labouring population is fixed, capital can expand the scale of its reproduction and promote the advancement of society's productive powers, by raising the organic composition of capital. Even though it cannot directly produce labour power, capital must be able to draw on a supply pool of this commodity in the form of a *relative surplus population* if it is to expand. The industrial reserve army is another name for this supply pool of labour power. On the other hand, if capitalist accumulation were always accompanied by an uninterrupted rise in the organic composition of capital and an accompanying increase in relative surplus population, the capitalist mode of production would never be able to organize a society according to its own principle, due to the presence of an always increasing mass of capitalistically unemployable workers. Moreover, if productive workers were always available at or near a subsistence wage, capitalism would not introduce new technologies nor would it go through its familiar *cyclical process of accumulation*.

Capital accumulation does not always involve a rise in capital's organic composition. Capital does not continuously generate an absolute surplus population which it does not employ. On the contrary, an *extensive accumulation*, which involves no rise in the organic composition, and which depends on the absorption of a surplus population created in the preceding depression, will later be shown to be the more normal pattern throughout the prosperity phase of a business cycle. So long as the supply of labour power is plentiful, capital has no commodity-economic incentive to explore a new technology. If an improvement in the technical method of production has to do only with circulating constant capital, as in the use of better-quality raw materials or fuel, for instance, it will be immediately adopted by all capitalists. In this context, extra surplus value hardly ever arises; for it is virtually costless for all capitalists immediately to adopt such improvements.

Technical progress, which involves a physical alteration of fixed capital, must be viewed differently. An industrial plant, which typically lasts for ten years or so, cannot be scrapped until it is worn out or until rising wage levels make it unprofitable. Since a large value has already been advanced, and has not been recovered in the form of money, no capitalist enterprise can abandon the existing plant in the first few years of its operation, even if a more efficient method of production is discovered and adopted by some firms. It follows that, from the point of view of annual reproduction, a plant of a given size may be viewed as akin to a free gift of nature, provided capital does not fail to add to its depreciation fund so as to prepare for its eventual renewal. The capital-goods sectors may then concentrate on the production of circulating constant capital so as to enable the scale of social reproduction to *widen*. Thus, during the prosperity phase of the typical capitalist business cycle, which we shall examine more closely in the doctrine of distribution, new investments in circulating constant capital, rather than in fixed capital, set the pattern of expansion. However, such investments eventually strain the labour market by draining the relative surplus population formed in the preceding depression.

The shortage of labour power, the crucial element of production, which capital cannot directly produce, will sooner or later impede the extensive accumulation of capital, when the demand for labour power by capitalist industry begins to exceed its supply. The price mechanism of the market is powerless to resist the persistent rise of wages and the consequent fall in the rate of surplus value. This is not the case with other commodities, which capital can directly produce. If the price of any other commodity rises, capital automatically responds by producing more of that commodity, and this adjustment will continue until the price rises no more. Thus, the law of value asserts itself through the motion of prices and so determines the real cost to society of the production of ordinary commodities. This mechanism does not apply to the supply or value of labour power, which must be determined otherwise.

The upward tendency of wages during the typical capitalist prosperity phase is checked by an *economic crisis* which issues in a depression. It is the shortage of labour power which causes a sharp rise in wages and leads to the *excess of capital*, the state in which a further accumulation of capital is accompanied by no additional appropriation of surplus value, as the desired growth rate of capital value exceeds the natural growth rate of the working population. When some of the firms in the leading industries find themselves unable to make new investments, a negative multiplier process is set off, which reverses the normal operation of capitalist society's social reproduction and disrupts capital accumulation. Additional means of production, produced in the expectation of a normal demand, can no longer be sold; thus, suppliers are obliged to reduce their output below the normal capacity and cancel orders for new means of production. Since accumulation funds cease to be spent and the circulation of commodities is generally inactive, the existing stock is difficult to sell and the reproduction of the capitalist production relation is called into question, as growing numbers of productive workers lose their regular employment. The impossibility of investing in circulating constant capital and variable capital means that plants are left idle. Although there is then an appearance of overproduction throughout capitalist society, this is merely symptomatic of the more fundamental disequilibrium of an excess of capital.

The fact that capital value can be maintained only in the form of money may be traumatic, but it does free industries from their attachment to a no-longer-viable technology. Indeed, *innovations* tend to occur in a cluster in the depression phase of recurring business cycles and are thus integral to the cyclical accumulation process of capital. When the reproduction process of capitalist society is temporarily paralyzed, the aggregate social capital is compelled both to innovate or rationalize existing plants, so as to discard the obsolete technologies embodied in them, and to introduce technical progress, by investing in new fixed capital, thus raising the organic composition of capital. In this, the *deepening phase of capital accumulation*, accumulation is said to take place *intensively*, because a society-wide technological restructuring of existing plants is forced upon capital.

The adoption of a new production method becomes easier in the phase of depression that follows a crisis because many of the existing plants have already depreciated much of their value, leaving a relatively small portion of advanced capital value unrecovered. Moreover, the disruption and contraction of the social reproduction process destroys not only the value and the use value of the presently advanced productive capital, but also the value of commodity capital. Indeed, prevailing prices do not justify the continued production of new commodities at normal capacity with the existing technology; thus, as the circulation of commodities contracts dramatically, the cost of maintaining existing plants typically becomes prohibitive. In this context, the undepreciated value of existing fixed capital has dropped virtually to zero. The cost of sacrificing it is thus small, relative to the advantage of adopting a new method, given that it is generally difficult to sell commodities at the prevailing prices. Extra surplus value is, therefore, vigorously pursued by the more capable firms, which adopt innovative technical methods that drastically reduce their necessary labour time and, therefore, production costs. Even though any extra surplus value earned must disappear, as the new method of production is more and more widely adopted, a gain in the productive powers of labour remains and a relative surplus population is reformed.

Not all technical progress is labour-saving, but the technical progress which is significant, from the point of view of the actual process of capital accumulation, is the one which saves the input of labour power relative to the means of production, raising the organic composition of capital generally. (An absolute reduction in the demand for labour may not occur, but the proportion of variable capital to constant capital normally falls.)

Since the accumulation of capital requires that readily employable labour power should always be present in the form of a commodity, capital is periodically compelled to resort to intensive accumulation, which reforms the relative surplus population that will be absorbed or drained in the subsequent phase of prosperity based on extensive accumulation. By thus raising its technical composition, capital creates the basis for a new capitalist production relation.

This alternation of extensive and intensive accumulation, in the course of business cycles, characterizes the *actual process of capitalist accumulation*.

The ability of capital to resort periodically to intensive accumulation accounts for the extraordinary resiliency and dynamism of the capitalist mode of production. This structural flexibility of capitalism, which enables it to incorporate more and more advanced production technologies whenever it is necessary to advance its chrematistic purpose, allowed capitalism to establish itself as a historically significant institution. If this flexibility were absent, capitalism would not have overcome its first decennial crisis resulting from an excess of capital.

As long as labour power remains a commodity, with a well-defined value, the law of value will be able to manage the capitalist mode of production effectively as a process of value formation and augmentation. The *law of population*, therefore, supplements the law of value, by defining the value of labour power, thereby establishing the ability of the capitalist mode of production to contain labour power in the form of a commodity. Through its law of population, capitalism establishes itself without depending on any alien principles. Capital is thus able to ensure its self-contained and self-sufficient status, by restructuring its technological base and, in the process, generating a relative surplus population.

In the cyclical course of capital accumulation, wages sometimes (in depressions) fall below the value of labour power and sometimes (during periods of prosperity) rise above it. When productive workers receive wages well above the value of labour power, and labour power becomes increasingly uncontrollable as a commodity, the existing technology no longer permits extensive accumulation to continue. The *value of labour power* is only revealed by the level of wages which prevails during the period of average activity, which occurs as part of capital's development of a particular complex of industrial technology.

As it evolves, capitalism revolutionizes the technology prevailing in society. Because the technology is more advanced in each succeeding accumulation period, wages are bound to rise more in each successive prosperity phase. Nor will they fall so much in each successive depression phase of capital accumulation. This is not merely an empirical or historical phenomenon; it is a development which the theory of capital demonstrates is a necessary consequence of capitalism's operation.

The rebuilding of fixed capital embodying a new technology is typically accompanied by the enlarged plant sizes of capitalist firms. The technology appropriate to the larger-scale operation of the more competitive firms is the one which saves the input of labour power relative to the material means of production, thus reducing production costs, while renovating the technological base of the economy. The organic composition is raised by investment in new and heavier classes of fixed capital, embodying more advanced technologies. Such investments require greater concentrations of capital. Since greater and greater concentrations of capital are required to purchase the method of production which embodies the most sophisticated knowledge of science and technology, the stronger capitalists prevail over the weaker, thus increasing the *centralization of capital* in each succeeding depression period as well. In this way, the leading competitors expand the scale of their operations to a greater extent than that which occurs as a result of the concentration of capital made possible by ordinary accumulation. Centralization accomplishes almost overnight a concentration of capital which would normally take years to develop, and makes it easier to adopt a more indirect method of production.

Unlike the concentration of capital, which is the necessary consequence of any accumulation, the centralization of capital depends on contingent factors as well; thus, although some instances of centralization occur in every depression period, the extent to which capital is in fact centralized cannot be logically determined. Moreover, capital which is centralized may later be split into parts by 'the division of property within capitalist families' (Marx 1969, p.586). Therefore, we cannot claim that this tendency towards the centralization of capital is sufficiently strong as to accomplish an inevitable monopolization of firms throughout the economy.

The only innovation under consideration here is one of a 'quantitative' nature, such as the introduction into the cotton industry of a new spinning machine with a greater number of spindles, which merely raised the organic composition of capital, rather than a technological innovation of a 'qualitative' nature, such as the dramatic innovations in the iron and steel industry in the last quarter of the nineteenth century, which allowed that industry to replace the cotton industry as the key industry during the imperialist era.

The compatibility of the reproduction of use values and capitalist production relations establishes the *self-dependence* of the capitalist mode of production in much the same way as Hegel's doctrine of essence, which, after proceeding through the dialectic of *intro-reflection, appearance, and actuality*, ends with the category of *unconditioned self-dependence* or *absolute actuality*, thus guaranteeing the *self-sufficiency* of the absolute. Once the viability and reproducibility of the value relation has been established, the dialectic of capital proceeds to the third and final doctrine of distribution, which corresponds with Hegel's doctrine of the *notion*.[17]

Part III

Dialectical Theory of Capitalism: Distribution

4
The Theory of Profit

There is a close correspondence between Hegel's doctrine of the notion and the doctrine of distribution in the Uno–Sekine dialectic of capital. In each dialectic, the third and final doctrine exhibits what the object of study is capable of accomplishing once the consistency of its mode of existence with its substantive content has been revealed.

The primitive form of the *notion* of capital has its origin in the sphere of circulation as the abstract form of merchant capital, which sought, by arbitrage or the sale of its commodity, a money value greater than it advanced in purchasing the commodity. Such an operation is not a *self-mediating process*. In the doctrine of production, however, capital becomes a *self-valorizing process* and, hence, a more adequate expression of the notion of capital. By the time the dialectic has reached the doctrine of distribution, the notion of capital has already established itself as an *absolute actuality* in Hegelian terms and is now ready to show what it is *subjectively*.

In Hegel's *Logic*, the *subjective notion* is the first to appear of a triad, which is completed by the appearance of the *objective notion* and the *idea*. In the dialectic of capital, the subjective notion of capital, the objective notion of capital and the idea of capital reproduce this pattern of development. Moreover, the Hegelian dialectic of *development* (*Entfaltung*, self-exposition or self-fulfilment), which governs the formation of the capitalist market, reproduces the triadic pattern of *universality, particularity*, and *individuality* in Hegel's final doctrine. Following Sekine, industrial capital is *universal*, in that it produces all use values; *particular*, in that it produces differing use values; and *individual*, in that it forms a unified whole, producing different use values.[18]

Capital concretizes itself in a manner which allows particular capitals, through competition, to establish a *general rate of profit*, which governs all spheres of the commodity economy: industry, agriculture, commerce and banking. Capital differentiates itself not only into branches of industry with distinct organic compositions, dictated by differing use-value considerations, which, in turn, dictate different production techniques, but, as well, into commercial and interest-bearing capitals. This differentiation is unified, however, through the *law of average profit*, which distributes surplus value in proportion to the magnitude of the money value of capital advanced, while capital's Hegelian-style *actuality*, or *self-dependence*, is guaranteed by its *law of population*. In this context, it seems perfectly legitimate that all capitalists, whether productively engaged in the manufacture of use values or unproductively engaged in commerce and finance, should share equally in the pool of surplus value, which now takes the form of interest, not profit. The dialectic ends when the notion of capital, which governs all forms of circulation and production, has progressed through the categories of profit, rent and interest, until it itself becomes a commodity, relieved of any material content and possessing the distinctive use value of being a pure self augmentation. It is the division of average profit into interest and entrepreneurial profit which externalizes the relations of capital. Capital is converted into a commodity, which allows it to distance itself, at least subjectively, from the production of use values. Capital, which now automatically bears interest, cannot stop circulating, for to stop would be to forego the interest that can always be earned when it is in motion.

The doctrine of distribution demonstrates that capital's reified, fetishized forms are simply the outward manifestation of a self-contained and self-determined inner logic. In the doctrine of distribution, this inner logic of capital reveals itself, not in the sense that it tends to become transparent, but in the sense that the theory has been developed to the point that it now is possible to expose all the connections between its outward manifestations and its inner logic.

The content of the *absolute idea* of capital is the whole capitalist system that has been presented herein. Just as Hegel's dialectic of *subjectivity, objectivity, and the idea* was able to develop until it became the *notion of the absolute idea*, as the *idea which thinks itself* (Hegel 1975, pp.221, 292–3), so does the notion of capital pass through the same stages, until, with the development of the form of interest-bearing wealth, it returns to its origins in the sphere of circulation as the absolute idea of capital, having made explicit what was always implicit within it and having demonstrated that it too requires no alien principles to unfold autonomously.

The doctrine of distribution focuses on market or price relations, thereby relegating the value relation, for the most part, to the background. Nevertheless, merely because the capital-versus-capital relation occupies center stage, we should not presume that the value relation no longer holds, or that the price mechanism and the law of value operate independently of each other. Indeed, the economic forms of profit, rent, and interest cannot be properly understood and demystified without a prior knowledge of the doctrines of circulation and production, which explain the necessary inner connections of capitalism. In the absence of the knowledge provided by these two doctrines, the rate of profit appears to be a mere mercantile form, indifferent to the productive base of society, since the market automatically effaces any trace of a specific mode of production, establishing, in its place, a universal relation of equality among traders. Without a prior understanding of the earlier doctrines, no explanation can be given as to why, in the third doctrine, rent makes it appear as if a thing, land, produces value; while interest, the most fetishized form of all, makes it appear as if capital can automatically create value, independently of the production process.

INTRODUCING THE THEORY OF PROFIT

In the doctrine of production, the dialectical exposition required that we explain the *value relation* as prior to the *price/market mechanism*. This value relation remained invariant to the differentiation of use values produced in different industries. Values and the rate of surplus value were thus not quantitatively determined with explicit reference to the existing technology or, in other words, the *technological complex*, because capitalists were viewed as operators of capital *as such*. There was no valid reason, in that context, to distinguish between the varying techniques capitalists employed to produce different use values. The legitimate assumption was that a still implicit technology would, in due course, be introduced to allow capital to produce all commodities as value, without wasting society's productive labour. It was both necessary and methodologically correct, at that stage, to presuppose a set of prices and a rate of profit consistent with an optimal allocation of productive labour, while holding implicit the exact mechanism by which the capitalist market realized that optimal state in which all socially wanted use values are produced in equilibrium quantities.

Although prices and the rate of profit were not entirely absent in the doctrine of production, our focus was on the worker-versus-capitalists relation, values and the rate of surplus value. In this context, c, v, and s were all understood in terms of embodied labour, while constant capital was assumed to be used up in one market period. This allowed us to demonstrate that the value relation between workers and capitalists could be formed and held independently of the particular industrial specialization of individual capitals. Although a relation between different capitals was always implicitly assumed and, sometimes, had to be explicitly acknowledged (particularly when discussing the turnover time of capital and the efficiency of value augmentation), this capital–capital relation was never allowed to divert attention from the more fundamental workers-versus-capitalists relation.

In the doctrine of production, the formation and augmentation of value were constrained only by use values in general, and not by particular types of use value. In the doctrine of distribution, in contrast, the contradiction between value and use values arises in another form, as a contradiction between the capitalist indifference to use values and the unavoidable technical variations which accompany their production. Capital is now finally ready to differentiate itself into heterogeneous forms to produce different use values, while still preserving the unity of circulation and production established in the first two doctrines. To do so, capital must develop its own market so as to produce all the distinct and diverse use values demanded, each of which requires its own specific technique(s), in a manner that is consistent with its own chrematistic principle. Thus, capital's principle of the distribution of surplus value must be preserved, as it adapts, or conforms, to the manifoldness of use-value production. If the value composition of capital is later to be shown to differ necessarily from one industry to another, the enforcement of the law of value and the production of all commodities as value will also require the establishment of a set of normal prices of commodities, which are divergent from their values, together with a rate of profit, which deviates from the ratio s / (c + v) of surplus value to capital advanced.

In the theory of profit, the subjective notion of capital takes the form of specialized units of capital, in different fields of industrial production, in order to produce a wide range of use values. Here, the commodity-economic principle according to which surplus value is distributed as profit to individual units of capital must be made apparent. The market or price mechanism must be explored, together with the technological and institutional conditions that must be maintained in order to allow the society-wide, competitive capitalist market to operate effectively, so as to permit *capital-as-such* to realize a self-perpetuating system. As well, it will be demonstrated that neither the price mechanism nor the law of value can operate independently. Because the costs to individual capitalists and society vary, it is only to be expected that two commodities with the same value or real cost will exchange at prices which depart from values; but it will be shown that values and prices are 'tethered', or systematically related.[19] The marginal producer, in any given industry, thus sells at a market price which, in equilibrium, is equal to the production price; but once these prices have been established, we can also calculate, in value terms, the cost to society of the capitalist production of the said commodities.

THE CONCEPT OF COST PRICE AND THE RATE OF PROFIT

In the doctrine of the subjective notion, Hegel covers the same ground as conventional Aristotelian logic. Without denying the validity of that logic as it applies to formal structures, Hegel exposes the emptiness of these abstract rules of argument until they are applied to the cognition of real truth, in the dialectical comprehension of a dialectical object. Sekine points out that the laws and categories of formal logic bear a similar relation to the Hegelian categories of the *notion as such*, the *judgment* and the *syllogism* as the formal, empty neoclassical economic theory does to the dialectical knowledge of capitalism. Neoclassical economic theory attempts to understand capitalist chrematistics, without recognizing the dependence of these chrematistics on the motion of capital, as it employs the capitalist market and the general rate of profit to ensure that use-value production is carried on in all the appropriate sectors that capitalist society requires. Whereas neoclassical theory deals only with the reified surface of the capitalist market and, therefore, sees only thing-to-thing, price relations, the dialectic sees not only these, but also the production relations, which ground these relations and activities, thereby ensuring capitalism's continued viability as a historical society (Sekine 1986, pp.17–18).

Value and surplus value can only be realized by the sale of the commodities in which they are embodied. Even industrial capital must first purchase its productive elements as commodities in the market and later sell the products it has produced as commodities in the market as well. Thus, industrial capital now reappears in its original mercantile form. The activity of industrial capital in the market is necessarily mercantile, even though the operation of buying and selling is interrupted by the process of producing a use value. Being mercantile means being indifferent to the specific form of use value one produces. Industrial capital, which advances a certain sum of money in productive elements, and realizes surplus value by the sale of its commodity, has no substantive interest in the use values which it produces. Any use value that realizes the most surplus value, in the form of profit, will be produced as value, and no value, or surplus value, can be deemed produced, unless it is realized by the sale of the commodity in the market. Sekine (1975, p.867) warns the unwary that

> [t]he law of value, which says that the value (or real social cost) of a commodity is determined by its labour content, does not imply that value can be determined by technological supply conditions alone. Indeed, the real content of value cannot be determined before the form of value or price (the size of the container, so to speak) is given.

According to Hegel, the *germ* of a plant contains its *particular*, such as roots, branches, leaves, etc., but initially these exist only as potentialities and are not realized until the germ uncloses. This unclosing is the *judgment* (primary or cell division) of the plant (Hegel 1975, pp.231–3). Similarly, the theory of prices, which is based on the differentiation or specialization of capital, as it produces all the use values that capitalist society requires, is the *judgment* or unclosing and attendant division of capital, in Hegelian terms.

The *rate of profit* measures the efficiency of a capitalist operation. Therefore, if this rate is low in one sphere of investment and high in another, capital automatically tends to move from the former to the latter. In consequence of the free mobility of capital, the rate of profit tends to be equalized in all spheres of production, thus establishing what is known as the *general rate of profit*. Capitalism would tend to specialize in the production of one use value or another, in any case, in order to achieve greater efficiency, but the capitalist market dramatically reinforces this tendency, by establishing this general rate of profit. The general rate of profit prevailing at any given time in the capitalist market determines the manner in which the totality of surplus value will be distributed to each and every capitalist enterprise. The surplus value which capital as a whole has produced is distributed to individual units of capital, in proportion to the magnitude of capital advanced. Because it constitutes a standard of average performance, this profit is called *average profit*. The *annual rate of profit (or efficiency of value augmentation)* of an individual firm may be defined by the formula

$$r = en / (1 + k),$$

where e = the rate of surplus value (s / v), n = the annual frequency of turnover of capital, k = value composition of capital (c / v).

Earlier it was implicitly assumed that normal prices were proportional to value. Such an assumption cannot be maintained when the diversity of use-value production is explicitly taken into account. Therefore, when evaluated in normal prices, the *rate of surplus value* (e') and the *composition of capital* (k') differ somewhat from their true, value-evaluated magnitudes (e and k); but such quantitative discrepancies need not obstruct the present analysis.

Capital impartially calculates profit, as the difference of the selling price of a commodity over the cost price (h), or purchase price, of the productive elements, labour power and means of production consumed in the formation of that commodity. Capitalists endeavour to buy productive elements as cheaply as possible and to sell their products as dearly as possible. Indeed, the *capitalist conception of cost* contains not only production costs, but also circulation costs, for all of the capital cannot be advanced in the form of productive capital; some must be held in the form of circulation capital in order to avoid interruptions to productive activity. Since the whole money value of capital advanced is either directly or indirectly useful to the production of surplus value, it seems only reasonable to the capitalist that surplus value or profit emanates from the entire mercantile operation of capital.

If the value of circulation capital is not yet reflected in the cost of the product, it is because the role that commercial capital plays in the turnover of capital has not yet been discussed. To avoid such complications, we shall assume for the present that the cost price includes only the market representation of the value of productive elements (the c + v component of the value of a commodity). Hence, the difference of the selling price (p) over the cost price (h) of a commodity yields surplus value (s = p − h) as a residual, prior to any deduction for pure circulation costs.

The capitalist is correct in recognizing that variable capital does not by itself produce a commodity. *Constant capital*, which is composed of circulating and fixed items, is also required. Not only that part of fixed capital which is currently consumed and depreciated (and, thus, has its value included in the cost price of the commodity), but also the total value of fixed capital, which functions physically as a single body, is indispensable to the production of the commodity. Moreover, while it is true that, in the doctrine of production, the pre-existing value, c, and the newly formed value, v + s, in the product, c + v + s, were clearly distinguished, this distinction means little to capitalists. They see themselves as being engaged in mercantile activity and thus do not regard the value of a commodity as the embodiment of socially necessary labour. The advance of variable capital (v) in wages, which is not recovered until the sale of the commodity, requires of a capitalist an initial outlay of money in just the same way as the advance of constant capital (c) in means of production.

Even though the variable-capital component of the product does not form income in the same sense as the surplus-value component, capitalists are still not justified in regarding the variable-capital component of capital as a cost similar to the constant capital component (as old value transferred to the new product). Nevertheless, the capitalist regards both advances of money together as the *cost price* (c + v) of the commodity. Surplus value, as profit, then appears as merely the mark up or margin of the selling price over the cost price. The *capitalist conception of profit* erases any trace of the relation s = ve (or surplus value equals variable capital times the rate of surplus value), in the value-formation-and-augmentation process. Surplus value, having been emptied of its substantive content, now appears as profit in the capitalist market.

Capitalists only augment value inadvertently while pursuing the maximum profit obtainable from the production of a use value. They fail to comprehend that *surplus value* derives from the use value of productive labour, when it is exercised beyond what is necessary to reproduce the value of labour power. For them, profit seems to arise from the mercantile operation of capital as a whole. They advance capital, K, to buy a variety of productive elements as cheaply as possible, and, later, they sell their products, not only as much above the labour cost, v, but as much above the cost price, c + v, as possible. Although the surplus-value component of the commodity value embodies productive labour, a real cost to society, this component appears to the capitalist to cost nothing.

Even though the recovery of the cost price in the value of a commodity is a categorical imperative for him, the capitalist is unable to objectively measure or determine whether the profitability of his business is adequate. Individual capitalists can only subjectively compare and compete with other capitalists. They cannot compare their performance in terms of the absolute magnitude of profit earned (s), but only in terms of the proportion (r) of profit to total capital advanced (K). The *rate of profit* (r = s / K), therefore, emerges as a standard of self-evaluation and mutual comparison. Only with this index can individual capitalists determine what would constitute the appropriate mark-up above their cost prices. The money value of a commodity is, thus, divided into the cost price, or money value of c + v, the productive elements consumed, and the profit, s = rK. Hence, the rate of profit serves as the principle which regulates the mutual relationship of capitalists among themselves.

The rate of profit, or ratio r = s / K, was referred to as the efficiency of value augmentation in the doctrine of production. Although this ratio remains unchanged, we must now refer to that ratio using the language of the market. In its abstract form, as the ratio of surplus value to the value of total capital advanced, the rate of profit allows capital to disengage surplus value from its productive foundation in order to adopt a form which is compatible with the mercantile principle of the market. We must now examine in this light the three strategic factors that determine the rate of profit.

Since capitalists do not know about the concept of the rate of surplus value, they do not consciously try to raise it. They raise the rate of surplus value inadvertently in the course of their pursuit of a higher rate of profit. The rate of profit thus becomes the *subjective notion of capital*, in Hegelian terms. Every individual firm strives for a maximum rate of profit by the mercantile practice of buying cheap and selling dear, but if all firms competitively strive to buy their productive elements as cheaply as possibly and to sell their products as dearly as possible, all commodities will tend to be traded at *normal prices* in the market. Since market prices are given from the point of view of individual capitalist–entrepreneurs, these maximize profit by minimizing the cost price of their commodities. This, in turn, entails employing the elements of production in the most economical fashion. In a purely capitalist economy there are only three ways to reduce the cost price of a commodity. A capitalist may (1) raise the rate of surplus value (e) to its maximum; (2) reduce the value or organic composition of capital (k) to its technical minimum; or (3) accelerate the annual turnover of capital (n). When individual firms compete in pursuing the highest rate of profit, the rate of surplus value tends to be equalized throughout the economy; but the equalization of the other two factors is limited to a specific industry due, in part, to technical factors, as we shall see.

The *cost price of a commodity* includes the labour cost, or the purchase price of variable capital, and the non-labour cost, or the purchase price of constant capital used up. The *labour cost per unit of a commodity* can be reduced in three ways: (1) by letting employed labourers work longer and harder; (2) by paying them lower wages; or (3) by introducing a labour-saving method of production.

If a particular firm imposes working conditions which are obviously inferior to that of other firms, the workers employed by that firm will tend to seek employment elsewhere. Workers will also tend to leave firms which pay wages significantly lower than the social average. In the long term, then, the efforts of individual capitalists to reduce the labour cost of production by the methods cited above lead to the establishment of a socially uniform standard of working conditions and wages throughout the economy and do not enable particular capitalists to profit permanently from a higher-than-average rate of surplus value.

The introduction of a labour-saving method of production permits extra surplus value to be earned by a handful of innovative firms, until the technique is more widely adopted. However, the extra surplus value must eventually be eliminated with the propagation of the technique. Thus capital, in its individual pursuit of a higher profit rate, reduces the labour cost per unit of the commodity and unwittingly maximizes the production of both absolute and relative surplus value. The *rate of surplus value*, which is the ratio of surplus to necessary labour, will then tend to be both maximized and equalized throughout the economy.

The *organic composition of capital*, which influences the rate of profit, refers to the value composition of capital, advanced in both fixed and circulating constant capital, and not merely the capital tied up in circulating items. Capitalism cannot equalize the value composition of capital from one industry to another, but individual capitalists do strive to maximize their profits by minimizing their costs, including their non-labour costs of production. To do so, they must minimize not only the money value of constant capital currently transferred to the new product (since this reduces the non-labour component of the cost price); they must also minimize the money value of constant capital tied up in their current operations, because that keeps the value or organic composition of capital from rising. Without actually knowing what effect the value composition of capital has on the rate of profit, the capitalist, in his quest to maximize profit, purchases constant capital and consumes it as economically as possible. The opportunity to buy more cheaply than one's rivals tends to be eliminated through competition, but both of the cited practices tend to reduce the organic composition of capital to the minimum possible with the prevailing method of production.

The efforts of individual capitalists to maximize profit raise the annual frequency of the turnover of capital (n) to its technical limit. Although the capitalist, in pursuing a maximum rate of profit, strives to attain indifference to the production of use values, the technical variability in the production of different use values tends to frustrate this goal. The value composition of capital must vary from one industry to another, because of the different techniques of use-value production employed in each.

THE LAW OF AVERAGE PROFIT AND THE MARXIAN THEORY OF PRICES

Since the competitive pursuit of a higher profit rate by individual capitals equalizes the rate of surplus value (e), but cannot eliminate differences in the organic composition (k) of capital, the duration of production periods and the annual frequency of turnover (n), profit rates would necessarily differ across sectors if normal prices were actually proportional to values. In the doctrine of production, where the efficiency of value augmentation was first defined, values and money values meant the same thing. It was pointed out, however, that, if the value composition of capital were found to differ from one industry to another, the enforcement of the law of value would then require both that the normal prices of commodities diverge from their values, and that the rate of profit differ from the abstract ratio s / (c + v). In that context, however, the necessity of a transformation, whether of values into prices or of surplus value into profit, could not yet be tackled. The formation of value was, at that level of abstraction, still viewed from inside the production process of capital, as it were. There, it was sufficient to know that capital produced all commodities as values, without wasting society's productive labour, so that as much surplus labour as possible could be devoted to the production of surplus value. Indeed, it was perfectly legitimate, in that context, merely to presuppose a set of prices and a rate of profit that would be consistent with an optimal allocation of productive labour, while holding implicit the exact mechanism by which the capitalist market would later achieve such an allocation.

Capital, in its production process, produces commodities as value quite indifferently to their use values; yet value must be embodied in a specific use value. Now, when capital comes forward to the market in order to distribute surplus value as profit, it finds itself differentiated into a number of industries or spheres (branches) of production, each of which supplies a particular use value. Capital is, however, now ready to confront and overcome this unavoidable diversity of use values as it subordinates all to its uniform quest for profit maximization. The theory of prices and profit must demonstrate the compatibility between capital's indifference to use values in the production of commodities as value, and the pricing of capitalistically produced commodities as distinct use values in the capitalist market. Thus, in the process of forming a general rate of profit, capital must clear the hurdles posed by inter-industrial differences in the technical methods of production.

The capitalist economy cannot allow persistent profit rate differences in different industries, because all capital would then be invested in high-profit industries and none in low-profit sectors. Capital must, therefore, eliminate inter-industry inequalities in the rate of profit, resulting from different value compositions in different industries. If capital is to produce all the use values which capitalist society demands in the appropriate quantities, the rate of profit, the rate of surplus value, and production prices must all be established with reference to the full specification of technological data, which we shall call the *technological complex*. The latter exhibits the way in which varying techniques are combined for the production of different use values. The production by capital of commodities as value cannot occur in isolation from the production of commodities as use values.

The simplest case of the capitalist market can be imagined as consisting of one capital good (X), one wage good (Y) and one luxury good (Z). In this case the technological complex (T), assuming the same turnover time of capital in all the three branches and the absence of fixed capital, can be formulated as follows:

$$
\begin{aligned}
(X_x, L_x) &\to X, & (50, 20) &\to 150, \\
(T) \quad (X_y, L_y) &\to Y, & (40, 30) &\to 80, \\
(X_z, L_z) &\to Z, & (30, 40) &\to 90, \\
X_x + X_y + X_z &\le X
\end{aligned}
$$

where X_x and L_x are the quantities of the capital good and labour to produce the capital good, X_y and L_y the quantities of the capital good and labour to produce the wage good, X_z and L_z the quantities of the capital good and labour to produce the luxury good, and X, Y, Z are the quantities respectively of the capital good, the wage good and the luxury good produced.

The weak inequality attached states the condition of reproduction. In terms of the numerical example provided, the output of the capital good is in 150 units, while the production of all goods consumes only 120 units, showing that the technology numerically illustrated satisfies the condition of reproducibility. This numerical example is so constructed that the capital–labour ratio of the wage good sector (40 / 30) agrees with the same ratio for the economy as a whole (120 / 90). In this way, we can let the wage good sector represent the sector with a socially average value composition of capital, the capital good sector the one with a higher-than-the-social-average, and the luxury good sector the one with a lower-than-the-social-average value composition of capital. (More will follow with regard to the definition of these value compositions of capital.)

As capital now faces the need to distribute its surplus value as profit, the precise mechanism by which the capitalist market enables the production of all socially wanted use values in equilibrium quantities must be disclosed. A general rate of profit cannot be formed unless production prices, which are generally *not* proportional to values, are established as normal (or equilibrium) prices in the capitalist market.

The *condition of reproduction* must also be satisfied, which means that capital goods cannot be used up in greater quantities than they are being produced in the same period. A capitalist economy is reproducible, in the long run, only when this condition is consistently fulfilled. No society can continue to reproduce itself if the productive consumption of one capital good permanently exceeds its current production. Even if we assume a suitable reallocation of labour, if one capital good cannot be currently produced at least as much as it is consumed, then the existing technology must be deemed *unproductive*. Capital cannot allow this to happen without entering a crisis.

Capitalism also faces the difficulty that its market cannot determine equilibrium prices unless each and every worker engaged in the production of commodities tends to spend the whole of his income on wage goods (and does not save). The essence of capitalism lies in the fact that capital is able to produce all commodities as value, with indifference to use value, because it has access to 'commodified' labour power. However, although labour power appears in the form of a commodity, it is inseparable from its natural owner and thus cannot be reproduced in the factory as integral to the production process of capital. Labour power must be reproduced through the individual consumption process of the workers themselves during their domestic life. Yet, when workers leave the domestic sphere and enter the capitalist market to buy wage goods necessary for the reproduction of their labour power, they must act no differently than any other purchaser of capitalistically produced commodities. They must indeed function as free, equal and independent traders.

The only constraint to which capitalism subjects workers is that they must each tend to spend all the money wages that they earn from the sale of their labour power to purchase wage goods in the quantities which are necessary and sufficient for the reproduction of their labour power. This ensures that labour power will continually be sold as a commodity, and, thus, that capitalism will preserve itself. In the capitalist commodity market, the budget constraints of all workers are added together into what may be called the *fundamental constraint of the capitalist market*, which is the identity that equates the wages paid to all workers with the money value of all wage goods produced. Workers need not actually be paid precisely their subsistence, or the value of their labour power, throughout an entire period or business cycle. What the fundamental constraint implies is that workers do not receive wages which allow them to save for any extended period. In reality, workers tend to save during the prosperity phase of the capitalist business cycle and to 'dis-save' during the depression phase of that cycle. The capitalist market competitively determines a general rate of profit and production prices subject to this fundamental constraint, and not subject to an arbitrarily prescribed wage-basket. The law of value would have no dominion, if society were nothing more than a collection of convict-labour camps or of cattle farms, but such a society would not then be capitalist either.[20]

With the above in mind, let us formulate a system in which a general rate of profit (r) and production prices (p_x, p_y, p_z) are to be determined; a system which we may call a P-operation on T:

$$P(T) \quad \begin{aligned} (p_x X_x + w L_x)\,(1 + r) &= p_x X, \\ (p_x X_y + w L_y)\,(1 + r) &= p_y Y, \\ (p_x X_z + w L_z)\,(1 + r) &= p_z Z, \\ p_y Y &\equiv w(L_x + L_y + L_z) \end{aligned}$$

where the last identity is the fundamental constraint. If the numerical example of the technology provided above is applied, and if we assume that $w = 1$, we find that $r = 0.7338$, $p_x = 0.5477$, $p_y = 1.125$, $p_z = 1.0871$.

While the capitalist market determines these equilibrium prices and the general rate of profit, it also determines behind the scene the labour values of the three commodities (λ_x, λ_y, λ_z) and the rate of surplus value (e) by solving the following system, which we may call the Λ-operation on T:

$$\Lambda(T) \quad \begin{aligned} \lambda_x X_x + L_x &= \lambda_x X, \\ \lambda_x X_y + L_y &= \lambda_y Y, \\ \lambda_x X_z + L_z &= \lambda_z Z, \\ \lambda_y Y &= (L_x + L_y + L_z)\,/\,(1 + e) \end{aligned}$$

where the last equation says that the value of the wage good produced is equal to the total hours of necessary labour, which, clearly, is the counterpart in the value space of the fundamental constraint. In terms of the numerical example, we here find that $e = 1.368$, $\lambda_x = 0.2$, $\lambda_y = 0.475$, $\lambda_z = 0.511$.

Now that equilibrium prices and values are both quantitatively specified by means of the two systems, $P(T)$ and $\Lambda(T)$, we must once again and conclusively account for the relation that binds these two concepts (prices and values) together in the dialectic of capital. Traditionally, discussions of the notorious transformation problem, purporting to explain this connection, have sown more confusion than they have shed light on the resolution of this controversy, not least because the term 'transformation' has been carelessly employed. The virtue of Sekine's approach in *Outline of the Dialectic of Capital* is that he maintains a clear distinction between the *dialectical or conceptual transformation* and the *quantitative or mathematical transformation*, in the sense of a mapping of variables in one space to corresponding ones in another.

As we move from the doctrine of production to that of distribution, we are first faced with the *transformation of value into production prices and that of surplus value into profit*. This reflects a *change in the self-conceptualiza-*

tion of capital, in the sense that the activity of industrial capital is no longer viewed from inside the production process, but rather from outside of it, as it manifests itself on the surface of the capitalist market. The latter requires the concept of the rate of profit, a mercantile form indifferent to the productive base of society, as a universal relation of equality among individual units of capital. However, the rate of profit, as the subjective notion of capital, requires the aforesaid transformation of the concept of surplus value into profit, which also entails the transformation of values into prices. This type of transformation has nothing to do with the concept of mapping in mathematics.

In a dialectical system, the terms 'transformation' and 'conversion' (*Verwandlung*) do *not* refer to a *mapping or mathematical function*, but rather to a logical development that occurs as the process of self-synthesis advances. In the dialectic of capital, for example, the same concept reappears a number of times, but, each time, it is increasingly more concretized, that is, more specified, and, so, for sake of clarity, it is given a new name to indicate its change in status. As the concept of capital is made more synthetic, things that were discussed more abstractly and more one-sidedly in earlier contexts must be reworked, so as to make them fully adequate to the new context in which they now appear. This is what we may legitimately call a *dialectical, or conceptual, transformation*. For example, the conversion of the value of labour power into wages means that what was referred to, in earlier contexts, as the value of labour power is now re-specified, or more fully specified, and is, therefore, renamed as money wages. Similarly, the dialectical transformation of surplus profit into rent implies that a surplus profit, which arises in a particular context (specifically, in relation to the differential fertility of land) is, in this new context, renamed as differential rent. There are many other instances of such usage in Marx's *Capital*, in Uno's *Principles of Political Economy* and in Sekine's *Dialectic of Capital* or in his *Outline of the Dialectic of Capital*. None of these cases implies a mathematical transformation, such as a mapping of a point from, say, the polar to the Cartesian coordinate system.

There can be no inverse transformation in the development of the dialectical logic of capitalism's self-synthesis because, for example, the concept of value logically precedes the concept of production prices and never the reverse. The *transformation of values into prices* occurs as we move from the doctrine of production, in which the production of commodities is viewed strictly as the production of value (and use values are not technically distinguished), to the doctrine of distribution, which takes the (technical) distinctness of the use values that appear in the capitalist market into explicit consideration.

Once the dialectical–conceptual or qualitative transformation has taken place, however, the *quantitative or mathematical transformation* from the value system into the price system, and from the price system back into the value system can and must be made. Values and prices that could not previously be quantitatively determined (because the technological complex could not yet be made explicit) in the doctrine of production can now be completely revealed, thus providing us with full information on the technology involved in the production of all use values. In the doctrine of distribution, the self-organization and self-presentation of the logic of capital has reached the point where what was earlier held implicit can be brought out into the open and treated in a legitimate and non-arbitrary fashion.

There is no question here of one system being mathematically prior to the other. Production prices of basic goods and the rate of profit can be mathematically derived from the values of basic goods and the rate of surplus value and vice versa. An inverse transformation is both possible and necessary, because a quantitative relation between the rate of profit and the rate of surplus value can now be established. The details of this procedure are explained in various places elsewhere (for example, Sekine 1997, II, pp.21–5).

No claim is made that the two systems cannot be solved independently of each other. Given T, both the P-operation and the Λ-operation can be performed on it separately to yield the *price space $P(T)$* and the *value space $\Lambda(T)$*. From this, it does not follow that one of them is redundant; for both spaces provide us with essential information concerning the operation of the capitalist economy. It is important to emphasize here that values are *not* merely first approximations of what will later become equilibrium prices. We do *not* calculate values just to derive equilibrium prices from them. What really happens in the price space is that capital determines equilibrium prices (production prices) simultaneously with the general rate of profit, thus letting the law of value enforce itself through the law of average profit. *Equilibrium prices* ensure that all commodities are produced in socially necessary quantities, that is to say, in accordance with the existing pattern of social demand. Thus, no commodity is either overproduced or underproduced when the capitalist market reaches a state of *general equilibrium*. Such a state implies that productive resources available to society are optimally allocated to all branches of industry. Even neoclassical economics dare not deny this obvious fact.

Recall that, in the doctrine of production, it was already demonstrated that productive labour alone is formative of value. In that value space, capital could reveal how much productive labour was being allocated to each branch of industry in a given (implicit) state of general equilibrium. That information was indispensable and must be kept in mind even after we leave the value space if we are not to lose sight of the fact that we are theorizing a genuine capitalist economy that can actually produce all socially necessary use values, just as any economy must do if it is to remain viable. To ignore this information or to equivocate with regard to it is to detach the market from the real, material foundation which supports it, thus sabotaging any attempt to fully comprehend the capitalist mode of production. One is then forced to fall back on the speculative construction of imaginary economic models that have no bearing on real economic life, however crucial this activity may be to the perpetuation of liberal ideology and the neoclassical school of economics.

In the course of its development, neoclassical economics has gradually divested itself of the classical vestiges of real cost and measurable utility, ending with its refusal to recognize any concept of values as distinct from that of prices. What this has amounted to is the ideological suppression of the reality of society, as Karl Polanyi might have put it. Alternatively, one might say that neoclassical economics refuses to recognize that any human society exists outside the capitalist market. Whence follows the *economistic* idea that human beings, when not obstructed, will always behave as efficiency-seeking automata or as maximizers of gains and minimizers of losses, together with the neoliberal dogma that all human societies are necessarily capitalist or nascent capitalist ones.

Values are indeed unnecessary or redundant for the upholders of such a faith (for example, the followers of Samuelson and their cousins, the neo-Ricardians), but they should not be so for historical materialists. Marxian economic theory, which necessarily entails the recognition of the transience of capitalism as a historical society, cannot possibly disown the concept of value without contradicting itself. It is precisely to avoid this insipid error that we must preserve the value space in the dialectical theory of capitalism. Rather than wasting more time on the ludicrous value-controversy, which preoccupied 'radical' economic theory during the last quarter of the twentieth century and which economic historians of the future will find both perplexing and appalling, let us confirm the Marxian thesis that the production price of the commodity with a higher-than-the-average value composition of capital will be higher than value, and the production price of the commodity with a lower-than-the-average value composition of capital will be lower than value.

In terms of the numerical example provided above, the value composition of capital in each of the sectors can be calculated as $(k_x, k_y, k_z) = (1.18, 0.63, 0.35)$, and it so happens that the average, weighted by the labour inputs, of these capital compositions, $k = 0.63 = k_y$. So the wage good can be deemed to represent a commodity produced with the average value composition of capital. This is because of the expedient assumption that, in this particular numerical example, the capital–labour ratio of the wage good sector, $X_y / L_y = 40 / 30$, is made the same as the capital–labour ratio for the whole economy, $(X_x + X_y + X_z) / (L_x + L_y + L_z) = 120 / 90$. So all we have to show to confirm Marx's above claim is that the relative price of the capital good to the wage good $p_x / p_y (= 0.49)$ is higher than their relative value ratio $\lambda_x / \lambda_y (= 0.42)$, since $k_x > k_y = k$, and that the relative price of the luxury good to the wage good $p_z / p_y (= 0.97)$ is lower than the their relative value ratio $\lambda_z / \lambda_y (= 1.08)$, since $k_z < k_y = k$. The numbers shown in the parentheses confirm the expected results.

(Note: Recall that the definition of the value compositions of capital are:

$k_i = \lambda_x (1 + e)(X_i / L_i)$, $i = x, y, z$, for each sector, and
$k = \lambda_x (1 + e)[(X_x + X_y + X_z) / (L_x + L_y + L_z)]$ for the economy as a whole.)

Let us call what appears inside of the square brackets the *capital–labour ratio*. You can see that in this model the value composition of capital is proportional to the capital–labour ratio, because the value compositions are always $\lambda_x(1 + e)$ times the capital–labour ratio.)

These exercises are designed to show that equilibrium prices, which need *not* be proportional to values (which may be higher or lower than what may be termed value-proportional prices), do not, however, deviate from proportionality in an arbitrary and lawless fashion. Equilibrium prices may be said to be *tethered* to values, the degree of deviation from proportionality being constrained by the extent of the differences in the methods of production or the variability of techniques, as measured by the value composition of capital, between one sector and another.

In no way should this be taken to mean that values must first be determined in order to arrive subsequently at equilibrium prices by applying to values some deviation coefficients. There is no such chronological or logical order. Both production prices and values presuppose a state of general equilibrium, which, once reached, determines both values and production prices simultaneously. It is absurd to talk about such values and production prices prevailing in an economy that does not periodically approach equilibrium.

In the above argument we see that the relative price of the capital good to the wage good must be $p_x / p_y = 0.49$ in order for the socially necessary quantities of all three goods (including the two in question) to be produced in the capitalist market. But it turns out, at the same time, that one unit of the capital good then requires 0.2 hours of socially necessary labour to produce, and one unit of the wage good, 0.475 hours of the same to produce, so that the value ratio of the two commodities must be $\lambda_x / \lambda_y = 0.42$. The excess of the value ratio over the price ratio is explainable by the fact that the method of producing the capital good is more capital intensive than that of producing the wage good. There is clearly nothing that offends economic rationality if, in equilibrium, the two commodities are exchanged at a ratio of 1 : 0.49, while the ratio of the labour embodiment of these goods has to be 1 : 0.42, for technical reasons. The two ratios are both correct and economically meaningful.

THE LAW OF MARKET VALUE

The *law of value* refers to the most fundamental reality of capitalist society in that its viability ensures and is ensured by the tendency for all capitalistically produced commodities to embody no more, and no less, than the socially necessary labour required for their production. The law has been studied in its concrete mode of enforcement in the capitalist market, as the *law of average profit*. Capital eliminates the variations in profit rates which occur in different branches of industry, as a consequence of differences in capital composition and the turnover speed of capital, by the *conversion of values into production prices*, such that, in whatever branch of industry capital is invested, an *average profit*, consistent with the *general rate of profit*, tends to prevail. The latter law enforces the law of value by determining production prices, which are, in general, *not* proportional to values. However, the law of average profit must in turn be supplemented by the *law of market value*, in order to allow for intra-industry differences in the conditions of production.

We have, so far, assumed that, whatever the use value, it can be produced with a single technique (or method of production). However, this is not the case even in pure capitalism. For although, in the process of competition, all capitalists do endeavour to adopt the most profitable of the available techniques, not all of them can be expected to operate with a single technique, in any given industry, at any given time. Even though capital produces commodities as value, with indifference to their use-value properties, it cannot produce that value without, at the same time, producing a specific use value. Since the production of a use value is a people–nature relation, it is subject to a variety of human and natural constraints, which are contingent from the point of view of the commodity economy and which, therefore, cannot be explained by its logic.

No capitalist industry consists of identical firms. Individual firms are different in size, in location, in managerial organization and in the technical methods of production that they employ. Furthermore, in agriculture, lands of differing fertilities have to be employed for the production of the same commodity. In manufacturing industries, innovative techniques may be introduced and yet for some time they will be operated, side by side, with inferior techniques that are only slowly being replaced. Although some of these factors tend to be standardized or made uniform by competition, the development of capitalism does not necessarily eliminate the singularities of different productive units, even within the same industry. Contingent factors, such as the ease of access to the prevailing system of communication, by which information is spread, the geographical location of a rise in demand, and the degree of dependence on skilled labour, employed to supplement deskilled labour, will affect how firms respond to a prior shift in demand. It follows that inequalities in profit rates, arising from the differences in the conditions of production, under which capitals in the same branch of industry compete, will not be completely eliminated either, no matter how intense the competition may be. The labour theory of value is robust enough not to be impeded by such contingent factors as multiple techniques, labour with different skills, or even joint production, as Sekine (1986, pp.156–202; 1997, II, pp.33–42) has definitively demonstrated.

If multiple techniques are employed in any given industry, for example, the dialectic of capital can specify which of them emerges as the *market-regulating technique*, in the light of which it distinguishes between *individual production prices* and the social or *market production price*. Individual firms employing a technique more productive than the market-regulating one will earn a surplus profit over and above the average profit, since their individual production price will be lower than the market production price. Individual firms employing a less productive technique will earn less than the average profit, since their individual production price will be higher than the market production price. This does not in any way indicate a defect of the theory of value; rather, it reflects the fact that the theory of value, in its concrete mode of enforcement in the capitalist market, can overcome this particular form of the contradiction between value and use value. The labour theory of value does not get into difficulties in any of the cases mentioned because it has the capacity to surmount these use-value obstacles by adopting the principle of market value.

The determination of values and production prices presupposes that an adjustment of supply can be made to social demand, as required by the commodity economy. The flexibility of this adjustment is guaranteed so long as commodities are supplied as the products of capital. If, for whatever reasons, the demand for commodity A increases and that for commodity B declines, more of A and less of B must be produced, so that resources flow from the B-industry to the A-industry. We must now answer the question as to which producers of A and which producers of B respond to the shift in demand by either expanding or contracting the supply of these commodities. Suppose that in each industry superior, normal and inferior techniques are being used. If the extra demand for A is satisfied by producers equipped with the inferior technique, then the market-regulating technique of the A-industry is the inferior technique. If, in response to the declining demand for B, those with the normal and the superior technique in that industry contract their outputs, then a suitable combination of these techniques will become the market-regulating technique for commodity B. In this way, the producers who set the market value and the market production price for a given commodity can be identified. They are called *marginal suppliers or producers*. Since a unique technique or combination of techniques can be specified as market-regulating for each commodity, a unique market value (or market production price) for it can be obtained on that basis.

The market value (or market production price) of any commodity depends on the conditions of production under which a commodity is supplied in response to changes in demand. The *market value* (or market production price) is determined *not* by the amount of labour actually spent per unit of the commodity, but by the amount of labour necessary to produce the *marginal supply* per unit of that commodity. The difference between the actually spent labour and the labour required to produce the marginal supply of the commodity gives rise to a *positive or negative false social value*. (Society in its role as consumer deems that socially necessary labour has been spent when, in fact, it has not.)

It is, however, not correct to assume, as in neoclassical analysis, that the marginal technique is always the least productive one, unless these multiple techniques reflect such extra-market factors as the differential fertility of land. The theory of market-regulating value (or production price) must be general enough to allow for all the possible ways in which a given variation in demand can be responded to by producers operating under different supply conditions. For example, if the burden of a marginal productive adjustment falls entirely on a particular technique, it is the quantity of socially necessary labour required by that technique which determines the value of the commodity in question, regardless of what proportion of the total output is produced by this technique and what proportion is produced by alternative techniques. Positive or negative surplus profits will then, in most cases, accrue to non-marginal producers.

Market production prices (the individual production prices prevailing at the margins of all industries) enable the marginal suppliers in all branches of industry to realize the *general rate of profit in equilibrium*. The same rate of profit tends to be earned by all capitals operating at the margin of any industry, even though, inside each industry, capitals employing different techniques continue to earn profit rates at variance with the general rate of profit. The constantly fluctuating market price of a product of capital is now attracted to its market production price, which may be higher or lower than the individual production prices of some producers. (The term *market price* refers to the price of a commodity which, though it fluctuates constantly, tends to move towards an equilibrium price or production price. It does not refer to the price form of market value, which is rather the market production price.) Behind the market production price stands the market value, just as individual values are linked to individual production prices. The *law of average profit* enforces itself through market values and market production prices.

The realization of a uniform rate of profit in different industries presupposes the free mobility of resources and consequent provision of all use values in the socially necessary quantities. Thus, the concepts of value and production price are meaningful concepts only when they tend to settle to definite levels in view of an adequate mobility of resources. An *adequate mobility of resources* does not mean that all currently employed productive resources should be able to change industries in response to the slightest variation in demand conditions. It requires only that the supply of all commodities can be adjusted to their varying social demand without involving an over- or an underemployment of productive resources.

The presence of fixed capital, together with other inelastic factors, often makes it impossible for well-established firms to switch industries at short notice. However, an unambiguous definition of values and production prices requires only a small reallocation of resources at the margin of each industry, which will in turn ensure the adaptation of supplies to a small change in the pattern of social demand. This is equivalent to saying that all industries are, in the language of neoclassical economics, *constant-cost industries*, because a sufficient number of marginal firms are capable of moving from one industry to another.

The mechanization of industry in capitalist society increasingly substitutes unskilled for skilled labour such that the marginal output of any industry tends to be produced solely with unskilled labour, given that such labour is much more mobile inter-industrially than labour with specific skills. If this were not the case with all industries, it would not be possible to say that capital produces commodities as value, indifferently to their use values, or that productive labour can be applied indifferently by capital to the production of any commodity.

Through the operation of the law of market value, capital continues to produce all the commodities it requires as value, even though each commodity is a use value, and is, as such, subject to a variety of contingent natural and human restrictions in its production. When no commodity is either overproduced or underproduced, however, it turns out that every commodity embodies only socially necessary labour, which constitutes its value. A *general equilibrium of all markets*, which together constitute a society-wide capitalist market, would be a meaningless concept if it were not backed up by an *optimal allocation of resources*. Of all economic resources, however, only productive labour constitutes a real cost to society, as has already been stressed. Therefore, an equilibrium price necessarily reflects the substance of value, or socially necessary labour, which alone is the real social cost of production of any commodity. *Socially necessary labour* is the quantity of labour which flows at the margins of all industries in order to produce the general equilibrium level of output of all goods, thus establishing the value of these goods. Although in an equilibrium state of the capitalist market the production prices of commodities are not proportional to their values, that does not contradict the fact that an *optimal allocation of labour* is accomplished only by the formation of a general rate of profit and production prices.

5
Business Cycles

Capital produces commodities as value by adapting not only to static differences in industrial methods of production within and across industries, but also to the dynamic technological changes that capitalist society as a whole undergoes over time. If, indeed, the pursuit of surplus profit always left an existing technology unchanged, but merely enabled its fullest exploitation by driving the capitalist market to an equilibrium, the resilience of capitalism would be so limited that it would not even withstand one serious depression. The adaptation of capital's chrematistic to dynamic technological changes occurs in the *deepening* phase of actual accumulation, which, on the surface of the capitalist market, appears as one of the recurring rounds of technological innovation that are part of the *depression phase* of each successive business cycle. This adaptation is mediated by capital's routine pursuit of surplus profit.

Capital preserves itself as a Hegelian *actuality* because, when all other means fail, it can periodically resort to the production of extra surplus value under the form of surplus profit to renovate or renew its technological foundation, thus providing itself with a fresh start. In Hegelian terms, the *judgment* must periodically yield to the *syllogism* in order for capital to achieve the dynamism necessary to sustain itself indefinitely. The capitalist pursuit of profit may be viewed as the *syllogism*, which brings 'the notion and the judgment into one'. The *syllogism of capital* explains why the rate of profit is what it is, here and now, by revealing its *substantive reason* or *ground*. In its secular decline, the rate of profit is *individual* or *actual*, because it reflects not only the chrematistic notion of the aggregate social capital, together with capital's division into competing units (the *judgment*), but also the material ground upon which its activity unfolds (Sekine 1986, pp.17–20; Hegel 1975, pp.230–3 and 244).

All capitalists pursue *surplus profit* (or *pure economic profit*, in neoclassical economics) whenever there is an opportunity. If, in all industries, only one technique were employed, no producer would retain a surplus profit when prices converged to production prices. In other words, surplus profit would arise only in the course of adjustment of market prices to equilibrium prices. When technical conditions of production differ among producers even within one industry, *surplus profits or losses* accrue to producers whose *individual production prices* differ from the *market-regulating production price* of the commodity. Correspondingly, the difference between their individual values and the market-regulating value would remain as *positive or negative false social value*, to the extent that the amount of labour they actually spent differed from the socially necessary labour, which constituted the *substance of market value*. Thus, even in equilibrium, surplus profit or loss, representing positive or negative false social value, persists, to the extent that the technical conditions of production continue to differ in the same industry. Often, such differences are due to the inelasticity of some factors of production, which cannot be standardized by competition among capitals. The extreme case of such *factor inelasticity* arises with regard to the supply of land. In that case, surplus profit is converted into rent. For instance, when two capitalist farmers operate under conditions that are identical except for the fertility of land, the one operating on the better land produces more than the other. Once this windfall is ceded to the landowner, the two capitalists will compete on equal terms in the capitalist market. The *principle of market value* applies when the owner of an inelastic factor remains the capitalist himself, such as a capitalist who owns a larger factory than a competitor and benefits from the attendant *economy of scale*. In this case, nothing prevents the disadvantaged capitalist from seeking an improvement in his conditions of production so as eventually to acquire the same surplus profit now enjoyed by his competitor. In this context, surplus profit acts as a lure or an incentive, beckoning all to attempt to be the best in the market.

The distinction between the surplus profit convertible into rent and that remaining in the hands of the capitalist lies in the fact that, in the former case, the difference in conditions of production is permanent and beyond the control of capital, while, in the latter case, it is not. Among the transitory intra-industrial differences in the conditions of production, there are those that are immediately eliminated by competition and those that linger for a longer or shorter period of time. Of the latter type, there is a special kind which has to do with the introduction of a new technique into an industry. This type is sometimes referred to as a *quasi-rent*. If a few capitalists innovate with respect to their method of production in advance of the majority, they earn surplus profit, since their method will now be more efficient than that of the majority of their competitors. This surplus profit will be eliminated in due course as more and more of the remaining competitors adopt the improved method of production. A certain length of time is always involved in switching methods of production. This length of time will not remain arbitrary or contingent, because it will be subject to the regulation of the capitalist market. Moreover, by the time this kind of surplus profit is eliminated, not only will all capitalists operating in the same industry be back on equal footing with regard to the technique they employ, but that technique will have become more productive.

The type of surplus profit just described reflects an *extra surplus value* rather than a false social value, because it is not lacking in value substance. No society can shift from one technique to another without some delay and real cost, and so these must be deemed in some sense socially necessary. This quasi-rent is quite unlike an ordinary surplus profit (or pure economic profit) because, although it will eventually be eliminated by competition, real progress in capitalist society's overall technology will by then have been realized, together with a fall in the general rate of profit (of which, more later). By the time the new method of production completely displaces the older method from an industry, the value of the commodity will have been permanently lowered; society will then be able to produce a unit of a commodity, say, cotton yarn, with substantially less socially necessary labour. A society, in other words, stands to gain from the reduction in the cost of producing cotton yarn that results from the adoption of more efficient machinery.

A significant innovation usually entails a greater degree of *roundaboutness* or indirectness in the process of labour and requires the formation of more means of labour to produce a given quantity and quality of use value. In Marx's terms, this is referred to as a *rise in the technical composition of capital*. Whether we refer to the technical composition or the *capital–labour ratio*, we must admit that we are not advancing a directly measurable concept, because constant capital can never be reduced to a homogeneous and malleable physical mass. In order to make such conceptions as technical composition, or roundaboutness, more amenable to theoretical use, it is necessary to evaluate constant capital in terms of value, or stored-up labour. Then the value ratio of constant to variable capital, or the ratio of the quantity of stored-up to current labour, to the extent that it also represents a rise in the indirectness of the process of production, can be adequately defined as the *organic composition of capital*. The quantity of stored-up labour should be viewed as equivalent to the quantity of current labour which would be required to produce the same capital goods as exist at present.

A gain in the average productivity of labour is typically accompanied by a rise in the organic composition of capital. The latter, once again, is the value composition of capital insofar as it reflects the underlying technology of production. Innovative machinery, with a greater productivity, frequently requires more labour to build than the current machinery. Certainly a new industrial technology in the era of liberal capitalism typically required a heavier fixed capital outlay, which also transferred the value of the circulating means of production (such as raw material) more efficiently to the commodity product. This raised the organic composition of capital. The dialectical theory of capitalism must assume that new industrial technologies introduced by competitive firms producing cotton-type use values are all of this type.

A new technology that does not involve a greater degree of roundaboutness need not be considered here, because the adoption of such a technology would not raise the organic composition of capital, nor would it reward the innovators with extra surplus value (if we ignore such legal questions as the protection of innovative techniques by patents, which, because they interfere with the operation of capital's logic, cannot be considered in pure theory). Such a new technology would not entail any cost to society, but most new technologies of the capitalist and even the Fordist eras did entail heavier fixed capital in order to transfer the value of the means of production more efficiently to the commodity product.

Capitalist society cannot bring about major advances in productive techniques except on the basis of a *rise in the organic component of capital*. When the total of invested capital rises, the variable capital component grows absolutely but declines relatively. The fixed capital component, by contrast, grows both relatively and absolutely. Advances in productive powers, due to improved production methods, raise surplus value, but not enough to counteract a *fall in profit rates*. The same may be said of improvements in the turnover speed of capital. Profit rates receive an upward push from advances in society's productive powers, but, at the same time, the technical and organic compositions of capital rise to such a degree that they permanently depress the general rate of profit, as surplus value must now be shared by an increased mass of constant capital.

The mere invention of a new technique does not mean that society can immediately replace all existing machines with new ones. That would mean that an intolerably large part of the productive labour previously spent on the existing machines would have been squandered. That said, capitalist society does not countenance any unnecessary delay in the introduction of the new technique either. An optimal time for the switching of techniques arrives when sufficient quasi-rent has been earned by the innovators to compensate for the value of the existing machines to be scrapped. In other words, at that point, the old method of production can be completely replaced by the new method without causing any loss to society, because the loss of those who fell behind has been compensated for by the surplus profit already earned by those who have already innovated. The need to identify the time required in switching techniques arises because a method of production is often embodied in fixed capital such as machines, which transfer their value to the product piecemeal over a number of market periods. For precisely the same reason, innovations tend to occur in a cluster rather than in isolation. Generally speaking, the development of the capitalist method of production does not occur in continual and uninterrupted technical progress, because the presence of fixed capital militates against such a process. Nor can capital wait until all of the existing plants and machinery are consumed before they are replaced.

The question of innovation can only be fully comprehended in a macro- rather than a micro-context; that is, on a social scale rather than within a particular industry like cotton spinning. Innovation cannot be explained simply by reference to an individual capitalist's desire for surplus profit or extra surplus value, for the introduction of new productive methods does not proceed constantly. The actual process of capital accumulation must alternate between *widening* and *deepening* phases, due to the presence of fixed capital. The two phases appear, on the surface of the capitalist market, as the *prosperity* and *depression phases* of business cycles. Fixed capital embodying the prevailing technology can be renewed only as it nears the end of its durable life. Thus, technical innovations tend to occur in a cluster during the deepening phase of capital accumulation, i.e. the depression phase of the capitalist business cycle, when capital is compelled to make them by the necessity of the actual process of capital accumulation. Capital introduces a new method of production as part of an industrial rationalization, which involves a *renewal of fixed capital* (plants and equipment), in order to extricate itself from a *periodic economic crisis*. The widespread adoption of such innovations then create a relative surplus population or industrial reserve army of labour greater than that which is generated by the mere inactivity of business. This relative surplus population is slowly drained as capital accumulates with a new generation of technology. Since capital accumulation, in the *prosperity or widening phase*, can count on an adequate supply of labour, an expanded scale of production does not require further innovations in productive methods. Capital meets no inherent limit to the expansion of production and the accumulation of capital, so long as it is well supplied with the labour power it cannot directly produce, in the form of a surplus population.

In order to avoid returning to this subject later, I will introduce loan capital here, although its appearance will only be dialectically justified in the following chapter. The *social unity of production* is made possible by loan capital. While it cannot always be maintained, it functions optimally in the period of average activity in the business cycle, when each sector produces close-to-equilibrium outputs relative to the existing pattern of social demand, and society's idle funds are effectively utilized so as to enable the maximum production of additional surplus value. In this context, the circulation of central banknotes maintains an appropriate quantitative relation with the existing gold reserve, and the production of monetary gold, which detracts from the production of other use values, is reduced to the minimum required to meet the monetary requirements of capitalist society. Loans are generally self-liquidating, because the creation of bank credit is followed in due course by the formation of idle funds. Moreover, the shortening of the circulation period, made possible by bank credit, maintains an appropriate relation between the formation of inventories and their absorption. In this fashion, the normal prices of all commodities are stabilized at their production prices.

The prosperity phase is itself divided into the three sub-phases of *recovery*, *average activity* and *precipitancy* (or overheating). In the recovery phase, labour power is readily available, and, due to comfortable cash positions, banks are forthcoming with loans at low interest rates. Different parts of the economy expand at varying speeds, because profit rates are far from uniform. Since the market is not yet stable, the expansion of outputs under given market prices, rather than the maximization of profit, is the prudent course. In this context, when the inter-industry allocation of resources cannot as yet follow the movement of market prices, and it is not yet clear what production prices will be when the economy has fully recovered, loan capital, as it responds to demand, plays an important role in channeling funds to the appropriate spheres of production, and, in so doing, contributes to the rebuilding of capital in various industries and the eventual equalization of profit rates.

Once productive facilities have been rebuilt in most industries, and the demand for commodities and employment of labour have recovered sufficiently, the market prices of commodities tend to rise towards a new system of production prices. In this context, loan capital need play only a subsidiary role in assisting the equalization of profit rates. Rather, industrial capital, guided by positive or negative surplus profits, accomplishes this by its own movement. The recovery phase ends as the demand for and the supply of labour power tend to be equalized and the phase of average activity begins.

The thesis that a capitalist economy tends towards a state of general equilibrium is confirmed in the average phase, since during this phase labour power tends to be in a state of equilibrium – the state in which as much of it is supplied as is demanded. Since the demand for labour power is not excessive, the level of money wages reflects the value of labour power.

It is not possible for only one capitalist industry or for one individual capitalist firm to achieve a balance of demand and supply in the labour market, because labour power is a special commodity which capital cannot directly produce. Yet, in the cyclical process of capitalist accumulation, which is a macro-economic process, the phase of average activity never fails to recur periodically and, during this phase, the capitalist market again approaches the theoretical image of general equilibrium, because the demand for and the supply of labour power tend once again to be equalized. Thus, the repeated appearance of this phase in the course of business cycles provides the law of value with its *ontological foundation*.

Following Marx, the Uno–Sekine approach theorizes a state of general equilibrium, which presupposes an optimal allocation of resources to all branches of industry. A general equilibrium was neither an invention of Walras nor a mere bourgeois fantasy; however, it is crucial to grasp its unique theoretical status within the dialectic of capital. Because equilibrium is theorized as a necessary consequence of the operation of the logic of capital, it is integral to the definition of capitalism. Nevertheless, it is also crucially important for the Marx–Uno–Sekine approach to ground the *micro*-concept of general equilibrium on the *macro*-concept of the cyclically recurrent phase of average activity (which comes to the same thing as having successfully grounded the law of value on the law of population, as the dialectic of capital has already done). To say that the actual process of capital accumulation cannot fail periodically to pass through the phase in which rates of profit tend to be equalized is to say that capitalism periodically approaches a state of general equilibrium. The latter is theoretically grounded (as opposed to being empirically so), because its appearance in the dialectic of capital is permitted only on the basis of a solid macro-foundation which has been developed to justify and support it.

The law of value, by far the most important component of the definition of capitalism by capital itself, cannot be adequately accounted for in the absence of a *general equilibrium* of the capitalist economy, under which a uniform rate of profit prevails and productive labour (as the only original factor of production that constitutes a cost to society) is optimally allocated to all branches of production (within a given set of technical parameters), so that no commodity is either overproduced or underproduced relative to the existing pattern of social demand. Under a general equilibrium of the capitalist economy, all commodities are produced in their socially necessary or equilibrium quantities, by means of socially necessary labour, and are then sold at their production prices.

Value links what is specifically capitalist and, hence, historically transient, with what is trans-historically present in all societies. Thus, it links the *commodity-economic* with the *real economic*. The allocation of resources is primarily a matter of the social organization of production, or the social division of labour, in Marxian terminology. This trans-historic need of human society is largely regulated by the commodity-economic logic of capital in mature capitalism. A material commodity, which is regularly traded in the capitalist market for a profit, is a use value, and, hence, must be a product of a social division of labour. It is, thus, consistent with the nature of Marxian economics (or the dialectic of capital) to claim that value is by far the most fundamental of the concepts required to comprehend capital. If all societies were capitalist, we would not need it; if no society were capitalist, we would not need it either. To understand value is to understand the *differentia specifica* of capitalism as a unique and historically transient society.

The buying cheap and selling dear of commodities in an impersonal market, through the medium of money, is radically different than the exchange of mere use values, which are not commodities. A general equilibrium in the competitive capitalist market results from such mercantile behaviour and not from consumers substituting one use value for another. The capitalist trader buys and sells commodities as an arbitrageur or speculator, in pursuit of the maximum mercantile or abstract-general wealth, moving commodities from where demand is low to where it is high, with complete indifference to the specific characters of the use values involved. Similarly, the capitalist manufacturers of commodities produce whatever commodities fetch them the most profit for their capital outlay, producing what is most in demand first and allocating resources optimally to all industries. In this way, an equal rate of profit and a general equilibrium will eventually be achieved, so long as use value life remains compatible with capitalism's commodity-economic management.

It is now appropriate to account for the only instability that can properly be treated within the scope of the theory of pure capitalism: the eruption of a *periodic crisis*, which, it could be argued, was manifested historically during the early and mid nineteenth century as a *decennial crisis*, though it cannot be said that any historical crisis was the direct result of the unobstructed operation of capital's logic in the absence of any contingent factors. A crisis signifies that the widening phase of capital accumulation has reached its limit as the reproduction process is thrown into disorder, because capital can no longer manage the market for labour power. It does *not* demonstrate, theoretically, the inevitable collapse of capitalism, but, rather, the necessity that capital must periodically make a painful transition from the *widening phase* to the *deepening phase* of accumulation in order to cope with an *excess of capital*, in Marxian parlance. When capital accumulates extensively, with a given technology, during the widening phase of accumulation, it unilaterally absorbs the existing supply of labour power until the price of labour power rises to such an extent that the further accumulation of capital becomes unprofitable.

Capitalists, who have invested considerably in fixed capital, cannot scrap it before it is sufficiently depreciated, just because wages have risen. Nor can they collectively agree to introduce a society-wide technical progress at the first sign that the labour market is becoming tight. Individual capitalists cannot introduce major innovations at this point for the following reasons: First, they would have to allow for the often prohibitive cost of scrapping their existing plants, which are still competitive. Thus, capitalists are bound to attempt to accumulate without raising the organic composition of capital. Second, depreciation funds are typically still insufficient, and the cost of borrowing, at elevated interest rates, is too high, to undertake a major plant reconstruction. Third, if a significant portion of accumulation funds must be withheld to provide for an imminent major investment, then the purchase of labour power and raw materials, which are also becoming more costly, will have to be postponed, thus slowing down the current expansion of output, and allowing other capitalists to encroach freely upon the innovating capitalist's established share of the market. It is obvious that no intelligent capitalist can, under these circumstances, risk a major plant innovation. So long as labour power is available and not prohibitively costly, capital will try to continue its expansion with the prevailing technical method. However, as the widening phase of accumulation proceeds, the relation between capital-istically producible commodities and labour power will necessarily become increasingly strained, and this is exacerbated when loan capital is forced to constrain the production of commodities. The economy must then enter the phase of *precipitancy* or *overheating*.

The pure theory has already demonstrated that a mature capitalist economy, in which all use values are produced as value, isolates money from other commodities. Active money then is used as means of circulation while idle money is socially shared among capitalists to maximize their production of surplus value. In this context, loan capital develops from out of industrial capital and acts as its external and independent regulator. Only banknotes that are backed by gold, a reproducible commodity or value object, can measure the value of other commodities, while acting as gold's proxy. The banking system intends to follow the prior development of the reproduction process, but, ultimately, it cannot remove the latter's cyclical instability. While it endeavours to stay abreast of the motion of capital's reproduction process, it is rarely and only fortuitously successful. It typically lags far behind the needs of the reproduction process, as it perceives only its external aspect, which relates commodity products among themselves, and remains blind to the relation between these products and labour power – the relation on which the process itself is anchored. Thus, regardless of how skilful the management of the banking system, it can never ensure full stability of the reproduction process, which cyclically alternates between prosperity and depression and erupts into periodic crises in between.

During the period of average activity, the equivalence of banknotes and gold money is guaranteed, because loans are self-liquidating, giving the impression that the central bank's gold reserve serves no useful purpose. When no one demands the conversion of banknotes into gold, the banking system will tend to underestimate the importance of its reserves and will recklessly pursue surplus profits. Although they cannot extend more loans safely, banks will attempt to satisfy the unflagging capitalist demand for credit which is beyond the capacity of the reproduction process to absorb. Thus, excessive bank credit eventually shortens the circulation period of industrial capital more than is socially warranted, leading to a deficiency in commodity inventories, and causing banknotes to be issued in excess both of the quantity necessary to circulate existing commodities at their production prices, and of what is justified by the potential formation of idle funds.

When the reproduction process is forced to operate at peak capacity to produce commodities, which are sold as soon as they are produced, the prices of scarce industrial materials must rise sharply. The speculative holding of these commodities causes prices to rise still further. The production of absolute surplus value then becomes increasingly difficult, because wages rise faster than the prices of wage goods. Workers must be offered higher wages, because labour power is scarce relative to demand, the surplus population having been completely absorbed. This outcome is inevitable because of the special nature of labour power – the one commodity capital cannot produce.

If the market prices of commodities rise above their production prices, the production of gold becomes less profitable. Hence, the expansion of this sector falls behind that of other sectors, as the gold reserves of the banking system can no longer be increased at the same pace as the continuing growth of the reproduction process of ordinary commodities. Commodity prices then rise in the face of a relative decline in gold production, and banknotes turn into means of circulation and payment, unfounded on the measure-of-value function of money.

So long as the rate of profit and the rate of interest rise together, the relation between industrial and loan capital remains complementary but, when bank credit continues to expand in this phase of the business cycle, while the production of gold increasingly falls behind, the rise in real wages, together with other costs, depresses the rate of surplus value and the general rate of profit. The rate of interest necessarily rises as the rate of profit falls, until the two rates achieve parity. As the producer of use values, industrial capital is constrained by a particular technological relation and cannot expand more than this technology permits without confronting an *excess of capital*, a situation in which the rate of profit falls below the rate of interest, thus forcing society's reproduction process to a standstill. Outstanding loans then become unrecoverable and loan capital must cease to operate.

Loan capital, through its rising interest rates, eventually checks the unsupportable expansion of industrial capital, which eventually finds it impossible to form accumulation funds, while still maintaining a positive rate of profit. If all profits, after fixed deductions, must be applied to the payment of interest and the repayment of past loans, the operation of industrial capital becomes completely futile, since it cannot meet current obligations without further borrowing in order to remain solvent. Not only the market rate of interest, but the repayment ratio and the degree of indebtedness also increase when the marginal investment of capital yields no positive profit.

An excess of capital brings accumulation to a standstill in a wide range of industries, disrupting society's reproduction process. In this period of crisis, the internal contradictions of the capitalist mode of production break into the open. The potential for incompatibility between the production of commodities *as value* and the production of commodities *as use values* is actualized, as the level of capitalist economic activity plummets. Under the circumstances, the law of value, working through the motion of prices and supported by the micro-behaviour of individual capitals in intra- and inter-sectoral competition, remains wholly powerless to lead the economy to a general equilibrium. Capital cannot continue to accumulate while operating under the prevailing value relation.

An industrial crisis occurs because of an excess of capital, but it only breaks out into the open because of high interest rates. Banks may safely create their own credit, by discounting bills and making loans, only insofar as the reproduction process and the existing technology of use-value production support it. When society's reproduction process ceases to expand, it cannot generate the idle funds which banks might otherwise convert into credit money so as to make it available in any sphere of use-value production. If bank credit exceeds the potential idle funds of the economy, so that the prevailing reproduction process fails to generate funds as expected, bills will not be honoured and loans will not be returned as credit periods expire. Bank deposits too will be withdrawn.

When society's reproduction process faces a fundamental disequilibrium, so that commodity exchanges can no longer be regulated by value, bank credit collapses and central banknotes in circulation become worthless. Their conversion into gold becomes imminent. In the state of an excess of capital, which halts the further extension of loan capital, the deficiency of gold production is thus suddenly exposed. During the period immediately preceding the crisis, conditions were not favourable for the production of gold. Since gold production appeared dispensable, accumulation was very slow in that sector, relative to all other sectors of commodity production. In the state of an excess of capital, when the extension of loan capital is halted, the previous excess of credit money and the present insufficiency of gold production both become apparent. In this period of crisis, circulating cash, whether gold or gold-backed banknotes, suddenly becomes scarce.

By the time gold returns to its proper place as authentic money and the sole measurer of value, the imbalance between the gold-producing sector and other spheres of use-value production has widened considerably. The more the production of gold was neglected in the immediate past, the greater is the shock to industrial capital, as a consequence of the general fall in prices from a level much above production prices before the crisis to a level significantly below them, although, admittedly, the fall in the prices of producers' goods, favoured by speculators, is greater than the fall in the prices of workers' consumption goods.

Although the banks which have managed to survive the crisis have built up adequate gold reserves, the disruption of the reproduction process and of accumulation discourages lending. Banks in possession of cash cannot lend to an industry which no longer has any prospect of generating idle funds, even at a usurious interest rate; they need dependable borrowers who can convert idle funds into capital. Just as money refuses to buy commodities which are wastefully produced, so does loan capital refuse to accommodate an overextended reproduction process. The latter is forced to retrench by a monetary crisis that involves the destruction of excessive capital. This destruction of capital in the wake of a crisis is a violent reaction to the attempt by capitalist production relations to reach beyond their technical limit, which is a consequence of the regulation of the productive activity of industrial capital by the loan capital it has itself generated.

THE DEPRESSION PHASE LEADING TO A SOCIETY-WIDE TECHNICAL PROGRESS

The business climate in the ensuing depression is characterized by an inactive market. A multiplier process of contraction causes the scale of social reproduction to shrink drastically, such that wages and employment decline dramatically as labour power becomes redundant. Overproduced commodities, warehoused speculatively for the optimal market conditions, must be dumped for less than their production prices in a desperate scramble for means of payment. The cyclical shortage of the labouring population, which entails a crisis and an ensuing depression, is not caused by a disequilibrium, whether in the form of an underconsumption or of a disproportion in the supply of certain kinds of commodities – producer goods or otherwise. It is not even an excess of wealth which brings about the crisis, but rather an excess of wealth in the value-augmenting form of capital. Similarly, what is scarce is not labour power, but labour power at sufficiently low wages to guarantee the profitability of capitalist operations. The aim of capital to maximize profit has temporarily come into conflict with the provision of use values to society.

When faced with a labour shortage, capital cannot suddenly undertake to generate a relative surplus population by introducing new methods of production so as to raise society's organic composition. Yet the accumulation of capital would be imperilled if the existing technology were permanently fixed, because the increasing pressure on the labour market would undermine the commodification of labour power. In the long run, capital can restrain rising wages and create a surplus population through the raising of society's organic composition of capital by means of a cluster of innovations. The fall in wages and supply prices in a depression cannot by themselves trigger a new round of expansion. The capitalist who operates a plant at half its usual capacity incurs significant costs in trying to maintain the use value of his idle productive capital. If the selling period is prolonged, the decrease in circulation and storage costs will not be in proportion to the decrease in the volume of commodities circulated. Something more is needed for accumulation to recommence.

The crisis brought on by the falling rate of profit and the subsequent contraction of the reproduction process ruins many capitalists; but it does not signify the breakdown of capitalism. More than ever, capital, which maintains its value only when it is in motion, must strive to augment value, if only to avoid losing it, together with the use value in which it is temporarily housed. Both unsold commodities and capitalist productive elements, whether machinery or materials, can deteriorate quickly if they are not used or sold. However, if the plant was renovated in the previous depression and has depreciated greatly throughout the succeeding period of prosperity, as capital accumulated extensively and output rose to capacity, and if the remainder of the plant's value cannot be quickly transferred to the new product because of the low output level, capital will not be concerned about maintaining the negligible value of the remaining fixed capital.

Capital earns less profit and forms smaller accumulation funds in a depression, but it also purchases less labour power and circulating constant capital. Moreover, banks do have funds which they would be happy to lend to the creditworthy, as conditions warrant it, while surviving firms themselves have depreciation and accumulation funds that are available for promising investment opportunities. However, investments must be made in such a way as to establish a clear advantage over others in the extremely intense competition that characterizes the phase of depression.

Capitalism can maintain labour power as a commodity and, therefore, survive a periodic depression only if it is capable of renewing its value relation by replacing the prevailing technology with a superior one. The imperfect subsumption of any use-value space under the logic of capital not only makes this periodic renewal necessary, but it also raises the possibility of the ultimate, historical transience of capitalism, even though the pure theory cannot demonstrate its inevitability.

When the market prices of commodities fall and stay well below their production prices, the expansion of gold production finally becomes favourable, putting an end to the fall of commodity prices. Industries which receive newly produced gold in return for their supplies to the gold-producing sector deposit some of it with the banks, adding to their reserves. In order to pay interest to their depositors, banks are motivated to provide credit, at a higher but still modest rate, to the more robust and competitive firms, which are prepared to invest in fixed constant capital, thus promoting technical progress. The improved technology allows these firms to achieve production prices even lower than the prevailing depressed market prices. This enables them to earn surplus profits reflecting extra surplus value. After a few capitalists in strategic industries do so, a multiplier effect of expansion begins to work its way throughout the economy. Abler capitalists renovate their plants, thus making the position of less fit firms, operating with obsolescent techniques, untenable. As innovations spread, market prices fall towards new lower production prices throughout the economy.

Many innovations occur simultaneously in this process of capital accumulation, and this raises the organic composition of the aggregate social capital on the one hand, while entailing an increased production of relative surplus value on the other. So long as the fixed capital which embodies the old technique remains insufficiently depreciated and preserves some significant value, it cannot easily be disposed of. A certain length of time, proportional to the remaining value of existing plants, must elapse before the old technique is displaced, but the competitive market environment ensures no undue delay. Thus, capitalism eventually establishes a new value-relation, thereby preserving itself as a self-dependent historical society.

Since the capitalist method of production does not directly regulate the supply of labour power, capitalism must periodically confront an excess of capital that ushers in the depression phase of the industrial cycle, during which the consequent plant innovation, involving a rise in the organic composition of capital, regenerates a relative surplus population that then permits an expanded reproduction in the ensuing phase of prosperity. This surplus population will not be absorbed until the reproduction process attains a peak that surpasses the previous one.

The law of average profit and the law of market value operate as the concrete modes of enforcement of the law of value in the capitalist market. Similarly, the *law of the falling rate of profit* operates as the more concrete manifestation of the law of relative surplus population, compelling capital periodically to renew its value-relation in order to preserve the commodification of labour power. It is not because land becomes less productive and labour power more costly that the rate of profit falls as capital accumulates through successive business cycles. It is because technology becomes more roundabout, raising the organic composition of capital in each successive cycle, that the rate of profit must fall. The law of the falling rate of profit operates such that the general rate of profit tends to fall, even if part of this effect is offset by a simultaneous rise in the rate of surplus value. However, since production methods do not improve constantly, and, hence, the organic composition does not rise without interruption, the tendency for the rate of profit to fall can only be detected if one compares normal or average profit rates during successive prosperity phases in successive business cycles.

The law of the falling rate of profit, which prevails to the degree that society really approaches pure capitalism, is correctly understood against the background of the accumulation process of capital. We cannot deduce it from the mechanical fact that the rate of profit is an increasing function of the rate of surplus value and a decreasing function of the organic composition of capital. In the widening phase of capital accumulation, the rate of surplus value declines with capital accumulation, while in the deepening phase the organic composition rises. The two factors are so combined as to bring down the rate of profit in the course of capital accumulation. What is fundamental to the law of the falling rate of profit is the fact that the speed with which the rate of surplus value declines in the widening phase of accumulation is the smaller, the higher the organic composition of capital. In other words, by adopting a more advanced technology, capital can more easily resist rising real wages and the consequent profit squeeze, even though the profit rate tends to decline secularly across business cycles.

Two more important aspects of the law of the falling rate of profit must be noted. First, the falling rate of profit does not imply that capitalism approaches a *stationary state*. The rate of profit never falls to zero, bringing capital accumulation to a halt. Rather, it falls asymptotically to a positive constant, as capital accumulates indefinitely. Second, there are cases in which technical progress involves more than a mere rise in the organic composition of the aggregate social capital. For example, the advent of a new steelmaking technology in the late nineteenth century produced effects far beyond a mere increase in the organic composition of capital. It entailed profoundly revolutionary or *qualitative* changes, far exceeding a mere *quantitative* progress in the organic composition of capital and in the industrial organization of capitalist society. The effects of such a historically unique event cannot be fully accounted for within the abstract context of a purely theoretical law of capitalism. The proper context in which to explain this event is the stages-theory of capitalism's world-historic development, which we shall discuss briefly later.

6
Rent, Commercial Credit and Loan Capital

The capitalist production relation is established when capital meets the direct producers, who have already been denied access to land, and purchases their labour power. In this commodity-economic relation of trade in labour power, land does not intervene. Indeed, land does not participate in the production of commodities as value. Even in the distribution of surplus value as profit among various units of industrial capital, as part of the process of the conversion of values into production prices, land plays no part. Thus, the fact that capital has to pay rent to make use of privately owned and monopolized land does not prevent it from forming and augmenting value in its production process. The intervention of landed property affects the distribution of surplus value already produced only in *quantitative* terms. It does not repudiate capital's distribution principle. That being said, it must now be recognized that, if the distribution of surplus value as profit in the capitalist market is comprehended only from the point of view of capital (as in the theory of profit), it remains only the *subjective notion* and is neither 'realized' nor 'objectified' in the Hegelian sense. In Hegel's *Logic*, the *subjective notion* must not only regulate its activities according to its own consistent, self-imposed principle; it must also reconcile or adapt itself to certain objective conditions that constrain its operations, in order to achieve harmony with that environment. It is the task of the *objective notion* in both the metaphysical dialectic and the dialectic of capital to make these necessary concessions.

While the production of commodities *as value* need not take landed property into consideration, capital must, nevertheless, now recognize that the *production of commodities as use values* cannot occur without using land as a means of production, nor can it ignore land's private, non-capitalist ownership, because it is this that ensures the continued separation of the direct producers from their natural means of production, which, in turn, supports the continued commodification of labour power (Sekine 1986, p.285; Sekine 1984, p.55; Hegel 1969, pp.705–6).

TAKING LANDED PROPERTY INTO CONSIDERATION

In the dialectic of capital, the various forms of rent cannot be deduced directly from the essentially passive nature of landed property. For it is capital, in its effort to limit the interference of landed property with its production process, which develops the various forms of rent in order to adapt and bind landed property to 'the economic form corresponding to the requirements of the capitalist mode of production' (Marx 1981, p.617). Rent is, thus, a concession of capital to the proprietors of scarce, 'monopolizable' natural powers, or means of production, which cannot be purchased as value objects, but which somehow must be made compatible with the operation of the capitalist economy. This interference is tolerated by capital, because it is preferable to such alternatives as the state ownership of land.

Capitalist society is made possible by the conversion of labour power into a commodity, which, in turn, depends upon the separation of the direct producers from land, the natural means of production. If capital had to depend on an agency such as the state to guarantee the reproduction of labour power, capitalist society would lose its self-dependence. A nascent democratic state, unlike landed property, would not find it so easy to rent land only to capitalists, while denying access to the direct producers. However, if the direct producers could gain access to land through the state, the commodification of labour power and, therefore, capitalism itself would be imperilled. Like the state, private landed property is alien to capital, but, unlike the state, landed property can be subordinated to the commodity-economic principle of capital. In fact, without the private ownership of land under capitalism, the 'self-containedness' of the commodity economy could not be maintained. The private ownership of land, outside capital's direct control, but alienated from the direct producers, must be accepted as a necessary evil by capital if the legitimacy of the commodification of labour power and the private appropriation of the products of labour, acquired from land or nature, are not to be called into question. If land is privately owned, there is a possibility of converting it into a commodity, and maintaining it in that form – something which would be impossible if land were publicly owned.

Capital did not create 'landlordship', or the legally sanctioned authority over the administration of land, but rather its modern form. In pre-capitalist societies, there was no clear concept of privately owned land. A feudal lord did not consider his manor to be his private property in the modern sense. A manor consisted not only of land but also of peasants, who had certain traditional rights to the use of the land. Landed property and the direct producers were inseparably wedded, allowing no room for capital to intervene. In capitalist society, by contrast, landed property and the direct producers meet only through the mediation of capital. This modern form of landed property emerged after the feudal mode of land-holding had already been largely eliminated and the *enclosure movement* had evicted the direct producers from the land. To complete the process of primitive accumulation, and to prevent the return of the direct producers to the land as they attempted to avoid selling their labour power as a commodity, much of the land was transformed into the exclusive property of private persons (legal owners). Because non-capitalist landlords so often refused to exploit the productive potential of depopulated land, capital had the opportunity to integrate it into a process of commodity production. The conversion of labour power into a commodity and the private (commodity-economic) ownership of land presuppose each other. With primitive accumulation, they are preconditions of capitalism rather than its creations. Capital secures the conversion of labour power into a commodity by rendering workers property-less, thus denying workers the right of access to the powers of nature.

The reproduction process of capital must subject itself to various external constraints, imposed by landed property, to achieve harmony with what is initially alien to it. Capital confronts a class of landowners, who are not capitalists, and who demand rent in return for granting capitalists the use of them as means of production for a specified period of time. Capital must adapt its method of distributing surplus value, while ensuring that its law of average profit is preserved, so as to accommodate the participation of landed property in the capitalist market.

Land-intensive industry or agriculture depends directly on the forces of nature, rather than indirectly, as does manufacturing, which purchases raw and manufactured materials as value objects. Since the powers of nature are neither the products of labour, nor automatically the property of capital, value objects cannot be substituted for land. No technical invention can substitute for arable land in agriculture, mines in the mining industry, or construction sites in the building industry. Because nature is so rich in variety, it is not easily amenable to commodity-economic exploitation. Although capital may be able to treat land as if it were a full-fledged commodity, it cannot make it either a reproducible commodity or capital.

Since land and landed property are difficult to manage commodity-economically, the full development of capitalist production relations in agriculture is difficult to attain historically. Typically, a large number of peasants continue to exist and to farm in a traditional fashion and on a limited scale, despite the efforts of capital to make them more fully subject to market discipline. Nevertheless, the economic function of landed property can be clearly exposed only in the context of the theory of purely capitalist society, which assumes both the absence of the peasant class and the presence of a fully developed capital–labour production relation. Marx (1981, pp.614, 618) recognizes this point unambiguously at the outset of his treatment of ground rent. The dialectic of capital takes its cue from Marx in assuming (1) that no landowner invests his own money to engage in farming himself; (2) that agricultural capital rents land from landed property; and (3) that no independent peasant class exists.

Even when land is converted into a commodity, it is not a reproducible product of labour (or commodity) in possession of value. If capital could freely purchase such a pseudo-commodity and did so widely, a significant part of capital would then blend with landed property, and the capitalist market would rapidly lose the ability to enforce its distributive principle. The pure theory must, therefore, make the following heroic assumptions. Capitalist farmers produce agricultural commodities by free choice on land leased from landed property. They are guided by the market and its commodity-economic logic, not by family tradition, just as manufacturing capitalists are. They pursue a maximum rate of surplus value by assembling wage workers in one place, by promoting a division of labour among them, and by introducing mechanical devices. Their workers are engaged in simplified labour processes, as are manufacturing workers, expending their productive labour with indifference to use-value considerations. Capital and labour move from agriculture to industry and back as easily as they do from one industry to another. Under these assumptions, the normal (production) prices of agricultural goods will be as strictly regulated by the law of value as manufactured goods. Although historical capitalism never closely approaches such conditions, it must also be recognized that too great a departure from them will undermine capitalism's viability.

The determination of the market value of products, including agricultural products, is a social act, albeit an unconscious and unintentional one. It is based upon the exchange value of the product, and not directly upon the soil or differences in its fertility. The dialectical self-definition of capitalism tells us that capitalism prevails to the extent that the market value of a reproducible commodity is determined by the quantity of labour that society in its capacity of consumer regards as necessary for the marginal production of that commodity. That is to say, if the demand for that commodity varies by one unit, the method of production or combination of methods which can supply the marginal unit of that commodity determines the market value and the market-regulating production price.

It is not unreasonable to suppose that the monopoly of the natural means of production by landed property in capitalist society could lead to the formation of monopoly prices for agricultural commodities. Although, in reality, some agricultural (and even a few manufactured) commodities fail to achieve a normal (or capitalistically rational) price for any number of contingent reasons, the viability of capitalism requires that the pricing of agricultural commodities will tend to be subject to the law of value. If this condition failed to apply to many agricultural commodities, not only capitalist agriculture, but also capitalism itself, would be imperilled.

THE TWO FORMS OF DIFFERENTIAL RENT

Capital first recognizes landed property as something which it not only does not develop from out of its own self-movement, but also as something which resists the encroachment of its commodity-economic logic. With the first form of differential rent, capital establishes a Hegelian-style *mechanical* (that is, an abstract, formal, indifferent and external) relation with landed property as an alien entity (Hegel 1975, p.261). Capital transfers surplus profits it cannot digest to landed property, because it represents the *differential fertility of land*, which is initially extraneous to capitalist chrematistic.

When surplus profits arise in manufacturing production, due to technical innovation, they constitute extra surplus value. These surplus profits, which have value substance, are eventually eliminated through capitalist competition, as the innovation is adopted generally by capital, thus causing the market-regulating production price of the commodity in question to fall. The same is true in agriculture. If the method of production is capable of being improved by capital, the law of market value deprives technically inferior capitals of an average profit. Surplus profits also arise in agricultural production because of a differential access to natural forces, which are in limited supply. The law of market value is flexible enough in its operation to adjust to capital's inability to change nature; thus, it allows all the capitals which are required to produce the socially necessary output of agricultural goods to earn an average profit, although they invariably operate on lands of different fertility. Capitalist society, in its capacity as consumer, must be prepared to pay the production price of the producer whose commodity was grown on the least fertile land that it was necessary to cultivate to supply the socially required output; since, otherwise, capitalists operating on the least fertile land would have to permanently forego an average profit, and would eventually cease production. Therefore, the *market production price of an agricultural commodity* must be determined by the least efficient method of production employed, and not by the most responsive technique, as is the case when capital is free to choose any technique. This is so even if the marginal supply response to variations of social demand is provided by agricultural capitalists who are located on superior land, because capital cannot, through competition, eliminate the differential fertility and quality of land.

Equal magnitudes of capital advanced on different lands of the same surface area earn a surplus profit, if that land is better than the least fertile. Of course, positive or negative surplus profits, reflecting positive or negative false social values, generally accrue to firms which produce with an individual production price different from the market production price; but the false social value arising from technical differences between capitals can be eliminated eventually by competition, whereas the false social value arising from differential access to natural forces is permanent. The surplus profits so produced, which accrue to some producers but not to others, cannot be internally digested by capital and thus cannot be eliminated in the course of capitalist competition. There is no rational commodity-economic principle to determine which capitalists should benefit from such an exclusive advantage and which ones should not. Therefore, labour which did not need to be expended for the production of an agricultural commodity (given that some capitalists had acquired privileged access to natural forces) is, nevertheless, deemed by capital to have been performed, just as it would have been in the absence of such an advantage. If surplus profits, arising in this fashion on the more fertile land, persist over time, the false social value, which capital cannot by itself eliminate through competition, is removed from it as *differential rent of form* I. Although this rent has no substantive economic content, given that land is not manufactured by commodified labour power in a capitalist factory, as are the other means of production which capital purchases, its appropriation by landlords unwittingly assists capital by establishing a more level playing field among capitalists, which reinforces the operation of the principle of average profit.

If landed property did not exist and all lands were open to cultivation on a first-come-first-served basis, capital would begin with the cultivation of the most fertile land and would then gradually shift to less fertile lands as the supply limit of each grade of land was reached. Consequently, the marginal supply of agricultural produce would always occur on the least fertile land. Capital would then be unable to abide by the law of average profit, since the surplus profits that always arise on the better lands would not be transferable to anyone. It is fortunate for capitalism, then, that capital is not free to cultivate only the best land first, given that capitalists do not have an unobstructed access to land, but must rent land from landlords.

Unlike profits, rents are revenues, which cannot be employed for capital accumulation. They provide for the ostentatious consumption of landowners, who are, nevertheless, not typically under the commodity-economic compulsion to pursue an unlimited maximization of income in the manner of *Homo economicus*, so beloved of bourgeois economic theory. Consider that not even capitalists aim to maximize their consumption funds. Hence, an already well-to-do landlord, who has much fertile land, may choose not to rent a substantial part of it to a capitalist, for any number of perfectly good reasons. Only a landlord whose land is relatively unproductive is under a great deal of pressure to rent most of it out to capitalist farmers.

One ought not to confuse a natural limitation in the supply of land with those limits to its supply that are imposed by landed property. Because the supply of the best-quality land is naturally limited, if the social demand for wheat is greater than that which can be provided from that land alone, the next best land will be urgently sought by capitalists for cultivation. However, lands of varying qualities are privately owned by non-capitalist landlords; thus, it is they who decide what quantity and quality of land they will offer and in what order. Inevitably, then, lands of varying fertility will be simultaneously cultivated by agricultural capital if the social demand for agricultural products cannot be fully satisfied by capitalists operating on the best quality land currently made available for rent.

An increase in the magnitude of capital investment on a given green area of land does not always decrease the return at the margin, because, in general, capital is not limited by the declining productivity of land or by the law of diminishing returns, but by landed property, which imposes external restrictions on capital investment. This is not to deny the *tendency for the marginal productivity of capital to decline*. Indeed, if that tendency were absent, one acre of land would be able to produce any desired quantity of wheat if enough capital was advanced on it. That would contradict the proposition that land is a natural means of production, limited in supply and susceptible of monopolization by landed property. Indeed, in the absence of a global tendency for the marginal productivity of capital to fall, a capitalist could, for example, produce any desired amount of wheat in his own backyard. In that case, the monopolization of land by landed property would no longer restrict agricultural production, and both landed property and rent would become theoretically irrelevant.

With *differential rent of form* I, landed property does not actively interfere with the determination either of the general rate of profit or of production prices. The capitalist market is left to its own devices, except that landowners remove the surplus profits arising from inequalities in the natural conditions of production, by converting them into rent. In this way, landed property merely assists capital in achieving a more competitive environment than it could achieve independently. The activity of landed property is, therefore, quite passive, in that it collects rent, which capital voluntarily surrenders. Only the contingent and, therefore, unpredictable manner in which landed property extends the availability of arable lands exposes capital to uncertainties.

The situation changes when we consider the second relation that capital establishes with landed property. *Differential rent of form II* echoes the Hegelian relation of *chemism*, because it is more intimate, penetrating or 'chemical' (Hegel 1975, p.265). The advance of capital on a given area of land is no longer strictly a matter of free choice for capital. Of course, capital maximizes surplus profits on any land if it is free to do so, but now the process can be either expedited or obstructed by landed property. The latter discourages long-term investments of fixed capital for the preservation and improvement of the soil, but it may also abet the speculative overinvestment of capital. If capitalists did not speculate, no production price of expediency would emerge, and, thus, differential rent of form II would not need to be paid. Its appearance requires not merely the differential fertility of lands, but also the capitalist pursuit of the maximum surplus profit.

With the presence of landed property, the regulation of the marginal supply of an agricultural commodity in response to changes in social demand cannot be determined by capital alone. Landed property can directly limit the supply of an agricultural commodity by refusing to make more lands available to capital when the social demand and price of an agricultural commodity rises. The conditions of tenancy contracts can also obstruct the mechanism of extra surplus value in agriculture and, thereby, delay technical progress there. Since capital can freely dispose of any surplus profit in excess of the contractual rent, it always seeks to maximize such a surplus profit. When the contract is renewed, however, landed property which observes the operations of its capitalist tenants will be inclined to increase the rent, depriving the capitalist, not only of surplus profits, but also of any of the 'undepreciated' portion of *land capital* (that is, any fixed capital incorporated into the soil, such as fertilizers, or inseparably wedded to the land and, therefore, immovable). Capitalist agriculture thus tends to exhaust the soil by failing to invest to maintain or improve it. If capital can lease land for longer periods of time, it will tend to invest more in the soil or in land capital with a long depreciation period and it will do more to exploit the productive potential of the land; but if lease periods are extended for too great a duration, the free mobility of capital into and out of agriculture may be seriously obstructed. To the extent that landed property obstructs the capitalist mechanism of extra surplus value, technical progress in agriculture is impeded and must fall behind that in manufacturing. The production prices of agricultural goods then fall below their value, and the rate at which the organic composition of capital rises is less in agriculture than in manufacture.

Capitalists who are operating on superior land will earn surplus profits, not merely because the soil is relatively more fertile, but also because the optimal advance of capital will be greater on such land, given its superior productivity The surplus profits gained from a more intensive investment on more fertile land will be converted into *differential rent II* as rental contracts are eventually renewed.

In manufacturing and commerce, capital can by itself absorb all the effects of speculation, so that, while individual units of capital may perish because of speculation, capital as a whole suffers the effects only temporarily. In agriculture, by contrast, not all the effects of speculation can be contained by capital as landed property takes advantage of them. If the price of an agricultural commodity shoots up, for whatever reason, windfall profits can be made by agricultural capitalists whose rent remains constant for the duration of a tenancy agreement. This typically leads to speculative investments necessary to raise output. Prices often fall before this larger output is harvested, which means that the speculative capitalists, typically operating on more fertile land, must sell at expedient production prices higher than the genuine production prices on the least fertile land in order to pay their rent and earn an average profit. If this situation persists for a sufficient period, the surplus profit now arising on even the least fertile land will be converted into rent.

Differential rent of form II arises on even the least fertile land, because of the capitalist activity of speculatively overproducing an agricultural commodity and of subsequently forming *expedient production prices*, which regulate the market, although they are higher than genuine market production prices. Although landlords cannot be blamed for this situation, which comes about as a result of capitalist speculation, they respond to it, when contracts are renewed, by raising rents even on the least fertile land, if the market-regulating price remains higher than the previous long-run equilibrium price for an extended period. Once a differential rent is contractually fixed even on the least fertile land, the normal prices of agricultural commodities cannot again fall to their individual production prices on that land. Thus, without directly interfering with the working of the capitalist market, the presence of landed property can lead to a permanent rise in the price of an agricultural commodity.

ABSOLUTE RENT

The third and last relation that capital concludes with landed property echoes Hegel's concept of *teleology* (Hegel 1975, p.267). Landed property no longer represents nature against capital, but justifies itself as a necessary participant in capitalist society. This is immediately apparent when landed property directly participates in the pricing of the capitalist market, collecting absolute rent and, at times, even a monopoly rent. Nevertheless, the cunning of capital is such that it is able to constrain the greed of landed property as it relates to the collection of such rents, by assuring the increasing affluence of the latter so long as the accumulation of capital itself progresses (Sekine 1986, pp.285–8). Thus, although industry was subordinate to agriculture in pre-capitalist society, capital and capitalist industry are able to dominate agriculture and landed property in capitalist society. It follows that the nature of landed property and (capitalized) ground rent in capitalist society cannot properly be comprehended until after one has grasped the *essence* and *subjective notion* of capital.

The private ownership of land is required to prevent the direct producers from returning to the soil to farm. If land is monopolized by private owners, even in the least fertile regions, capital too can never have free access to land. Part of surplus value must be ceded as rent to private landed property, not only to guarantee the principle of equal opportunity to all units of capital, as in a differential rent, but also to ensure capital's access to land in general. This absolute rent can be paid only if the prices of agricultural goods exceed their production prices on the least fertile land. By limiting the supply of arable land in order collect this rent, landed property directly interferes with the working of the capitalist market.

To say that a genuine commodity is a capitalistically reproducible one with a normal price implies that a capitalist industry can produce it with a *constant supply price* or, in other words, that it is produced by a *constant-cost industry*. If a diseconomy, external to the firm but internal to the industry, remains, even in the long run, the supply price of the commodity rises with its output and the industry is said to be an *increasing-cost industry*. In the dialectic of capital, such a possibility exists only in agriculture, where land, as a factor of production, is not at the free disposal of capital. When not enough land is brought into cultivation, because landed property refuses to make it available to capital, it is possible for the long-run supply curve to have an upward slope. If an autonomous increase in demand shifts the demand curve to the right, the supply curve of the relevant capitalist firms will also shift to the right, absorbing that increase entirely, unless landed property interferes with this process; in that case, the price must remain above the normal supply price, establishing a new equilibrium. The landlord has the power to decide, when the rental contract comes up for renewal, either to extend or to reduce the supply of his land for cultivation. He is not guided by the laws of capital or capitalist convenience when he chooses to increase or decrease the supply of land. Nor is it possible to predict whether the land he will offer or withdraw will be of superior or inferior quality.

The pursuit of extra surplus value in manufacturing occurs cyclically, during depression periods, as intensified capitalist competition compels the rationalization of industrial technologies. A new technology that significantly reduces the cost of production can only be advantageously introduced when the existing fixed capital is about to end its life. We have noted that the existence of landed property obstructs this mechanism of extra surplus value in agriculture and delays technical progress in production methods there.

Obstructions can also occur because of the fact that agricultural production is more ecological than technological. Unlike a manufacturing industry, which utilizes the forces of nature only through the mediation of value objects, agriculture is directly subject to a variety of natural constraints. The annual cycle of seasons, weather conditions and the fertility of the soil restrict the production of value and surplus value in agriculture and obstruct the development of the capitalist method of production. While the lengthening of the working day and the intensification of labour contribute greatly to the production of absolute surplus value in manufacture, agriculture must contend with daylight hours of a fixed duration and working periods which are interrupted by seasonal changes. The production period in agriculture, which forms an organic unity from seeding to harvesting, cannot normally be subdivided and assigned to different capitalist enterprises. Nor can it be shortened by specialization. Thus, the capitalist method of production does not develop in agriculture as easily as in manufacturing.

Since agriculture is directly tied to nature, and has a generally lower degree of roundaboutness, the process of mechanization therein cannot proceed as rapidly as elsewhere, even apart from the obstruction of the mechanism of extra surplus value by landed property. The production costs of agricultural commodities cannot be reduced by mechanization unless the scale of operation is large enough to permit it – and capitalist tenant farmers who are not plantation owners or contemporary corporate agribusiness oligopolies are unlikely to reach that plateau. Because of its necessarily slower growth, the level of development will be lower in agriculture than in non-agriculture, whether in terms of turnover speed or of organic composition, regardless of the initial conditions in each.

Recall, however, that the development of the capitalist method of production never proceeds with the same speed in the production of varying use values, due to differences in the organic compositions and turnover speeds. Moreover, technical progress does occur in agriculture, albeit relatively slowly. Since capitalist agricultural production is based on the employment of wage labour, it too must develop through cooperation and manufacture. Granted, agricultural production does not occur in fully mechanized factories. However, even within manufacturing industries, some can more easily be mechanized than others, and there are, as well, differences in the degree of roundaboutness.

Since the organic composition of capital is generally lower in agriculture than in manufacture, the surplus value produced in agriculture, where the value composition of capital is lower than the social average, and production prices are also lower than their value-proportional prices, is transferred to the non-agricultural (and, most significantly, to the manufacturing) sector, where the value composition of capital is higher than the social average. The intervention of landed property obstructs this mechanism by limiting the supply of agricultural land, so as to raise the prices of agricultural commodities above their market production prices and above what would be proportional to their values, in order to collect the price differential as rent, thus interfering with the capitalist distribution of surplus value to various sectors, as average profit and the conversion of values into production prices.

If the obstruction merely reduces the flow of surplus value from agriculture to manufacturing, landed property collects *absolute rent*. The value composition of capital in agriculture still tends to be lower than the social average, and the production prices of agricultural products remain proportionally lower than their values, meaning that surplus value still tends to be transferred from agriculture to non-agriculture, in a capitalistically rational fashion, but at a reduced rate. If the prices of agricultural products are raised to their values (value-proportional prices), the redistributive flow of surplus value from agriculture to manufacturing ceases altogether. When manufacturing receives no transfer of surplus value from agriculture, nor gives any transfer of surplus value to it, such that the activity of the agricultural sector makes no contribution to the formation of the general rate of profit, then the rent collected by the above mechanism is the *maximum absolute rent*.

It is, however, technically possible for landed property to limit the supply of land so drastically as to raise the market prices of agricultural goods above that which would be proportional to their values. Landed property would then earn *monopoly rent* in addition to absolute rent, and this would disrupt the operation of the law of average profit. Surplus value would then flow from more capital-intensive manufacturing to less capital-intensive agriculture, which is the reverse of the capitalist principle for the distribution of surplus value that the law of average profit strives to establish. Such a monopoly rent cannot be tolerated by capital, because it would compromise the regulation of capitalist society by the law of value, destroying the manufacturing sector and raising the spectres of a *Malthusian underconsumption* and a *Ricardian stationary state*.

In a purely capitalist society, landowners must not earn more revenues than they can reasonably consume. Since they cannot themselves convert their savings into capital, they must, in principle, spend their revenues on consumption. If they fail to do so, a *deficiency of effectual demand* will then develop. If the prices of many agricultural goods rise without limit as demand expands, due to the fact that the supply of land remains absolutely inflexible, then these products will be subject to a natural monopoly, and their prices will be *monopoly prices*. For example, a high quality wine, which must be produced on land with unique geographical and physical attributes, will become an object of *natural monopoly*, because it cannot be capitalistically reproduced beyond a certain quantity, regardless of the social demand for it. If most agricultural commodities were irreproducible in this sense, and therefore failed to possess a stable normal price, capitalist society would be impossible.

Fortunately for capitalism as a historical society, monopoly rents did not constitute a serious problem for several reasons. Only a handful of agricultural luxury goods were subject to natural monopoly. Moreover, there were always some landowners who would offer uncultivated land for rent, if rents rose dramatically. In the early period of capitalism, when landed property could not yet benefit fully from the capitalist tendency towards increasing rents, it instead often expropriated not only rent proper, but also a portion of profits and wages. In parallel with the accumulation of capital, however, the magnitude of surplus value produced in agriculture increased. Therefore, by the time capitalism firmly established itself, a minor elevation of the prices of agricultural goods over their production prices was enough to generate a sufficient absolute rent. It is never in the interest of landed property to exploit capital to its ruin, of course. Landed property only benefits when capital prospers in agriculture. Historically, landlords tended to recognize that prohibitive monopoly rents meant that their land would not be leased or that they would ruin the capitalists who provided them with their incomes.

The speedier the accumulation of capital, the greater is the basis of absolute rent. The more prosperous the capitalist class becomes, the more affluent the landlord class becomes, as both surplus value and rental incomes necessarily rise together as capitalism continues to develop. Yet the burden of absolute rent also becomes lighter as capitalism develops. While the development of capitalism necessarily widens the technological gap between manufacturing and agriculture, such that the organic composition of the latter falls relative to the former as a greater quantity of surplus value is converted into absolute rent, landlords, who derive their income from ancestral lands, not from moveable capital, are inclined to be *satisfied* (to borrow a term made popular by H.A. Simon) with their relative and increasing affluence and are neither subjectively motivated nor externally pressured to maximize their wealth. This seems to have been the case during the period of British liberal capitalism. Thus, for strictly theoretical purposes, it is legitimate to assume that even if the burden of absolute rent becomes somewhat heavier, rather than lighter, the working of the law of value will typically not be jeopardized by it, because a declining proportion of total surplus value (which increases with capital accumulation) will need to be converted into absolute rent, in order to ensure the increasing affluence of the landlord class.

Both the historical existence of capitalism and the pure theory, which strives to explain the principles or logic that capital employs in its effort to manage the material life of such a society, must presuppose a landed property that is sufficiently cooperative to capital. Unoists refer to the necessity of this relationship as the *teleological co-existence of capital and landed property*. The significance of the theory of rent, in particular, is to examine how capital negotiates the terms of its teleological coexistence with such an alien power as landed property. Landed property is not a chrematistic form of value augmentation, nor does it operate with the commodity-economic rationality characteristic of capital. The reactions of landed property in the regulation of arable land are, for capital, essentially irrational contingencies, which it must adapt to, while pursuing its own principle of maximal value augmentation. Capitalism must strive to make landed property conform to both its production methods and its distribution principle, so as to preserve the value regulation of economic life, while at the same time tolerating the fact that it cannot invest on any given piece of land without paying absolute rent to landed property, whether this land produces surplus profit or not.

Capitalist society, in its pure, theoretical form, must be deemed to be free from monopolistic 'exploitation' by landed property. Both monopoly rents and underconsumption can cause serious problems for capitalism; but they do so 'from the outside'. In other words, rather than being inherent in the commodity-economic logic of capital, they are extreme cases of the external constraints that landed property imposes on capital. If they become overwhelming, capitalism will be undermined. The purpose of the pure theory is to show (or define) how capitalism works when it is least obstructed by such outside factors. The logic of capital unfolds in its fullness only in their absence. While we abstract from such obstructions in pure theory, we do not deny their importance, not only in history, but also in the stage theory of capitalism's development and decline.

COMMERCIAL CREDIT AND LOAN CAPITAL

In order to save on the unproductive costs and time devoted to circulation, capital must first develop mechanisms for utilizing idle funds in the most efficient manner, thereby promoting an enhanced value augmentation and allowing more production to take place. Loan capital and commercial capital are permitted to share in the surplus value produced by industrial capital, because they reduce its circulation costs and circulation time. Like landed property, they support the production of surplus value, even if they produce none themselves. By providing credit, *loan capital* enables industrial capital to buy commodities, which it would otherwise not be able to purchase currently. By taking over the difficult and time-consuming operation of selling commodities for industrial capital, *commercial capital* enables industrial capital to concentrate on the production of surplus value.

The theory of money has already established that active money, as medium of circulation, presupposes idle money, as a store of value, and that the latter exists in the forms of reserve money, means of payment, and funds (or monetary savings). However, the development of capitalism changes the nature of idle money. Idle money is not merely hoarded, becoming capital only by chance; rather, it is necessarily formed, when part of industrial capital momentarily halts its motion. The circulation process of industrial capital, M—C...P...C'—M', begins with money capital, M, but ends with simple money, M', a portion of which can then be re-advanced as money capital, M. The reproduction process of capital generates idle money as a temporary asset, in the course of converting commodity capital into productive capital, as depreciation and accumulation funds, and, finally, as reserve money, held to guard against price fluctuations. Since the purchase of productive elements cannot always be made instantaneously, M, as M' – m, cannot all be re-advanced as capital at the same time. In the link M'.M of the on-going circulation process of capital, idle funds are necessarily held for varying lengths of time, because they cannot be immediately employed as money capital.

The introduction of *commercial credit* limits the dispersion of private (individual) capitalist enterprises, and strengthens the socially integrating aspects of commodity production. If cotton growing, spinning and weaving were integrated under the operation of one single capital, it would not be necessary for the product of each process to be circulated as a commodity and sold for money. It is the differentiation of capital into independent, specialized operating units that splits one technical process into sub-processes and compels capitalist society to hold unproductive circulation capital alongside productive capital.

'Loanable' money, M, arises automatically in the link M'.M of the on-going circulation process of industrial capital. An individual industrial capital which has produced C can sell it on credit if the M' now received would otherwise constitute idle money that it could not convert into money capital and is thus available as 'loanable' funds. In that case, rather than incurring the cost of storing C' needlessly over a lengthy selling period, industrial capital can dispose of it for a *trade bill*, provided that the purchaser of C' has a good credit standing. Here, industrial capital acts as *loan capital* to another industrial capital, which uses otherwise idle money as means of payment and is, thus, able to enter its production process immediately. Because this occurs generally, capital can purchase commodities more speedily, while economizing its holding of unproductive circulation capital (or, in other words, while minimizing pure and ordinary circulation costs). Purchasers can productively consume inputs offered as commodities, without having to pay cash for them until after they have received the proceeds from the sale of their own products. In this way, loan capital supports greater surplus value production. From out of this additional surplus value, the interest on loan capital can be paid. Although commercial credit does not abolish circulation capital, it reduces its proportion in the aggregate social capital, and thereby contributes to a more efficient operation of the reproduction process and, thus, to an increased production of surplus value in capitalist society.

The commercial credit which industrial capitalists extend to one another forms the basis of the entire credit system. No independent moneylending entity develops the form of loan capital. Although it arises as a subsidiary chrematistic of industrial capital, loan capital must necessarily develop into an independent capitalist operation, which separates idle funds from their owners and concentrates them in the banking system, where commercial bills may be discounted.

One important limitation of trade credit, which is overcome by bank credit, lies in the fact that it is tied to a very specific chain of transactions. A trade credit is given by someone who sells a commodity to someone who buys it, not the other way round. A silversmith or winemaker unrelated to the cotton trade can neither give nor receive credit from it. Nor can consumer credit be extended in this context. The latter practice developed in the post-capitalist era, to permit consumer durables to become leading 'commodities' in western society. By contrast, trade credit cannot be generalized indiscriminately, because it is closely tied to the technical sequence of use-value production. Trade bills are a limited form of credit-money, which have a narrow range of circulation. Neither workers nor capitalists can acquire goods for their personal consumption by means of trade credit. Moreover, industrial capitalists who collectively own society's idle funds cannot, by themselves, operate loan capital in a sufficiently objective fashion. Thus, so long as loan capital operates trade credits among industrial capitalists, outside of the banking system, the interest, M' − M = m, or the price paid for the use of funds, M, may be quite arbitrary. It may include capitalistically irrational and excessive or expropriatory gains, similar to those received by pre-capitalist moneylenders and usurers, rather than being limited to an appropriate and sustainable interest. Moreover, when individual industrial capitalists engage in M...M' that is not mediated by the banking system or the money market, it has no inherent necessity to repeat itself as capital.

Banks are bound to appear to extend industrial capital's limited operation of loan capital. Because they are relatively independent of them, banks can socially regulate the anarchic activities of individual units of industrial capital. With the formation of the money market, individual industrial capitalists find it increasingly difficult to dispose of their idle funds arbitrarily, because they must submit to the social discipline of the prevailing interest rate, imposed by the money market, both as lenders and as borrowers of funds. Banks, as financial intermediaries, make up the money market, in which the *rate of interest* for loans of given durations is competitively and impersonally determined. In this fashion, idle funds are converted into special commodities (in that they do not have varying material qualities) which are priced according to the prevailing rate of interest. The rate of interest reflects the market forces of demand and supply which, in turn, depend on the current conditions of society's reproduction process.

Not only industrial capital but bank capital too consists of individual capitalist operations, whereby the owners of investment funds convert them directly into their own capital, in their pursuit of average profits. Banks must be operated by individual capitalists as private bank capital. They purchase buildings, hire office personnel, and pay office expenses with their own money, M, in order to concentrate and 'socialize' (in capitalist terms) the special commodity C, or idle funds. The money saved by one capitalist becomes 'loanable' funds and is used by other capitalists for real investment during a specified period of time. In this fashion, capitalist society efficiently socializes the use of idle funds.

A bank that receives some significant sum of money as a *time deposit* may lend it out to a customer for the same period, charging him the *lender's interest*, which is a little higher than the *depositor's interest* on the same amount of money. Banks are thus traders of funds as commodities, profiting from the prevailing differential between the depositors' and the lenders' interest rates. 'Loanable' funds, concentrated in the banking system, are no longer restricted by a specific trade in use values, but constitute a common source of finance or credit to all industrial capitalists. Idle funds, generated anywhere in capitalist society, can be channeled to wherever funds are immediately required for investment, by the medium of the banking system.

Bank capital extends surplus-value production, reduces the burden of both circulation capital and circulation costs and increases the magnitude of productive capital, by converting the idle funds which industrial capital generates into loan capital. *Loan capital* then facilitates the purchase of commodities by industrial capital. Both trade credit and bank credit are issued on the basis of a commodity already sold. Money is lent to the purchaser, either directly, by the seller, or indirectly, through the bank. For one industrial capitalist to purchase a commodity on credit, however, its sale must already have been arranged.

Banks can discount good trade bills with *banknotes* or *demand deposits*. In discounting a bill, the bank is obliged to thoroughly investigate the soundness and creditworthiness of the parties involved, and may even charge a *risk premium* on top of the interest, if that is advisable. Banknotes are the bank's own promissory notes to pay cash on demand. By discounting trade bills, banks convert either actual or potential idle money into active money, which circulates in place of gold coins. Since banks are quasi-public institutions, intermediating the reallocation of funds among capitalists, banknotes can constitute *credit money*, which circulates more generally than commercial trade bills issued by individual capitalists. Capitalist society cannot be operated in a capitalistically rational and efficient manner with regard to credit unless capitalists, who can afford to wait without receiving payment, are able to provide 'loanable' funds to other capitalists who can make immediate use of them.

Issuing banks are eventually bound to realize that their banknotes need not be backed up by a 100 percent cash reserve in order to maintain their convertibility. This realization follows from the fact that banknotes are not only promissory notes to pay cash later, but are also *means of circulation and payment* in their own right and are thus equivalent to cash.

The banking system, which concentrates society's idle funds, is constantly supplied with them. If a loan is returned, another loan may be extended, so as to repeat the operation of loan capital. This results in a reduction of circulation capital and the circulation period by making commodity purchases easier, and permits a corresponding increase in productive capital, which promotes greater surplus-value production.

The tendency towards the equalization of profit rates and a general equilibrium, which is guided by the pursuit of surplus profits, depends on the inter-industry mobility of capital as it responds to the fluctuation of market prices. While it would not be easy for anyone to withdraw capital already advanced in the production of a specific use value and move it elsewhere, to produce another use value which yields a higher rate of profit, it is not actually required that individual capitals migrate from one industry to another in response to prior shifts in aggregate demand. The necessary adjustment can be accomplished if the existing firms in the more profitable industries expand their output, and those in less profitable ones contract it, through the mediation of the banking system.

The prevailing rate of interest plays a major role in the formation of a general rate of profit, because loans are made available to the spheres of industry where relatively higher profit rates are anticipated. Before capital moves into that industry from elsewhere, and before the capital within that industry builds its own accumulation funds sufficiently, an acceleration of production is nevertheless made possible by an injection of a portion of the aggregate social capital in the form of socialized funds, free of use-value restrictions, that loan capital makes available. In the short term, at the macro-level, the formation of new capital is accelerated in relatively more profitable industries and is restrained in relatively less profitable industries. In the longer term, the mobility of industrial capital, together with variations in accumulation rates across industries, can be expected to accomplish the necessary production adjustments and the equalization of profit rates.

Banks too, as capitalist enterprises, must earn average profits. If too much capital is advanced in banking, some banks will fail to earn average profits; if insufficient capital is advanced in banking, some banks will earn surplus profits. Hence, in banking too, a socially necessary quantity of capital tends to be advanced, following the law of average profit.

COMMERCIAL CAPITAL

As was argued earlier, the cost price of a commodity must allow not only for its production costs but also for its circulation costs; therefore, the total capital advanced to prepare a commodity for its eventual sale on the market necessarily includes circulation capital as well as productive capital. Industrial capital must accept the fact that it has to hold unproductive circulation capital in order to avoid interruptions in its production of surplus value. The holding of circulation capital in proportion to the length of the circulation period may be deemed the *ordinary cost of circulation*, just as the holding of productive capital in proportion to the length of the production period is accepted as the *time cost of production*. Pure circulation costs are neither part of direct production costs, nor borne for the purpose of avoiding interruptions in production. Their purpose is to reduce the burden of holding capital, productive and unproductive. Pure circulation costs are incurred so as to mitigate the time-related costs of both production and circulation.

The time and resources (as value objects) devoted to the buying and selling of commodities, which constitute either ordinary or pure circulation costs, do not depend on technical factors alone, but on many contingent factors too. Such contingencies will be removed by the necessary appearance of commercial capital. By handling a variety of commodities at once, *commercial capital* promotes much greater efficiency in the selling of those commodities than their industrial producers could manage. Unlike pre-capitalist merchants, it does not link a small group of producers with a small group of consumers, taking advantage of their limited information to gouge both. Instead, commercial capital earns an average profit by trading commodities within the reproduction process of capitalist society or, more specifically, by purchasing in large volumes all the commodities of the producing units of industrial capital at uniform wholesale prices, lower than production prices, and selling these commodities to large numbers of dispersed direct and productive consumers at uniform market prices, taking a more or less definite period of time to do so, and, in so doing, relating all producers and consumers in the capitalist market. Commercial capital thus 'socializes' commodities which are produced individually under different conditions, while reducing the length of the selling period to its necessary minimum and reducing circulation costs and the circulation capital so employed. Commercial capital earns its profit, not by immediately making the additional production of surplus value possible, but by enabling the production and circulation of a given magnitude of surplus value with less capital.

Commercial capital cannot even earn as high a rate of profit as industrial capital was assumed to have earned prior to its necessary differentiation from commercial capital without shortening the circulation period and thereby saving society's circulation capital and pure circulation costs. Nor does the introduction of commercial capital diminish the profitability of industrial capital. Commercial capital shortens the circulation period of capital so far that the total advance of capital in society is diminished (notwithstanding the conversion of pure circulation costs into commercial capital), thus increasing the uniform or common rate of profit accruing to both industrial and commercial capital. Commercial capital receives a share of surplus value, in the form of commercial profit, because of this important contribution.

An individual unit of commercial capital can more efficiently handle a much greater volume of commodity trade than an individual unit of industrial capital. The motion of industrial capital, because of its diverse techniques of use-value production and the attendant stringent use-value restrictions, could not by itself reach its goal of an absolute indifference to use values. Due to the presence of commercial capital, industrial capital is able to immediately plough back the proceeds into further expansion of the scale of its production, to the extent, of course, that loan capital is prepared to finance it. Thus, even though individual units of industrial capital still continue to produce specific use values, capital, as a whole, tends to be released from such restrictions. Commercial capital, by assuming, almost single-handedly, the burden of commodity-economic anarchy, assumes the position of the risk-taking capitalist, although it produces no surplus value itself. Of course, it is still the case that only industrial capital employs the labour power which produces surplus value, so industrial capitalists must still strive to produce commodities which are socially necessary or in demand.

While loan capital emerges from the M'.M link of industrial capital and remains essentially its subsidiary operation, commercial capital differentiates itself from industrial capital by specializing in the entire C'—M' phase of the circulation of the commodities of industrial capital, and thus tends to overshadow both the motion of industrial capital and loan capital, by submerging them effectively beneath the original, purely chrematistic and mercantile (M—C—M') form of capital. The money that commercial capital spends to purchase commodities from industrial capital is not a medium of circulation passing through the hands of the consumers of use values, direct or productive. Commercial capital pays industrial capital in advance for the commodities that it subsequently sells. It does not use its money simply as the means of circulation. Instead, it advances its money as capital in the chrematistic operation M—C—M', and in the process indirectly promotes industrial capital's surplus-value production, by expediting and systematizing the hazardous, complex and specialized process of selling commodities (C'—M') in the motion of industrial capital. By containing the C'—M—C of industrial capital in its M—C—M' circuit, commercial capital reasserts the fact that capital is in essence a pure circulation form. This self-recognition of capital is, in Hegelian terms, the *Cognition* (Hegel 1975, p.283) of capital. Of course, the attempt to view the M—C...C'—M' of industrial capital in the same way as the M—C—M' of merchant capital suppresses the fact that C in M—C...C'—M' represents elements of production, including labour power and C', the product of capital, whereas C in M—C—M' is just any commodity.

Prior to the differentiation of commercial capital from industrial capital, the account of the equalization of profit rates had to assume that industrial capital sold its commodities to consumers, whether direct or productive. If industrial capitals were to act as their own merchants, selling their own commodities, they, like merchant capitalists, could not individually 'socialize' their commodities, given that each would be caught between restricted groups of producers and consumers. They would be unable to independently determine the socially necessary magnitudes of circulation costs or circulation capital. Thus, nothing approaching a perfectly competitive capitalist market would ever materialize, and the general rate of profit and production prices, through which the law of value is supposed to be able to enforce itself in the capitalist market, would also remain empty categories, because, although capital might ideally pursue them, it would not have the power to achieve them.

The full activity of commercial capital is necessary if the capitalist market is to become *actual* in Hegelian terms. Since commercial capital, like other forms of capital, competes for surplus profits, but is no longer constrained by specific use values, as is industrial capital, the rates of commercial profit tend to be equalized. Moreover, although, in any given capitalist market, there is a finite limit, beyond which the annual frequency of turnover, n, cannot be raised, this limit is not known to individual capitalists, commercial or otherwise. Thus, competing commercial capitalists turn over as quickly as possible, and, in so doing, they raise not only the turnover frequency of capital, but also the common rate of profit.

The presence of commercial capital must be implicitly presupposed if the general tendency for profit rates to become uniform in the capitalist market is to prevail. The statement that an average profit accrues to all capitalists who only advance socially necessary capital would be meaningless unless the socially necessary quantity of circulation capital could first be ascertained. This quantity must not be arbitrarily imposed, from the outside, on the capitalist economy, but must evolve through the working of the capitalist market itself. For each commodity, the market must standardize, not only the length of the circulation period, but also the pure circulation costs, which will be deducted from surplus value. When the society-wide capitalist market develops, not only do both the circulation capital and the pure circulation costs required for the sale of any given commodity tend to become standardized, but they also tend to be generally reduced to their socially necessary minimum through the competition of commercial capitalists. Just as industrial capital converted technically necessary elements of production into its cost of chrematistic, commercial capital determines the socially necessary magnitudes of circulation capital and circulation costs. The theory of the equalization of profit rates already implied such magnitudes, but industrial capital could not itself develop a society-wide trading market to shorten and standardize circulation periods. It is left to commercial capital to accomplish this task.

7
Interest-Bearing Capital Closes the Dialectic

Landed property, which monopolizes natural resources, does not itself extract surplus products from the direct producers in capitalist society. Rather, it appropriates a portion of the surplus value already produced by capital, through the imposition on the latter of the various forms of rent. It can do so because the production of use values as commodities by capital cannot avoid the use of a land, a means of production, which is neither a product of capital nor directly convertible into capital, and, hence, cannot be purchased as a typical capitalist commodity in the market. Capital must, therefore, make property in land comprehensible to itself by rationalizing it as the ownership of a commodity like any other. However, even if capital deems land a 'commodity' in the same sense as an antique or an object of art, which are also not capitalistically reproducible, its price will nevertheless remain arbitrary and thus incompatible with capitalist rationality. Though land is not a capitalistically reproducible value object or a genuine commodity, capital can accept its presence only if it is deemed a commodity in possession of a capitalistically rational price, which the present owners have previously purchased or inherited as a property from its original purchasers. Only when the original acquisition of productive land by landed property, which could not have occurred without coercion, is successfully concealed by this fiction, can landed property become an acceptable partner to capital, and therefore entitled to a portion of surplus value on a continuing basis.

The concession of rent to landowners enables capital to develop a new self-image, that of interest-bearing wealth. This practice rationalizes the principle that in capitalist society the owner of a property which is not a value object is nevertheless entitled to a rightful share of surplus value, in the form of a flow of periodic rental incomes. Although this alien idea is initially imposed on it, capital applies this principle to itself and begins to regard itself as an interest-bearing property asset, entitled to a share of surplus value, merely because it is capital, and not because it is the producer of that surplus value.

If land is to be rented, or purchased as a commodity, in a fully developed capitalist society, the money needed to pay for it can only come from the pool of idle funds awaiting conversion into capital. Such idle funds are converted into commodities and floated, as loan capital in the money market, to earn interest rather than average profit. If these funds are used for the purchase of land, they can be regarded as a special form of loan capital, which earns rent instead of interest. The land price can be calculated, capitalist-rationally, alongside the current rate of interest, as an asset which yields a series of rental revenues, rather than as an asset or principal which earns interest revenue.

LOAN CAPITAL AND COMMERCIAL CAPITAL

Capital is now ready to complete itself by adopting the commodity form and becoming an interest-bearing asset, but to do so it must first contain and thereby obscure or camouflage the technical manifoldness of its use-value production within its indifferent circulation form. In Hegelian terms, industrial capital must now conceptualize itself, not from the point of view of its bare *essence*, but from the point of view of its *appearance*. Specifically, this means that industrial capital must consider itself, not as the producer of a diversity of use values, but as the economizer of circulation costs.

In forging 'external' relations with landed property, capital has agreed to cede part of surplus value to it in the various forms of ground rent. This practice rationalizes the principle that, in capitalist society, the owner of a property is entitled to a flow of periodic incomes. Capital then applies this principle to itself 'internally', by viewing itself as a 'property' that yields a stream of interest (rather than rental) revenues. Interest-bearing capital is not only reified but also commodified, with a definite price attributed to it. It is a most atypical commodity in that it possesses a use value, but no material content. As such, it paves the way for the development of the joint-stock, corporate form, the shares of which are traded in the capital market. However, the theory of pure capitalism can only anticipate the development of such a form of capital. The distribution principle of capital in pure theory is thus completed with the concept of interest-bearing capital, which overcomes all use-value restrictions.

Once interest-bearing capital has been developed, capital, as a form of value formation and augmentation that is mediated by the production of use-values, is finally ready to return to its origins as a purely circulatory form of chrematistics. Although interest, which originated in merchant and moneylending capital, is not a new concept to industrial capital, the theory of capitalism cannot equate the interest which moneylending capital charged to pre-capitalist borrowers with the interest which arises from within the circulation process of industrial capital. Interest-bearing capital is the most synthetic and therefore complete concept of capital. It thus corresponds to the *idea* in the Hegelian dialectic (Hegel 1975, p.276; Hegel 1969, p.756).

The *idea of capital*, as interest-bearing capital, can only be reached after industrial capital delegates its circulatory functions to loan capital and commercial capital. Prior to the differentiation of commercial capital from industrial capital, the latter earned an average profit, R, by selling its commodity for a production price. However, when society's capital is advanced, not only in industry, but in banking and commerce as well, a common rate of profit, r, smaller than the general rate of profit, R, must distribute surplus value to all units of capital, whether in industry, in banking or in commerce. Therefore, average or normal profit now refers to this common rate of profit, r, times the advance of any capital anywhere in the economy and not merely in industry. Any difference in the rate of profit now necessarily leads to a flow of funds, either from industry to commerce or from commerce to industry, with the assistance of loan capital. The marginal adjustment between the two sectors depends on the redistribution of socialized funds, originating in loan capital, which are capable of being utilized as money capital, whether in industry or in commerce. The mobility of capital should now be seen as the flow of loan capital to whichever sector earns a surplus profit over and above the common rate of profit. For example, if a surplus profit arises in commerce, some idle funds, generated from industry and socialized by loan capital, are not returned to industry in the form of credit. They are converted into additional money capital in commerce instead, so as to expedite the expansion of commercial activity. Conversely, if commerce is relatively inactive and surplus profits arise in industry, credit flows in the reverse direction, from commerce to industry. If a common rate of profit prevails, both in industry and commerce, the aggregate social capital will already have been allocated to the two spheres optimally. Thus, commercial capital, as a derivative of industrial capital and integral to capitalism, functions alongside industrial capital and earns average profits within the reproduction process of capitalist society, due to the prior existence of loan capital.

Our new definition of average profit does not make the concept of the general rate of profit, developed earlier, redundant. Commercial capital continues to sell commodities for their production prices, which imply the operation of the general rate of profit. Even the common or uniform rate of profit, r, and the redefined average profit or normal profit, calculated accordingly, presuppose production prices and a general rate of profit.

Commercial capital finally removes the use-value restrictions that even industrial capital shares with merchant capital. With the advent of commercial capital, the capitalist market completes itself, while making the equalization of the profit rates both ideal and real (or rational). Commercial profit reinstates the concept of 'profit upon alienation', associated with merchant capital. Profit is no longer viewed as the distributional form of surplus value, but appears to be an increment of value, derived from the trading activity of commercial capital. Indeed, unlike the M—C—M' of merchant capital, the same form, operated by commercial capital, represents a pure chrematistic, indifferent to the use values of particular commodities.

The concept of profit originally arose with that of the cost price into which capital was converted. Industrial capital attempted to act as a merchant in the capitalist market, by accepting profit as a distributive form of surplus value, but was subject to many use-value restrictions. Throughout the theories of profit and rent, industrial capital gradually overcame the technical variabilities and contingencies inherent in the production of use values. Only after capital established a teleological relation with landed property did industrial capital accomplish this, when it gave birth to loan capital and commercial capital. Unlike merchant and moneylending capital, commercial capital does not derive its 'investible' funds from outside industrial capital. Money that is advanced as commercial capital must first arise as idle funds, originating in the motion of industrial capital. More specifically, it must arise from the link, M'.M, which appears within the C'—M'.M—C phase of the motion of industrial capital.

Such idle funds, however, cannot become capital, unless they are first socialized by the motion, M...M', of loan capital. Only loan capital, which socializes the idle funds of industrial capital, can form additional money capital that can be advanced in commerce or industry. Loan capital constitutes the source of all new capital formation, but it is commercial capital, which advances the money that industrial capital originally spawns and which loan capital subsequently socializes. Because industrial capital does not sell its commodities directly to consumers, it releases much of its circulation capital as idle funds to the money market, where it may facilitate the necessary expansion of commercial capital. Alternatively, it may also provide loan capital, either to an industrial sector that is expanding during the period before capital actually moves into an industry from elsewhere, or before capital within a particular industry builds its own accumulation funds sufficiently.

The variation of profit rates compels capital to move from industry to commerce and from commerce back to industry. Capital is essentially indifferent, however, as to whether it earns profit by shrewdly trading commodities or by judiciously managing a productive plant. In both cases, profit accrues to a capitalist in proportion to his business acumen. For the reproduction process of capitalist society to maximize the production of surplus value, the circulation period of capital must also be shortened as far as possible and circulation costs, both ordinary and pure, must be reduced to their minimum. Loan capital and commercial capital accomplish this, but, for them to perform their functions, part of the aggregate social capital must always remain in the form of money.

The commodity exchanges, C'—M—C, which are absorbed by the M—C—M' circuit of commercial capital are no longer subordinate to the motion of industrial capital. When commercial capital operates the M—C—M' circuit formerly employed by merchant capital, it, for the first time, represents a pure chrematistic of capital, whether it is advanced in industry or in commerce, because it originates as loan capital and hence is automatically entitled to an interest over and above a normal profit. Although the interest on 'loanable' funds was earlier explained by the additional production of surplus value, made possible when they were lent to industrial capital, the same explanation cannot apply to the case in which the same funds are lent to commercial capital, since the latter does not produce surplus value.

Commercial capital does not see that the profit it earns springs from the additional production of surplus value by industrial capital, with the assistance of loan capital; thus, the link between profit and surplus value is broken. When commercial capital buys commodities from industrial capitalists and sells them later to purchasers, at a higher price, the commercial profit that it earns necessarily appears to consist of interest, which is equivalent to a property income, such as rent, and which would have been automatically earned, in any case, if the money had been invested in the loan market, and an entrepreneurial reward as compensation for its trading activity. Since commercial workers, who assist in the unproductive labour of business administration, formally (though not substantively) occupy the same position vis-à-vis commercial capital as industrial workers do to industrial capital, and since there is also no qualitative difference between the commercial labour performed by commercial workers and that performed by their capitalist employers, it appears that capital and labour are mere occupational categories that need not entail irreconcilable class-based conflicts of interest. Thus, no distinction can be made between exploited productive labour and the unproductive labour, which exploits. This is reinforced by the fact that commercial capital pursues a maximum rate of return, which is not directly related either to the rate of surplus value or to the organic composition of capital. The misconception that industrial profits are also not derived from surplus value flows from this. This overly formal thinking also makes it possible to view the capitalist as a special category of entrepreneurial worker, who earns a wage as his entrepreneurial reward. Such an ideological conception of industrial harmony mystifies the production of surplus value. Indeed, the activity of commercial capital both perfects and fetishizes the capitalist market, reinforcing the law of value, at the same time that it camouflages its operation.

The requirement that borrowers pay interest to lenders, as when commercial capital makes use of loan capital, develops into the rationalization that owners of capital should pay an interest to themselves, as if they were the borrowers of their own capital, at the prevailing market rate. An extended application of the same subjective procedure converts land into a commodity which possesses a capitalistically rational price. At this point, landed property need no longer be viewed as collecting rents at no cost to itself. For landowners, too, may be deemed to have purchased land as a commodity in the past, in just the same way as capitalists have advanced money as capital. Thus, landowners are entitled to rental revenues in the same way as capital owners are entitled to profit revenues. In this manner, landed property is deemed to comply with the commodity-economic rules of the capitalist market. The *form of interest-bearing capital* enables the unity, which has so far remained unaccomplished, of the object (land) and the subject (capital), and subsumes land, an entity outside the realm of capital, under its rule. Even land is thus made qualitatively homogeneous to capital.

While capital does not do away with the class relation between workers and capitalists, an ideology which ignores it tends to develop, more or less automatically, after land is converted into a commodity, thus establishing an apparent parity of land and capital. The historical character of capital, however, cannot be wholly expunged, so long as it is understood as a profit-seeking chrematistic. For, unlike interest, the category of profit is not fully supra-historic in its appearance. According to the revised trinity formula of the 'vulgar' economics of Marx's era, capital, land and labour were all viewed as representative factors of production, which together contributed to the production of use values. They were all alleged to have generated incomes because of their use-value productivities, whether these incomes constituted interest accruing to capital, rent accruing to landed property or wages paid to labourers.

The division of the normal profit of the aggregate social capital into interest and entrepreneurial reward appears to reduce society's surplus value either to an income – whether in the form of rent or interest – which is derived from the ownership of a property that provides non-human services, or a commercial labour-service income earned by capitalist–entrepreneurs. It now seems that the capitalist class joins the working class in earning an income for its labour services, but it also joins landed property in that it receives interest because of its ownership of capital as a property.

The part of society's total profit, which is interpreted as interest on capital, is completely different, both quantitatively and qualitatively, from the genuine interest that loan capital actually earns. The rate of interest established in the money market reflects the prevailing prices of funds, which have been converted into commodities. The *interest on capital* implies a subjective and ideological, but not actual, conversion of the aggregate social capital into loan capital, in light of the prior determination of the rate of interest in the money market. Thus, unlike the first fraction, the second distinctly expresses the *fetishism of capital consequent upon its reification as a property*. It appears as a mystical, wondrous, automatically interest-bearing and self-expanding asset, in money form.

When economists associate interest (or profit) with capital, wages with labour, and rent with land, they overlook some crucially important facts. Capital confronts not land, but landed property, which has already been adapted to the capitalist mode of production. It does not confront labour in general, but the labour of property-less workers, whose labour power capital purchases and consumes at will. Wages, therefore, do not represent remunerations for concrete labour services rendered, but the price of labour power. Nor are workers' wages freely disposable income for workers, as profit is for capital.

Interest-bearing capital appears as a sum of money that promises a certain flow of future incomes. In this form, capital is already potentially a commodity. It is, therefore, impossible for capital not to anticipate the *joint-stock corporation*, as an ideal mechanism for realizing its conversion into a commodity even if the use-value conditions, which would support the creation of such a firm, would also begin to undermine the operation of capitalism. Only those sectors in which incorporation is not required, because use values are still relatively small and capable of being produced by relatively small and dispersed firms in near perfect competition, can perform the ideal conversion of capital into a commodity. Thus, a *capital market* has no place in the theory of pure capitalism. Idle funds which become available only for a definite period of time are thus wholly channeled into money markets.

The incorporation of a firm was originally a method of organizing enterprises of a scale that exceeded the resources of small individual capitalists. Early in the development of capitalism, joint-stock companies were common in overseas trade, transportation and public utilities. In manufacturing industries, however, they did not emerge until much later, in the final imperialist stage of capitalism. The advent of the iron and steel industry then required large firms, which could be organized only as joint-stock companies. The consequent cen-tralization of capital, however, reversed the tendency of historical capitalism to move toward its pure form, which we have theorized as the dialectic of capital. Capitalism's mode of accumulation too had to change, and this meant that finance capital became the dominant form of capital. To examine such concrete-historical circumstances, one must move beyond the purview of the pure theory. For example, an actual joint-stock company sells its shares in capital (equity) markets, which evolve as adjuncts to money markets. The operation of capital markets presupposes a class of rentiers in possession of idle funds, which arise independently of the motion of industrial capital. The pure theory cannot explain the economic foundation of such 'money capitalists', whose continued existence does not depend on the necessary unfolding of commodity-economic logic. For Unoists, this phenomenon is best explained in the context of the theory of the imperialist stage of capitalism's historical development, as part of the discussion of the rise of finance capital and the joint-stock company.

With the return of capital to its original commodity form, the dialectic of capital closes its circle. By converting itself into a commodity, which has the use value of yielding interest, capital understands, from its own point of view, that it must maintain its motion unceasingly, as a perpetuum mobile. Since interest-bearing capital is a commodity that generates interest, leaving it idle would mean forgoing interest and failing to exploit its use-value potential. Only when capital realizes that it is a ceaseless motion – not because it has to produce surplus value, or to seek surplus profit, or even to economize on circulation costs, but simply because it is capital – is the ultimate nature of capital finally exposed. With that recognition, this dialectical system completes itself as a self-enclosed whole. All previous determinations of capitalism are *sublated* in the above result, which simultaneously returns us to the beginning of our investigation. The commodity, in a fashion not unlike that of the *absolute idea*, 'the idea that thinks itself' (Hegel 1975, p.292), has taken us full circle, by displaying all of its antecedent categories as the self-differentiation of its unceasing operation in the world of abstract theory, where the only use-value resistance capital has to meet are idealized cotton-type use values that it can entirely overcome by its autonomous motion. Thus, the commodity is not only the simplest logical category, or *abstract-universal*, which anticipates the genesis of capital, but it is also the most synthetic, logical category or *concrete-universal*, whereby capital finds its ultimate expression.

The dialectic of capital has completely exposed the inner logic of capitalism, leaving no 'thing-in-itself' unknown. Capitalism reveals itself as self-regulating, self-defining, self-reproducing and self-concluding. Because mature historical capitalism tended increasingly to approach its ideal form as an all-encompassing commodity economy during the liberal era, it appeared to many that what ultimately were to prove to be historically transient, commodity-economic forms were actually going to envelop all alien, non-capitalist factors and so materialize both a permanent natural order of economic life and a universal harmony of (class) interests.

While genuinely needing class divisions in order to exist, capitalism's conjuring away of class conflict does raise the possibility that such conflicts might genuinely be transcended. Notwithstanding the antithetical historical materialist proposition that the class-divided nature of capitalism is a common property of all hitherto existing sedentary societies as well and does not specifically distinguish capitalist society from others, what is specific to capitalism is that the fruits of the direct producers' surplus labour cannot be appropriated by capital through the direct application of extra-economic coercion. Socio-economic relations under capitalism are thus already free from extra-economic coercion, in principle. The conversion of labour power into a commodity subjects the direct producers to impersonal, commodity-economic compulsion to engage their labour, while tending to make it impossible for anyone to appropriate their surplus labour by other than commodity-economic means. (Instances of extra-economic coercion may contingently occur even under capitalism, but they are not essential features of capitalism and ultimately obstruct its operation.) The specifically capitalist social relation cannot be reduced to the master–servant relation that might prevail in a pre-capitalist class society. From the point of view of the dialectic of capital, which has exposed the commodity-economic basis of the capitalist ideology, there is no doubt that if not only capitalism as a unique form of class society, but also class society per se is to be abolished, the commodity form of labour power must be discarded, without, at the same time, restoring any form of the extra-economic coercion of the direct producers.

Part IV

Capitalism and History

8
The Stages Theory of Capitalist Development

MERCANTILISM

The Unoist approach characterizes the first period of capitalism as the mercantilist stage. The nature of this stage is best understood if one focuses on seventeenth- and eighteenth-century Great Britain, prior to the Industrial Revolution, because that country was most successful in laying the foundations of the capitalist mode of production. Britain's mercantilist polices are deemed to be most germane to the task of characterizing mercantilism as a material type.

The dominant form of capital in the formative stage of capitalism was merchant capital. In the theory of a purely capitalist society, and in the mature liberal capitalism of the nineteenth century, which is the inspiration for that theory, the dominant form of capital is industrial capital, while merchant capital (or, more correctly, commercial capital) plays a subordinate role, given that it is concerned only with reducing circulation costs for industrial capital. In the stage of mercantilism, however, merchant capital was not confined to commercial or trading activity, but was also involved with finance, speculation, and both the direct and indirect exploitation of labour. Moreover, the rising merchant class formed a hegemonic alliance with an increasingly commercialized landlord class (Albritton 1991, p.68) and the nascent absolute monarchy.

One must distinguish between mercantile activity generally and merchant capital. Mercantile activity started in the ancient world with the beginning of long-distance trade between sedentary agricultural societies. In and of itself, it has no tendency to turn into capitalism. Throughout most pre-capitalist history, mercantile activity was peripheral to community life. Carrying on foreign trade mainly in surpluses and luxuries, the merchant as middleman tended to leave the division of labour within communities undisturbed. This mercantile activity does not lead inexorably to capitalism. Historically, mercantile activity began to turn into merchant capital (as the latter term implies the advent of the formative stage of capitalism) only to the extent that it is no longer content to focus on long range or external trade, but also has begun to penetrate traditional societies from the outside, thus promoting greater internal and foreign trade. The increasing penetration of mercantile relations into a society slowly altered the division of labour therein by initiating and promoting the process of formally subsuming its labour-and-production process, which, in turn, created the conditions that would make possible a more substantive subsumption in the future. Throughout the seventeenth century and for much of the eighteenth, however, workers still maintained a degree of independence from capital, because labour power was only partially commodified and the labour-and-production process was not substantially subsumed under capital's commodity-economic form of management.

Before and during the stage of mercantilism, a substantial foreign trade in wool and woolen cloth flourished. As mercantilism developed, the commercial policies of Britain thus served the royal interest less and less and instead began to be shaped by Parliament, which was under the influence of manufacturers and merchants of woolens. Merchants and landed property succeeded in winning state support for the progressive enclosure of the commons, which made possible the raising of sheep for profit. Many of the rural poor became a conveniently impoverished and vulnerable 'industrial reserve army' of underemployed workers as a result of these enclosures. This was an essential prerequisite for the further development of capitalism.

The domestic handicraft production of woolen articles, organized as a *putting-out system* by merchant capital and focused primarily on international trade, typified the proto-industrial activity of the mercantilist stage. In Britain the manufacture of wool was carried on throughout the nation. Thus, it was in this sector of the economy that the formal subsumption of the labour-and-production process was most successfully realized. Indeed, the establishment of a wool industry independent of – rather than subordinate to – agriculture was made possible by the putting-out system. Although it eventually engulfed the production of other commodities, the putting-out system developed first, and most extensively, in wool production, because this sector never fell under guild control, given that the spinning and weaving of woolen cloth were not highly skilled activities, and could thus be carried out in rural households.

In the putting-out system, capital did not directly supervise production, nor did it simply hire wage labour in the labour market. Instead, capital provided inputs to cottage producers, who controlled their own labour process and received a piece wage for the product, which capital then marketed. Since agricultural labour tended to be irregular and poorly paid, the spinning and weaving of woolen cloth provided supplementary income for rural cottage dwellers. Merchants organized the putting-out system with the aim of maximizing their profits, but, unlike factory production, the household, as a unit of production, could not be organized or managed by capital. Moreover, the fact that the basic unit of production was the family or household severely limited the development of technology and the division of labour. It also drastically inhibited capital's ability to directly control the labour process and to discipline workers.[21]

It has been customary within the Marxian tradition to employ the categories of *cooperation, manufacture* and *modern mechanized industry* to indicate the level of development of the specifically capitalist method of production. The method of manufacture which began to develop the capitalist division of labour arose from a prior phase of cooperation that entailed the assembling of many workers in a factory and was followed by modern mechanized industry in mature industrial capitalism. Merchant capital gradually moulded capitalist production relations from the seventeenth to the eighteenth century. The process whereby the medieval specialization in trades was transformed into the manufacture division of labour in the capitalist factory was a process in which traditionally independent handicraft workers and artisans were gradually converted into unskilled, wage-earning partial operatives with hardly any professional training. The concrete manifestation of this process may, to some extent, be observed in the manufactories of merchant clothiers.

Although it was the predominant form taken by capitalist production in seventeenth- and eighteenth-century Britain, manufacture was not the leading method of production during that same period. This new method of production implied a more advanced stage of the conversion of labour power into a commodity, but the manufactory, as an imperfect concretization of the manufacture division of labour, remained subordinate to the commission or putting-out system of merchant capital. The age of modern mechanized industry arrived before the manufacture division of labour ever constituted a historical epoch of its own. Indeed, since commodities were still largely supplied to international markets, manufacture would not have been sufficiently flexible in the face of unpredictable changes in distant demand. Rather, it was to the advantage of capital to maintain the merchant method of procuring the outputs of formally independent small producers, who, as handicraft workers, were still in possession of some means of production of their own.

The capitalist separation of manufacturing from agriculture, either under the commission (putting-out) system operated by merchant capital, or, even more so, under the manufactory production of commodities, entailed the formation of extensive market relations within the nation. The home market drew agriculture into commodity-economic relations, while simultaneously creating an extensive population of direct producers in rural districts. The growth of a labour market was also made possible by this separation of a large number of direct producers from the land. These workers, whose connection to an agricultural base was severed, were progressively deprived of such means of production as raw materials, tools and workplaces and eventually could not function as independent producers. Gradually, merchant capital expropriated small producers in both town and country, whether operating in handicrafts or in rural domestic industries. The erosion of the position of independent artisans forced more and more of them to seek employment in the putting-out system as well.

In manufactories, the productivity gain due to the division of labour was quite restricted by the still predominant handicraft techniques. Nevertheless, even under the putting-out system, the production process began to be parceled up and subdivided, as direct producers lost their means of production. While this subdivision of the handicraft industry into partial operations had a relatively minor productivity effect, merchant capital did derive considerable expropriatory gains from the direct producers. Thus, it can be said that merchant capital, operating the putting-out system, left the direct producers in their old occupations and yet converted them into wage workers, not so different from the workers found in manufactories.

The putting-out system constituted a qualitatively distinct mode of capital accumulation requiring its own stage specific explanatory theory. For some considerable period of time, the progress of technology was compatible with this nascent form of commodity-economic management. As a system of profit-making, it entailed minimal fixed costs and was sufficiently flexible to remain economically viable, despite the low level of development of the productive forces and the primitive and unstable market environment (Albritton 1991, p.122). Under these conditions, the putting-out system was more flexible and resilient than manufactories that typified Marx's manufacture division of labour.

The development of the putting-out system did not motivate merchant capital to shift its orientation away from foreign trade. Both the putting-out system in manufacturing and a quasi-commercialized agriculture engaged in foreign trading activity, albeit in a highly protectionist fashion that incorporated much of that trade into a colonial system. While large profits were made through all sorts of foreign trade, it was those branches that interacted directly with domestic production that were most crucial to the development of capital and capitalism. Thus, the putting-out production of wool and the export of woolens constituted the most important branches of production and foreign trade, respectively, for the further development of capitalism.

The formative period of capitalism corresponded with the world-historic process of transition from medieval, feudal societies to modern, bourgeois society. This transition was accelerated by the accumulation of merchant capital, which grew by resorting to the method of 'expropriation'. However, only the state could expedite the transformation of small producers into modern wage workers, because merchant capital, which did not directly operate the reproduction process of society, could not enforce such a process by itself. The state hastened the transformation and, in the process, transformed itself into a bourgeois state. The emerging nation state in the form of the absolute monarchy assisted the development of capitalism by securing the fiscal base of the nation and by facilitating the creation of a national market for the burgeoning commodity economy. The state supported the movement for enclosures, which destroyed traditional social relations to the advantage of the upcoming bourgeoisie. That a feudal regime would itself contribute to the destruction of feudalism was characteristic of mercantilism, a stage of capitalism that was prior to the self-dependence of capital.

Since merchants had no direct access to the political machinery of the state, they sometimes had to appeal to fiscal greed of the kings, and, at other times, to make concessions to the interest of the landed aristocracy. Although the mercantilist economic policies of seventeenth- and eighteenth-century Britain evolved from the creation of a system of royal charters to monopolies and then to the passing of the Navigation Acts and, finally, to more general commercial policies, they consistently aimed at assisting the primitive accumulation of capital by merchant capital.

The state policy of the mercantilist stage was typically dedicated to ensuring that the commonwealth grew as a result of more wealth flowing inwards across the border than that which flowed outwards. Mercantilist foreign trade was essentially an aggressive, commercial projection of the nation outward into a highly competitive and hostile international trading arena. If the state had not protected the emerging domestic market, its infant industries and monopolistic trading companies, capitalism would not have survived or developed.

Protectionist customs duties and laws not only protected British agriculture, but British manufacturing in general, especially wool manufacturing. Imports, which would compete with domestically produced British goods, were banned or highly taxed even if they came from the colonies, whereas exports such as corn were often subsidized. The Corn Laws protected British agriculture by preventing the importation of cheaper food grains and, in years of good harvest, even subsidized exports. The effect of these laws was to raise the price of bread (Albritton 1991, p.101).

Trading firms chartered by the British crown, such as the Hudson Bay Company or the East India Company, and taking the form of joint-stock companies, were typically given exclusive control over certain colonies or regions and over the trade in particular commodities. The building of colonial systems to advance national interests and reap super-profits became imperative. The British, who were most successful in this enterprise, developed their colonies as British possessions, colonized by British settlers and serviced and protected by the British navy. Direct trade between colonies and the rest of the world was forbidden by the Navigation Acts (1651–63), which stipulated that colonial exports had to be carried on British ships to British ports before they could be re-exported on British vessels. British merchants could, in this fashion, monopolize the carrying trade with their far-flung colonies and make further profits from the entrepôt function of re-exporting colonial commodities from Britain. In this way, British ports, and especially London, became great entrepôt centers for the re-export of colonial commodities. By these methods, Britain came close to monopolizing the world's supply of such commodities as sugar and tobacco and, as a consequence, British monopolies made very high profits.[22] At the same time, Britain received raw materials and consumer goods at lower costs than other European powers, which were less successful in establishing their colonial systems.

British colonies received few of the benefits of this colonial system. Colonies were not permitted to develop industries which would compete with those of Britain. Moreover, in colonial industries controlled by Britain, the use of forced labour was common. Both slave and indentured labour were used to produce cheap agricultural products which would not compete with British agriculture. Indeed, the slave trade, as an integral part of the notorious 'triangular' trading relationship, was extremely profitable. Britain dominated the slave trade throughout this period (Albritton 1991, pp.92–4).

Great Britain, which in the middle of the seventeenth century had contended with the Netherlands by way of the Navigation Acts, confronted France towards the end of the century with more general commercial policies. Thus, the commercial policies of Britain no longer directly served the king's interest, but were shaped by Parliament, which was under the influence of the wool manufacturers and merchants. Britain had previously prohibited the export of raw wool in order to ensure that the domestic wool industry, the products of which had long been the most important export item of the country, should be adequately supplied with materials; but now the prohibition not only aimed at providing the domestic industry with cheaper materials, but also at denying foreign competitors fair access to British raw wool. This unambiguously mercantilist measure was intended to achieve the monopoly of the British wool industry in the international market. Various measures were also adopted against cotton goods from India, which were regarded as competitors of British woolen goods. Commercial policy, aimed at protecting the domestic wool industry, constituted the core of British economic policies in the late mercantilist period.

The economic policies of merchant capital tended to undermine the ground upon which it stood. Nevertheless, there was no economic dynamic at work in mercantilism or in the putting-out system that made the transition to industrial capitalism inevitable. To determine what causes a transition from mercantilism to liberalism or from liberalism to imperialism would require that we move to another, more empirical–historical level of analysis that is, nevertheless, informed by what has already been learned from pure theory and stage theory.[23]

LIBERALISM

The period in which capitalism definitively established itself and achieved maturity is characterized by the Uno school as the liberal stage. This period is best represented by mid-nineteenth century Britain after the Industrial Revolution had already transformed economic life in that nation to such an extent that Britain's economic hegemony could not be successfully challenged. The bulk production of cotton articles in modern mechanized factories was the typical industrial activity of this stage. Industrial capital, divided into relatively small, independent and competing enterprises, was the dominant form of capital. It was under this form, moreover, that capitalism became a historical society, in the sense that its reproduction process was primarily regulated by the logic of capital. Industrial capital accumulated by exploiting the surplus labour of wage workers within society's reproduction process that it itself managed, unlike merchant capital, which had remained outside it and thus profited mainly from expropriations of existing wealth.

Once having adopted the exchange relation as the principle that governed its reproduction process, capitalism's commodity-economic management of material economic life displayed an increasing regularity and coherence. Moreover, the accumulation of capital no longer needed fraud and spoliation, nor an extensive reliance on the mercantile skill of buying cheap and selling dear. The coercive policies, which were needed at the birth and in the early formation of capitalism up to the end of the eighteenth century, now became not only dispensable but also repugnant to the newly emerging social order.

The liberal capitalist economic regime did not evolve overnight, nor did it impose its factory-type mechanization on all productive spheres in society. It was by divorcing industry from agriculture, which had occupied the productive center of traditional societies, and by inserting commodity-economic relations between industry and agriculture, that the new system of capitalism gradually evolved and, with it, the irrevocable conversion of labour power into a commodity. Capitalism in Great Britain had prepared the ground for this process in its wool industry of the seventeenth and eighteenth centuries, and completed it with its cotton industry in the nineteenth century. The completion of enclosures, which denied rural workers the opportunity to supplement their income by working off the land, coupled with the New Poor Law (1834), made it possible for the British cotton industry to achieve the closest historical approximation to the total commodification of labour power that prevails in the theory of pure capitalism (Albritton 1991, p.138). During this period, the majority of workers were ultimately forced to sell their labour power to capital in the leading cotton industry and elsewhere. Even so, that industry imported its raw materials from, and exported many of its products to, many other nascent capitalist nations; so, obviously, the British capitalism of that historical era did not realize a fully self-contained or pure capitalist economy.

While it is true that during the stage of mercantilism farms were already marketing their output, they were largely self-sufficient with regards to inputs (seed, fertilizer and tools). However, during the stage of liberalism, the farming sector began to buy significant amounts of commodified inputs, whether as fertilizer, animal feed, tools or machinery, just as the industrial sector was already doing (Albritton 1991, p.140). It was not, however, the changes in agriculture which were crucially important in establishing the stage of liberal market capitalism. For a market-capitalist society to be viable, capital must be able to switch readily from the production of one use value to another in response to price changes in a competitive market. As the theory of pure capitalism demonstrates, only industrial capital has the flexibility to produce commodities with indifference to use value. Thus, it is accurate to say that capitalism is fundamentally industrial. Agricultural capital can never achieve anything close to the total indifference to use value, because nature is so much harder to control than the artificial environment of a capitalist factory. Seasonal changes, weather patterns, pests and soil conditions all constrain value expansion in such a variety of ways that a fully capitalist agriculture is inconceivable. The marketing of agricultural goods is also more difficult than the marketing of industrial commodities, because the products of the land are so often perishable. Moreover, those who are attached to the land, whether agricultural capitalists, independent farmers or even farm workers, experience greater difficulty in moving, whether from the production of one agricultural commodity to another, from one farming community to another or from agriculture to other sectors entirely, in response to changes in demand (Albritton 1991, p.83). Recalcitrant use-value obstacles will always constrain capital's participation in agriculture, but, even in those cases where capital has significantly increased its participation in agriculture, it has done so only on the basis of the prior development of industrial capital, which must provide important agricultural inputs to assist agricultural capital in its efforts to overcome some of the use-value resistance offered by nature to capital's domination.

Capitalism is a society which tends to produce all material use values as commodities by means of material commodities and commodified labour power. According to the theory of pure capitalism, the total commodification of economic life necessarily presupposes:

1. the complete separation of workers from all natural and other means of production, which compels them to sell their labour power for a wage which is just adequate to buy back and consume that portion of the commodities they have produced to reproduce their labour power;
2. the free mobility of deskilled and homogenized labour, which permits supply to move easily to meet a prior shift in demand;
3. the widespread mechanized factory production; and,
4. the complete absence of either collective human resistance to the logic of capital or active state economic policy intervention to support it (Albritton 1991, p.133).

A familiarity with the dialectic of capital and with the stage theory developed by Uno and later critically appropriated by Albritton definitively confirms that Britain in its liberal market-capitalist period was the closest historical approximation to a pure market-capitalist society. During the course of the Industrial Revolution in Britain, the introduction of the fly shuttle, the spinning jenny, the water frame, the throstle, the self-acting mule, the self-acting power loom and the use of steam power combined to establish the ascendancy of the cotton industry, which, in turn, accelerated the mechanization of other industries. Even the transportation system did not remain unaffected by this mechanizing trend. The replacement of firewood by coal provided a new and superior source of energy to fuel the resulting revolution. Since capitalist factories were directly or indirectly powered by coal, the use values which could be most easily produced with these coal-based techniques were the ones which capital attempted first to commodify.[24]

The factory, as a basic unit of production, has many profit-making advantages over the family-based putting-out system. Large numbers of workers could be brought under one roof, thereby not only making it possible to reap the advantages of their combined labour or of *cooperation*, but also preparing the way for the development of an advanced division of labour, with each worker being typically assigned one repetitive task. In the phase of *manufacture*, the division of labour could only proceed so far, because this method was based on handicraft; thus, the labour power of the workers still dictated the development of production methods. In other words, manufacture ultimately depended on human skill, no matter how minutely the production process was split into partial operations by the division of labour. Nevertheless, the workers' close proximity to one another prepared the way for the development of modern mechanized industry. The development of the factory system, together with the Industrial Revolution that accompanied it, completed the divorce of industry from agriculture, which had begun earlier in the wool industry of the mercantilist era. During the late liberal period, the direct producers, who had been gradually deprived of their means of production and skills over many decades, were finally largely reduced to the status of deskilled, property-less workers or proletarians.

In larger-scale capitalist industries of the factory-dominated liberal era, the tool, which was used as a means of labour and as an extension of the hand of a skilled worker, was replaced by machines that, as mechanized means of labour, had the power to operate with many instruments of labour at the same time. A central power source, such as a steam engine, could then be employed to power a coordinated, semi-autonomous complex of machinery, thus greatly magnifying productivity as it simultaneously advanced the division of labour.

This *factory system* was a prearrangement that the worker was compelled to fit into as just one small cog in a great mechanism. Workers thus lost control over the labour process, not just because the pace of work was determined by capitalistically controlled machinery, but also because the organization of work was dictated by the prior organization of the machinery. All motions in the factory came to be regulated by this machinery, which engulfed the workers, reducing them to the status of living appendages of a mechanical system. The machinery, which was owned by capital and designed by its agents according to scientific principles, appeared to increasingly deskilled and vulnerable workers as an alien, threatening and satanic force. The domination of things over humans was thus realized in its rawest and most brutal form in the capitalist factory of this era (Uno unpublished, II, ch.1; Albritton 1991, pp.130–1).

The trend towards deskilled, simplified, homogeneous, undifferentiated and disinterested labour, together with the mechanization of transportation and other improvements spawned by the Industrial Revolution, meant that personal differences among workers could be largely ignored, as deskilled workers were, more or less, interchangeable. This, in turn, meant that supply could shift rapidly to respond to a prior change in demand, because workers were not only far more mobile, but also required only minimal retraining to prepare to produce a new product. Workers were typically forced to relocate at their own expense if shifts in demand required that they move from one job to another.

Although there was no period of capitalist history when workers did not resist capital, the workers' labour power was most commodified and workers themselves were least able to collectively resist capital in the liberal era. The cotton manufacturing industry of the 1860s exemplified this, because workers had lost effective control over the organization and pacing of their labour process, but had not yet organized themselves into effective trade unions or political parties.

The leading cotton industry, like light manufacturing in general, was highly competitive. Compared to the iron and the railway industries, little investment in fixed capital was required, making it possible to enter the industry with a relatively small outlay. This ease of entry, combined with limited economies of scale, meant that this industry tended to expand by the proliferation of many small competing firms which were primarily partnerships. There was no technological imperative which promoted the formation of significantly large firms. Moreover, the Bubble Act of 1720 effectively blocked the development of joint-stock companies until the mid 1840s.[25]

In the liberal stage of capitalism's development, industrial capital adopted a method of production which greatly accelerated the advancement of society's productive powers. This consisted of reducing the labour time necessary for the reproduction of labour power, while the length of the working-day remained constant. That is to say, it consisted of reducing the value of labour power, while the consumption of its use value, labour, remained unchanged. Since this method (of the production of relative surplus value) had no physical limit, capital could realize its mercantile objective to purchase the elements of production as cheaply as possible and then later sell its product as dearly as possible. Even though industrial capital could, as a general rule, neither sell commodities above their values, nor buy commodities below their values, it could pursue the production of relative surplus value. Capital, in other words, could realize an unlimited value augmentation, which was firmly grounded on liberal society's material reproduction process. This was a significant step forward from the stage of development in which merchant capital accumulated by subordinating production from the outside, eventually eroding its own foundation. By contrast, industrial capital in the liberal period survived and flourished by introducing new production methods in successive depression phases of capitalism's recurring business cycle. This not only restored profitability for the firms that successfully introduced the new methods, it also developed society's productive powers to an unprecedented degree and with an unparalleled rapidity, while generating a relative surplus population which capital could draw on as it moved towards recovery and a new round of growth. In this fashion, capital escaped any constraint which might have been imposed upon it by a shortfall in the natural growth of the working population that would otherwise have been sufficient to prevent a new round of growth (Uno unpublished, II, Introduction; ch.1).

The advancement of the productive powers that provided human society with material progress was pursued automatically under capitalism, through the operation of the commodity-economic mechanism just described. The same driving force also contributed towards the further development of mechanized industry. Of course, it was not because of their commitment to any general principle that individual capitalists sought to improve production methods. They were motivated rather by the special profit (often called quasi-rent) which they could earn if they adopted a new method of producing the commodity with less input of labour, directly and indirectly, than others who continued to operate in the same industry with conventional techniques.

The period between the 1820s and the 1860s in Great Britain constituted the epoch in which industrial capital established itself, based upon the capitalistic development of the cotton industry. The latter became the dominant industry, spawning a similar capitalistic development in other industries. Business cycles, which characterized mature capitalist production, made their appearance in precisely this period. Indeed, the cyclical process of expansion and contraction was decisively influenced by the pattern of growth in the leading cotton industry. Of course, the phenomenon of economic cycles had been observed a number of times during the seventeenth and eighteenth centuries, but it was not until 1825 that a typical capitalist crisis occurred. Earlier crises did not originate in the core of society's reproduction process, but occurred for such contingent reasons as the bursting of commercial speculative bubbles, fiscal failures or other disruptions in financial relations. In contrast, the crises which occurred after 1820 were due, in large part, to a failure of the reproduction process itself. By this time, even financial relations were broadly determined by society's reproduction process, which now embodied the core functioning of capitalist society. Needless to say, since we are no longer in the realm of pure theory, we would expect that many contingent factors would contribute to each capitalist crisis and, thus, a far more complex and nuanced explanation would have to be given for each of them than that which is offered in pure theory. Even in Great Britain between the 1820s and the 1860s, when capitalism most closely approximated its ideal image, it is not possible to find a single crisis undisturbed by contingent factors. The influence of international trade on crises during the liberal stage was of fundamental significance and cannot be dismissed as easily as such contingent factors as railway speculation or crop failure. Industrial crises were, thus, caused by combinations of such external factors and disruptions originating in the domestic reproduction process. Nevertheless, the nature of the technology, the financing and the dominant ownership form all contributed to a pattern of development that was characterized by decennial economic crises. Indeed, periodic crises occurred in 1825, 1836, 1847, 1857 and 1866. The regularity of these recurring crises, which emanated, at least in part, from the reproduction process itself, adhered to a pattern that any student of the pure theory would already be familiar with. These recurring crises did not lead to the suppression of competition and its replacement by monopoly or oligopoly. Some concentration and centralization of capital took place as a consequence of each crisis, but not to such a degree that would lead to a handful of firms dominating the leading cotton industry.

The exaltation of freedom and equality celebrated by liberals was not and is not freedom in the abstract, but a freedom congenial to capitalism. Capitalist society cannot be legitimately equated with an imaginary community of free and independent small producers, who meet on equal footing in the marketplace to exchange commodities. In fact, independent small producers must always be ruined, or reduced to a rump, if capitalism is to develop.

Mature capitalism presupposes the creation of a class of doubly free workers, who have escaped the feudal master–slave relation to become free wage workers, but who, in the process, have been freed or ejected from productive land and its attendant access to the means of production. The state in late liberal capitalist England could play a much less active role in economic life, relying less on direct, physical coercion. It could even appear to stand above the fray of class struggle, offering equal protection to all property owners, because capital, its competitive market and commodity-economic logic impersonally and automatically regulated the production of commodities and the reproduction of the special commodity of labour power, while the rapid mechanization of industry increasingly deprived the working class of their traditional skills, thus making them more and more dependent on the commodity economy. Consequently, industrial capital was able to appropriate the fruits of the workers' surplus labour in the form of surplus value without having to resort to extra-economic coercion.

The society-wide, impersonal and seemingly impartial market appeared on the surface to offer economic agents economic freedom and equality of opportunity while, in reality, its inner logic acts to reproduce class inequality. Liberals have always been ideologically blind to the fact that a class of workers who have nothing to sell but the 'property' of their labour power could not possibly meet on equal footing in the market with those who own income-producing property outside their persons and who appear in the market exclusively as buyers of labour power. Other stages of capitalism and, of course, other types of hierarchical society have had to devote far more attention to the development of the appropriate ideological defences of class and other social divisions, whereas the market, by virtue of its misleading appearance, relieves the defenders of the system of much of this burden (Uno unpublished, II, Introduction).

The closer a particular social formation approaches pure capitalism, the less state support is required and the greater is the likelihood of a laissez-faire policy being advocated and implemented. It is, therefore, not surprising that in the liberal stage of capitalism laissez-faire policies were pursued. Due to the liberal faith in the self-regulation of the market, the economic policies that were favoured tended to eliminate restrictive trade practices (both at home and internationally), while strictly curtailing public finance. The Navigation Acts and the Corn Laws, together with royal charters with respect to monopolies, import duties and export bounties, were all eventually revoked. As the workshop of the world, Britain imported raw materials from all over the world and exported manufactured goods. Along with free trade went a degree of self-government for Britain's settler colonies, with which that country carried on the major part of her trade. Free trade, however, was not as completely free and equal as is sometimes supposed. Because of its tremendous advantages as the first nation to develop as an industrial capitalist power, Britain could commit to free trade so long as that country remained the dominant capitalist and colonial power and could, therefore, benefit, more or less automatically, from such a policy. Nevertheless, Britain did not welcome industrial competition from those colonies which did not have a large British settler population and, when Britain's economic hegemony was challenged in the late nineteenth century, there were immediate calls for protectionism.

The phenomenal expansion of the market for the cotton cloth produced by the leading industry of the leading capitalist state was due largely to its relatively low price. In the analysis of this cheapness, emphasis is typically placed upon the dramatic gains in productivity brought about by Britain's cotton factories. Albritton reminds us, however, that these low prices depended, in no small part, on the cheapness of imports of bales of raw cotton from the United States. This cotton was produced by slave labour such that the growth of slavery in the American South went hand-in-hand with the development of a cotton manufacturing industry in Britain that made use of free wage labour. Therefore, it cannot be argued, as it is in the theory of pure capitalism, that capitalism, in this crucially important historical context, developed by relying exclusively on 'free' wage labour, since slavery also greatly facilitated its development (Albritton 1991, pp.144–5). That said, it is only to be expected that British capital, as any capital, would import raw cotton and other raw materials from those regions where they could be obtained most cheaply, with complete indifference to the conditions under which these products were produced. Moreover, the maturation of liberal capitalism did tend to undermine the foundations of the slave economy.

IMPERIALISM

In the theory of pure capitalism, it is assumed that capital and its society-wide competitive market can overcome any and all use-value resistance in order to organize the material life of society solely by commodity-economic means. In history, capital was never able thus to manage the material life of any society, although the period of British liberal capitalism most closely approached that ideal. The survival of liberal capitalism depended upon the continued importance of light industry, as exemplified by the cotton industry, as the dominant type of use-value production. The operation of capital's commodity-economic logic did not, by its own autonomous motion, generate a growing reliance on the heavy, complex and expensive technologies that were introduced by oligopolistic joint-stock corporations in the late nineteenth century to dramatically raise productivity in the steel industry. Indeed, capital, as capital, does not engage in research with regard to new techniques as part of its profit-seeking activity. Even if it adopted a technology invented in a research center owned by it, capital would still be adopting something which did not emerge from its own activity. Although improvements in production technology were periodically introduced during the liberal capitalist stage, these manufacturing innovations were compatible with the continued management of production facilities by many, relatively small and competitive private enterprises, whereas the new steelmaking technologies developed in the latter part of the nineteenth century undermined liberal-style capitalism, because such small firms could not afford to introduce them.

Capital entered a new stage of historical development when the logic of capital had to confront and overcome a new set of use-value obstacles that required of capital that it develop new organizational forms, incorporate new technologies and seek support from the state in the form of new and more active economic policies to permit it to continue to accumulate. The stage theory of imperialism must, therefore, demonstrate how capital's logic was affected when the economic activity of capitalist nations began to be dominated by such heavy industries as the iron and steel industry rather than by light industries such as the textile industry, which had managed the liberal-era British capitalist economy in a fashion that was far more consistent with the commodity-economic logic that is reproduced in the theory of pure capitalism. Indeed, what may at first have appeared to be a rather inconsequential shift from cotton to iron and steel brought with it a complete reorganization of the dominant mode of capital accumulation and a qualitatively new stage of capitalist development, which reversed the tendency for historical capitalism to dissolve traditional social relations and thus move towards the ideal image of capitalism that appears in the pure theory. The reversal of the tendency towards a purely capitalist society reflects the fact that, once having developed, capitalism never achieved the capacity to reproduce itself in a fully autonomous fashion and, hence, more or less indefinitely. Thus, it was inevitable that it would eventually enter a stage of decay and finally collapse.

The stage of imperialism began in the last quarter of the nineteenth century, when countries such as Germany, the United States and France became developed capitalist powers and began to challenge Britain's economic hegemony. The long depression of the 1870s, which followed the Franco-Prussian War, put an end to free trade. Britain's challengers began to pursue state economic policies which have since been characterized as imperialist. These countries could not follow the leisurely development path taken by Britain in the seventeenth and eighteenth centuries, during the latter's period of primitive accumulation, when it had no rivals. Instead, they imported a fully mechanized cotton industry from Britain and, in the process, quickly created a class of property-less workers that an indigenous capitalism could then employ. With the coming of age of German industry, around the turn of the century, Britain lost her economic hegemony, and all capitalist countries began to be influenced by the economic activity of that country and of the United States. Since the rapid growth of the German steel industry was perhaps the most outstanding example of this new phase of capitalism's development, and since the Americans remained geographically, economically and politically isolated from the unfolding events in Europe that culminated in World War I (in which Germany's imperialist policies were directly implicated), this interpretation of Unoist stage theory will highlight the German case as the stage-specific dominant type. Given that the European capitalist powers were now moving along different trajectories, away from pure capitalism, it is necessary also to give due attention to the path that Britain in particular took, especially because it has contemporary relevance.

To become the leading European capitalist country during this period, Germany had to commodify labour power and to build its heavy industry under conditions which required that these processes be both more rapid and less complete than was the case with Britain. To launch itself on the road to capitalist development, Germany imported from Britain only the most advanced methods of mechanized industry. That country was wise enough not to try to follow the development path established by Britain, since the logic of capital had to contend with a qualitatively different level of technology and a different dominant type of use-value production, which were specific to this period. It was one thing for Britain to adopt economic policies of laissez-faire domestically and free trade externally when it had already developed its capitalist light industry to a considerable extent without foreign competition; it was quite another thing for its rivals to do so when heavy industries, such as the iron and steel industry, were playing an increasingly important role in economic life generally and when many countries were attempting not only to develop their capitalist industries, but to penetrate foreign markets.

It was the extensive construction of railways that first stimulated the demand for iron and steel products, but the advent of the new steelmaking technology gave further impetus to the use of these products. Steelmaking innovations, such as the Bessemer process (introduced in 1855), the Siemens-Martin process (1865) and especially the technique developed by S.G. Thomas and P.C. Gilchrist (1875) to improve the above two processes, allowed the German steel industry to become the leading steel producer in Europe. With the latter technique, the steel industry was no longer limited by the availability of high-quality iron ore. The construction of ever larger blast and steelmaking furnaces dramatically increased the amount of capital and size of plant required for the operation of such industries. Moreover, technical and economic rationality frequently demanded that one ironworks should operate several blast furnaces side by side and that the production of pig iron should be integrated not only with steelmaking and the rolling of steel products, but also with the utilization of chemical by-products, together with various upstream operations, such as the production of coke and the mining of coal and iron (Uno unpublished, III, Introduction; ch.1).

Since large-scale industries which manufactured such heavy use values as iron and steel products required a massive fixed capital investment in plants and heavy machinery and this, in turn, entailed the concentration of capital from a number of small individual owners, especially in Germany, the limited liability joint-stock corporate enterprise (which had previously been limited to public utilities and commerce) now became prevalent in manufacturing, in order that capital might take advantage of the economies of scale inherent in that form. By this time, individually owned firms were no longer competitive with 'capitalist-social' joint-stock enterprises in heavy industry.

A consequence of this movement away from competition was that many small capitalists were reduced to rentiers, and a petty-bourgeois class of white-collar workers expanded both inside and outside of industry. Like landlords, rentiers and white-collar workers could save a portion of their incomes, even though they could not directly convert these savings into capital themselves. Since heavy industries required the long-term mobilization of large amounts of capital – much of it in the form of credit – to purchase heavy machinery, and since it was no longer possible to finance these industries by the method of loan capital (or, in other words, by socially utilizing idle funds which were periodically generated by the motion of industrial capital), idle funds could not be left in the hands of rentiers and the middle classes if the accumulation of capital in heavy industry were to continue. Thus, the securities market and investment banking developed to concentrate and direct dispersed monetary savings into investment in heavy industries.

Capitalism always endeavours to make use of socially available funds for surplus-value production. In liberalism, only capitalists had long-term idle funds, which could be advanced as capital while loan capital provided short-term credit. In the imperialist stage, the joint-stock company enabled its large shareholders, with a relatively small original investment, to acquire enormous amounts of socially available funds, without relying on loan capital. This ongoing expropriation of rentier savings through the securities market made possible the reinvestment of a large amount of surplus value which would otherwise have remained idle and, thus, helped to preserve the viability of capitalism in the imperialist era.

The joint-stock corporate form enabled one firm to own shares in another firm, which in turn owned shares in another. In this fashion one firm could achieve control over many others. Thus, this form assisted in the centralization of capital, which was accomplished through pyramiding, interlocking directorates, cartels, trusts and other forms of oligopolistic and monopolistic organization. Cartelized groups of joint-stock corporations, which emerged in Germany in the 1870s and reached their zenith around the turn of the century, could not have raised either the necessary volume of capital or the organic composition of that capital had they continued to rely on the form of individual ownership (Uno unpublished, III, chs.1, 2).

The combination of many joint-stock enterprises in one organization controlled by finance capital promoted not only a large-scale mechanization of the plants, but also large-scale forms of business management. These tendencies could not be explained by reference to the concepts of the *concentration* and *centralization* of capital, derived from pure theory, and evidenced by the development of light industry in the liberal stage. The cotton industry, for example, would not have developed to the point that it would have required such a mass of fixed capital. Although the iron and steel industry would not have developed without the prior stage of liberal industrial activity, the steel industry cannot be viewed as a simple extension of the light industry of the earlier era. There was a dramatic and qualitative difference in the size and weight of fixed capital, whether in the form of the means of labour or in the form of raw materials, which the new industry required.

The Unoist argument that the mode of accumulation of finance capital necessarily required monopolies implies a rejection of the typical Marxist–Leninist view that monopolies appeared as a necessary consequence of competition. The appearance of oligopoly and monopoly cannot be explained as a necessary consequence of the continued and unimpeded operation of the logic of capital.

Only monopolistic companies had the resources to invest in the expensive retooling required to introduce technological advancements (Albritton 1991, p.184). Moreover, these large firms could take a more systematic approach to extracting greater productivity from the workers in their employ. The systematic application of Taylor's scientific management principles was employed to thwart workers' efforts to combine on the shop floor in an attempt to slow down the pace of work. Workers were isolated from one another in the steel industry and elsewhere both by the design of the machinery and by management directives intended to script their every move. In order to increase management control over the labour process and to push the workers to work as hard as they were physically capable of doing, the stopwatch was employed to break down each job into its component operations and to establish time limits for the completion of each step. Finally, various kinds of bonuses were established to reward those workers who established new higher standards of performance, which other workers were then pressured to meet (Albritton 1991, p.186).

The new credit system that evolved allowed a relatively small number of large capitals with privileged access to funds to dominate small capitals. The original paid-in capital that large joint-stock firms received could not be pulled out by individual shareholders. Even if shareholders sold their shares and personally withdrew from the business, others first had to buy these same shares, which meant that the company's real capital continued its motion undisturbed by the transfer of ownership titles. Thus, shares, being only 'fictitious' or 'commodified' derivatives of real capital, were merely titles to the periodic sharing of a firm's surplus value or profit in the form of dividends; but it was the real motion of capital that continued to generate these profits. Of course, if a very large number of shares changed hands, the control of the company based on the ownership of capital might actually change (Uno unpublished, III, ch.2).

Thus, since management power ultimately rested with the largest shareholders, the majority of small shareholders were mere dividend receivers. Large shareholders exercised control over an enormous concentration of socialized capital, though they had invested only a small portion of it. They typically enforced the dividend policy of the company in a fashion that was disadvantageous to ordinary shareholders[26] and attempted to retain much of its net earnings, instead of distributing them as dividends. In this way, the major shareholders, officers and senior executives, who often became major shareholders themselves, became the accumulators of capital and secured themselves against business fluctuations.

The small number of large capitalists managed and controlled not only single firms in which they had invested, but other firms in which their parent company held a majority of the shares. Alternatively, large capitalists might control a coordinated group of large firms, by having all firms own shares in the other firms of the group.

Those few large capitalists who collectively controlled these large firms could not keep the whole operation of any one firm under their direct control and, moreover, they typically had diverse interests or holdings in a number of large firms. Thus, they tended to hire professional managers to manage the day-to-day operations of each firm. A formal separation of management and ownership took place, in such a way that neither the large nor the small shareholders acted like the full-fledged capitalists of the earlier liberal era. This has lent credence to the view that the control of the modern corporation is really, and not merely formally, divorced from the ownership of its capital. However, the degree of control is not in direct proportion to the ownership of shares, inasmuch as the large shareholders with a relatively small investment exercised the ultimate decision-making power over an enormous sum of capital, whether they themselves actively managed the company's day-to-day operations or hired professional managers to perform these duties. Thus, the concentration of power among the leading shareholders should not be viewed as indicative of an absolute separation of control from ownership, but, rather, of the fact that what were once the tasks of individual entrepreneurs who managed society's reproduction process in the age of industrial capitalism have instead, from this period forward to the present, become a shared responsibility of major shareholders and senior executives (Uno unpublished, III, chs.1, 2).

Because such large investments of fixed capital were necessary, only large banks could risk financing the massive fixed-capital investments required for continued growth of heavy industry. Although banks thus played a crucial role in this new stage of capitalism, it should never be forgotten that it was industrial development, especially in those heavy industries which required a massive accumulation of fixed capital, that gave rise to this new role for banking. The evolution of such large and complex structures and their attendant management forms were dictated by the development of the capitalist production and reproduction processes that accelerated the central-ization process in which a few large capitals absorbed many smaller ones. Huge combines could not exist without similarly large credit-granting institutions that could effectively mobilize social savings in the service of monopoly capitals. The stock market and the major banks served this function.

Because the banks provided long-term credit for the immense fixed capital investments required by heavy industry, and thus had enduring relations with large firms, they had a strong interest in the long-term stability and profitability of such big borrowers and discouraged cut-throat competition among them. In the founding of any new company, a bank had to take the long view of its future association with that firm and eschew consideration of immediate gain. Prudence not only required that a few major banks close to financial markets grew to a size that would allow them to lend to a number of major corporate borrowers at once, but it also dictated that banks form close connections with several of the major competitors in the same industry and that bank officers directly participate in the management of affiliated industrial enterprises in order to protect their investment.[27] In turn, the company which welcomed interlocking directorates with a major bank could expect a readier access to funds. Banks, not being tied to specific use values like typical industrial firms, were less prone to destructive competition and more prone to mutual accommodation. Such European-style industrial banks ventured well beyond the practices of British-style commercial banks, since bank-affiliated firms became subject to regulation by the large banks (Uno unpublished, III, Introduction; chs.1, 2; Albritton 1991, p.185).

In the imperialist period, the activity of bank capital extended from the mediation of the buying and selling of funds as commodities to the selling of capital as a commodity. In the former activity, a bank earned the interest differential between loans and deposits as profit on their own capital, which remained extremely small relative to the money value of either loans or deposits. In the latter case, a bank would go beyond mediating the buying and selling of funds and would seek a founder's profit, which entailed significant investments of their own capital.[28]

The Uno school follows the classical Marxist convention of employing the term 'finance capital' to refer to the fusion or coalescence of investment banking and industry which assured the required conversion of society's idle funds into capital. Finance capital is characterized by its inclination to control the capitalist reproduction process on which it is based, while standing somewhat removed from it.

Even though the connection between finance and production is best represented by the type of organization prevailing in the German steel industry, the dominant industry in the leading capitalist nation of this stage, this does not exclude the possibility that finance capital might manifest itself in such a fashion that it appears to be unfounded on any particular productive base, as was the case in Britain. Investment in joint-stock companies hinges, not on the accumulation of industrial capital, but, rather, on the mobilization of idle funds arising in the hands of all social strata. Industrial firms in Britain were slow in adopting the form of the joint-stock company, because the accumulation of industrial capital based on the solid foundation of private enterprises had been fully successful. These enterprises made use of the financial market almost exclusively for short-term circulation credit and were opposed to state and corporate involvement in the economy, based on past bad experiences. Moreover, the investment of capital abroad had already begun to play an important role in Britain in the heyday of liberal capitalism. The fact that the securities market in London was originally involved with investments in foreign public bonds and private debentures, railway stocks, etc., acted against the more representative development of a capital market that would focus on domestic industrial finance as its main area of business, as was the case in Germany. These circumstances led to the evolution of financial markets which were biased against offering such services as that of underwriting shares for domestic industrial firms.

Britain, which had previously dominated the European steel industry, continued to be responsible for a number of the inventions that led to innovations in Germany's steel industry; but Britain had old, relatively small plants, located in what had become cramped, urban environments, which could neither contain the new, large-scale technologies nor integrate what had hitherto been separate industries. Germany had an advantage because, in many cases, that country could build from scratch on new sites. The Germans could copy and improve on the British model, incorporating the latest technologies and building on a grander scale. Britain's iron reserves were rapidly depleting while her German rival had access to rich deposits in Lorraine, Luxembourg and elsewhere.

The British steel industry too eventually achieved the necessary concentration and centralization by utilizing the joint-stock corporate form, but Britain did not generate monopolization in as systematic a fashion as Germany, where large firms in the coal, iron and steel industries formed interlocking cartels, with the collusion of the major German banks. British banks did not involve themselves in the issuing of industrial shares. The relationship of banks and industry remained strictly that of lenders and borrowers. No German-style fusion of banking and industry took place.

Yet capitalism in late-nineteenth-century Britain also entered the stage of finance capital. British investments in foreign portfolios were to forge a long-term capital commitment to foreign productive activities. Britain was realizing the dominance of finance capital in the sphere of foreign investment, while leaving domestic industry largely to its own devices. Indeed, Britain was already becoming a rentier state, as the productive base that its finance capital sought to dominate was to be found abroad.

Unlike free competition in the marketplace, which constantly replaces poor performers with better ones, through a process akin to natural selection, competition in the age of monopolies intensified the domination of more-centralized capital. Large capitals absorbed small ones, a development which, to a considerable extent, eliminated the free competition that, in principle, capitalism presupposes (Uno unpublished, III, Introduction; ch.1). Monopolies were necessary to sustain capitalism's viability in the stage of imperialism; but, once monopolies existed, there was nothing to stop these firms from conspiring to acquire excessive monopoly profits which were not justifiable even from the point of view of the special capital requirements of heavy industry.

Oligopolistic and monopolistic firms, operating principally in one or more of the leading iron, steel and coal sectors, and assisted by the major banks, were able to restrict output so as to raise prices above those which might be justified by their heavy machinery costs and above what a competitive market would have allowed in order to reap surplus profits, especially when tariffs protected them from international competition. Such firms could rely on the massiveness of fixed capital in their industry to provide an effective barrier to entry, but, if that failed, they could temporarily cut prices to drive out a potential rival. Monopoly prices acted as a further spur to vertical integration, since it made sense for a steel corporation to buy a coal corporation in order to avoid the monopoly prices of the coal industry.

It was, of course, understandable that oligopolistic joint-stock enterprises would attempt to stabilize their share of the market and limit competition. Large firms could not expand, contract, or otherwise easily and quickly adapt to market changes because they had to contend with massive fixed-capital constraints. The expansion of such an industry, which required massive funds for fixed capital, was not easy. Even when new facilities were in place, it sometimes took several years for them to become fully operational. Once capacity was expanded, a sudden rise in output might cause a shortage of raw materials, which could then lead in turn to an elevation in input prices. By the time the supply finally increased, the boom might already have passed. When the price of a particular heavy and complex use value rose during a prosperity phase, the production of it could not easily or quickly be expanded. Surplus profits therefore appeared. These excessive profits diverted surplus value away from the competitive sector, vitiated the law of average profit and prevented a maximization of social output, so that investment opportunities were prematurely exhausted, effective demand was severely curtailed and underconsumption became endemic. It was the movement towards oligopoly and monopoly that caused the market to lose its self-regulating mechanism.

The concentration of capital under the form of joint-stock company disrupted the periodicity of economic crises, which was more clearly observable in the age of mature industrial capital (1820–70). The working of the capitalist law of population too tended to be distorted, as the adoption of new productive methods and the consequent creation of a relative surplus population no longer occurred in the process of regularly recurring business cycles. The fundamental contradiction of capitalism, which stems from the commodification of labour power, and which manifests itself in the form of periodic crises, was now too intractable for the freely competitive market to resolve. This was compounded by virtue of the fact that the source of idle funds, which the money market regulated, no longer sprang directly from the motion of industrial capital. Finance capital, rather than loan capital, regulated finance, with the consequence that the dynamics of capitalist development began to depend upon its initiatives.

In this era there were not sufficient labour-intensive industries to provide an approximation of full employment at any time. Finance capital could enforce an intensification of labour in the factories under its control, because agriculture and petty industrial operations were plagued with surplus populations and disguised unemployment. A dual economy thus emerged, in which a highly modernized industrial sector existed side by side with the traditional sectors cited.

The lender–borrower relationship between banks and firms, which periodically stalled in key industries and burst into a panic or a crisis in liberal capitalism, was transformed into the coordinated investment policy of monopoly firms and large banks combined in an organic fusion. This may create the false impression that the anarchy of the capitalist economy was overcome within this new regime, but industrial crises did not disappear in the age of imperialism. Although firms were financially regulated, there was always a limit to the ability of specific industries and individual firms to absorb unemployed workers and, overall, firms were also often saddled with excessive output, whether in the form of means of production or of articles of consumption, which they could not transform into capital. The iron and steel industry frequently resorted to a major expansion towards the end of the prosperity phase, prompted by the enormous surplus profit that tends to be earned during that phase. This expansion could not be timed in such a way as to gradually absorb the industrial reserve army available at the beginning of a prosperity phase. It was not merely a glut of commodities that caused economic difficulties in the imperialist era, but the overabundance of productive capacity, caused by a great mass of newly built fixed capital that was suddenly no longer required to satisfy market requirements. A sharp fall in profit rates, reflecting a prior elevation of wages, which was the source of those crises generated by capital's own motion, tended to be submerged in the imperialist era beneath the decline of profit rates brought about by an overproduction of commodities.

Ensuing depression periods could cause severe falls in rates of return. The destruction of capital in imperialist crises was, therefore, far more disruptive than had been the case in the liberal era.[29] For example, the cost of reactivating a blast furnace, once it had been out of operation, could be prohibitive. A closed-down plant had to be scrapped or disposed of for a minuscule sum. Hence, it was as difficult to cut back during a depression phase, when demand was low, as to step up production during the prosperity phase, when demand was high. When high cartel prices inevitably collapsed, the political–economic crises which ensued did not necessarily create conditions that would usher in a new round of economic expansion on the solid foundation of a new generation of technology and a new and corresponding value relation. The market could no longer ensure that capital was cyclically renewed to launch a new phase of prosperity, since large firms could not be pressured to introduce innovations in a depression. The business cycles, which had formerly regulated the growth of capitalist production, were seriously deformed by the hypertrophy of fixed capital in heavy industry, which meant that both the movement of profit rates through business cycles and the process of averaging profits were significantly impaired.

The partial organization of the economy by monopoly capital aggravated its unevenness, which, in turn, increased pressures for imperialist external policies. Competition intensified even among the largest firms, or groups of firms, possessed of strong monopoly power. Because of this, the developed capitalist nations had continually to confront a situation in which the conversion of idle funds into capital produced no positive profits, while an excess of capital, which had only been a cyclical occurrence in the period of liberal capitalism, became chronic. If capitalism were to survive in the imperialist era, finance capital had to find a strategy which would enable the system to guarantee the reproduction of labour power and to overcome the problem of an excess of capital without relying on intolerable and politically dangerous economic crises.

The very large corporations that materialized in response to the great depression of 1873, and the cut-throat competition associated with it, clearly had an increased capacity to withstand depressions and to avoid ruinous competition, as compared to the small firms which had prevailed in liberal capitalism. Precisely because of their great size and the huge amount of funds invested in them, however, periodic crises became less acceptable and bankruptcy unthinkable, due to the far-reaching economic consequences if any of these firms failed. Economic crises also became less tolerable because of the extension of the franchise and the increasing entry of the masses into political life. Indeed, the expectation gradually grew that the state ought to act whenever economic crises threatened to cause mass suffering. Indeed, finance capital needed a great deal of state support in this era to create the conditions necessary to sustain the production of heavy use values by capitalist means. The laissez-faire polices of liberal capitalism were no longer viable. The age may be characterized by the high-tariff policies of Germany and by Britain's massive increase in the export of capital. These strategies considered jointly allow us to distinguish finance capital from mercantile and liberal capital.

Protectionism was absolutely essential as nascent capitalist economies of various nations embarked upon development trajectories at varying rates and with varying degrees of success. Germany did not need such infant-industry protection by the latter half of the 1870s, but the privileging of large-scale, export-oriented production by cartelized industries in that country meant that protectionism could not be dispensed with.

A bureaucratic, interventionist and authoritarian state, modeling itself on the monopolistic corporation that dominated the German economy, thus assumed an important economic role. This imperialist state implemented economic polices which benefited domestic monopolies and cartels. It erected tariff barriers, which allowed large firms to charge monopoly prices in the domestic market without fear of foreign competition. Monopoly profits were, of course, not unlimited because, when all countries erected tariff barriers, international trade was severely restricted. Even in the competitive sector, the state had to ensure that the rate of profit remained above the rate of interest and that workers' purchasing power was not grossly eroded by monopoly pricing. Concomitant with the implementation of protectionist policies, powerful nationalist ideologies took hold of European populations. Class-based ideologies thus lost some of their appeal to a working class which was divided by national and cultural boundaries.[30]

State economic and political intervention aimed to head off economic crises, but such crises did eventually occur. Recovery was slow and painful, because cartelized industries were in a position to maintain high prices and to avoid technological innovation, even in the face of a depression. This made technological renewal much more difficult for capital-starved competitive industries and led to a prolonged stagnation in the economy as a whole.

The imperialist state assisted finance capital in a variety of ways. It expanded its scope to include the provision of centralized electric power generation and a transportation and communication infrastructure, including road, rail, telegraph and postal systems. Germany's state-supported educational, scientific and research institutions became the envy of other nations. Major beneficiaries of this state intervention were the large industrial firms, requiring skilled workers, well-trained engineers, technocrats, scientists and managers, which German schools, polytechnics and universities produced in abundance. By applying the technical knowledge provided by educational and research institutions to agriculture, German farmers, using chemical fertilizers and large-scale modernization, were able to increase crop yields per hectare above that of their rivals. The *Sozialpolitik* policies of the state increased workers' purchasing power, thus ensuring the reproduction of labour power and countering the threat posed by the growing trade union and socialist movements. The state-sponsored extension of scientific management principles ensured that the spread of democratic ideals and institutions would not penetrate factory walls.

The Uno school provides scientific proof for the Leninist view that the excess of capital, relative to the domestic market, that arose mainly because of the high monopolistic prices maintained by means of tariffs could only be exported. Idle funds, which could not be profitably invested at home, were invested abroad by finance capital, in the colonies and spheres of influence of imperialist nations. Profits arising from foreign investment were reinvested to foster those industries abroad which would either benefit the export industry of the mother country, or, alternatively, secure a source of scarce raw materials for exclusive use of her finance capital. The thesis of Rosa Luxemburg's *The Accumulation of Capital* that capitalism could not survive without support of peripheral non-capitalist regions may not be convincing generally, but it is more than plausible for the imperialist period.

Every national capital wanted to export its capital, while protecting it from foreign capitalist competition. The export of capital to the colonies was frequently concerned with finding cheaper sources of raw materials, and this was often possible not merely because labour was cheap there and rent costs negligible, but also because states in the colonies were forced to grant monopoly privileges to a few large companies. These companies were thus able to earn super-profits by eliminating or severely restricting competition. As capital investment in the colonies grew, colonial states had to develop their capacity for repression, in order to violently secure labour power that was generally not yet commodified.

The health of the economy depended increasingly on state intervention, in the form of an aggressive expansion of national boundaries, either by the annexation of the neighbouring territories of other European powers or by colonial expansion outside Europe. In the 1890s, with the steady advance of organized monopoly in Germany, the interest of German banks shifted from portfolio investment in foreign securities to direct investment. By that time, large banks and heavy industries had already been integrated in an organic fusion inside Germany. Industries now ready to spread their activities abroad benefited from the assistance of their bank partners, which, through their network of branches in foreign countries and concomitant experience in international financial transactions, could provide expert guidance.

While Britain benefited from a large colonial empire, Germany's preference for direct investments often gave that nation an advantage over both Britain and France, which favoured portfolio investment. The enormous wealth accumulated over and above that which was needed by British industry in the first half of the nineteenth century had allowed Britain to become the principal exporter of capital to the Americas and continental Europe, but, perhaps for that very reason, British capital was exported in an unsystematic fashion. The British acquisition of new territories seemed motivated not simply by the desire to ensure the immediate export of capital, but rather by an anticipation of the future needs of finance capital. Obviously, Britain attempted to secure outlets for its manufactured goods, and resources that could be used as raw materials in its factories. It may have hoped as well to enlarge opportunities for direct investment. However, the primary motive of Britain's expansion was to enclose a territory and its resources for prospective use, where British monopoly capitals might operate unimpeded by the capital of other capitalist nations. Indeed, the annual returns on investment abroad and the enormous gains that accrued to the financiers who mediated such investments, amounted to colossal sums, which could be earned only because Britain possessed its overseas colonies and spheres of influence.

What made Germany, the most methodical investor, a much more aggressive imperialist power was the fact that that nation, in the course of consolidating organized monopoly within its border in the 1870s and 1880s, discovered itself painfully handicapped relative to Britain and France in the acquisition of exclusive spheres of action abroad, by virtue of its belated participation in the race for the partition of the planet.

A characteristic feature of the imperialist stage was the economic and political decline of the traditional landlord class, which had previously maintained agricultural sustainability by acting as the protector of the land and its resources. The political decline of that class and the rise of large corporations, especially agribusiness corporations (which subsequently became large landlords in their own right, especially in peripheral and colonial regions), began to undermine the separation of capital and landed property, which had provided for the soil's protection, while promoting a less equal playing field among capitalists, which impaired the functioning of the capitalist market. A consequence of these trends was the agricultural crisis of the 1875–95 period, which exacerbated the tensions between European nations and contributed to the instability of the imperialist stage. These developments contributed to the decay and eventual collapse of capitalism.

A mad scramble for territory by the capitalist powers led to the division of the rest of the world amongst them. Once this division had taken place, the map could only be redrawn if one imperialist state could seize colonial territory from another. Imperialist policies thus led to a military build-up

204 CAPITALISM AND THE DIALECTIC

and frequent clashes among the imperialist powers, which culminated in World War I. When the finance capital of one country tried to export its problems by building a formal empire abroad, it encountered the protective tariffs and colonies of the other imperialist countries. Economic nationalism, militarization, and technological innovations in heavy industry led to the growth of what has come to be known as military–industrial complexes in Germany, the United States, Great Britain, France and other leading capitalist nations. An arms race ensued as these powers began to direct massive amounts of capital to the weapons manufacturers and research facilities, so as to stimulate the research and development of ever more sophisticated and deadly weapons. The manufacture of military goods moved dramatically from craft to factory production. Corporate firms, employing assembly line techniques and producing on a cost-plus basis, rapidly became the principal producers of weaponry, replacing small state-owned facilities. The income tax was eventually introduced, as an allegedly temporary wartime measure, to increase funding for this arms race. The era of modern warfare and mass slaughter had thus begun.

Stage theory describes how the economic policies of the state externally assisted the operation of the commodity economy in its subsumption of a particular type of use value in each stage of capitalism's development. As use values changed over time, capitalism's continued existence depended on the development of new state economic policies in order to ensure that the commodity economy would remain viable. Once finance capital overcame industrial capital, the hitherto prevailing tendency of capitalism to rid itself of contingent impurities and move towards pure capitalism was reversed, thus signaling the fact that capitalism was no more a permanent society than any other historical society. The Unoist stage theory of imperialism, which explains the causes of the division of the world into colonial empires and the subsequent world war, demonstrates that, in its final stage, capital had no recourse but to turn to extra-economic solutions to escape from a crisis generated by the operation of its logic, when capitalism could not overcome the intractable use-value resistance posed by heavy and complex use-values.

9
Conclusion: Capitalists Beyond Capitalism

In this chapter I wish to recapitulate and extend the argument Sekine and I made in 'The Disintegration of Capitalism: A Phase of Ex-Capitalist Transition' (2001), in the light of developments that have taken place in the global economy more recently. Sekine (2007) too has published a preliminary work that deepens our understanding of the post-Fordist phase of the ex-capitalist transition, but his more definitive study is forthcoming.

Bourgeois economics possesses no rigorous definition of 'capitalism', which reflects its ideological position that all societies are by definition capitalist. Whereas the bourgeois approach presumes that *any* use-value space will support the operation of capitalism, the Uno approach recognizes that only comparatively few of these spaces – those in which many key use values are capitalistically producible as commodities – can be managed, subsumed under or integrated by the logic of capital.

Recall that the formation of the modern nation state, under the absolute monarchy during the mercantilist era, created the conditions that would permit the free mobility of labour within its borders and, therefore, a unified society-wide division of labour. Capitalism developed in this context because the competitive market was such an effective vehicle to manage the production of light and simple use values by relatively small, competitive capitalist firms within one society or, alternatively, in a trading community (which might typically include several neighbouring nations). The value principle and commodity-economic logic could only operate in such a context.

In any historical context, capital is incapable of overcoming all use-value resistance by its own autonomous operation.[31] Any use-value space outside theory will include some *externalities* or intractable use-value resistance which capital will be unable to autonomously manage. Only if these externalities can be *internalized* will the use-value space support a viable capitalism.[32]

If the existing *use-value space* lacks the material conditions that would make capitalist production a viable proposition and if capitalists thus cannot earn high enough profits, even in the absence of some institutional impediment which inhibits capital accumulation, we are up against a deep-rooted, systemic malady, which bourgeois policies, intended to 'internalize externalities' so as to make them amenable to the capitalist-style commodity-economic form of management, will not be able to cope with.

Unoists use the dialectical theory of pure capitalism (*genriron*) or of the capitalist mode of production and the theory of the imperialist stage as referents when evaluating the extent to which a historical society in which capitalist activity is widely engaged actually materializes a viable and, therefore, largely self-regulating and self-reproducing capitalist economy.

In our joint article (2001), by contrast, Sekine characterizes societies in which capital and its society-wide market and attendant commodity-economic logic can successfully manage and reproduce material economic life with limited assistance from the bourgeois state (which 'internalizes externalities' that capital cannot quite overcome) as examples of capitalism-II or of genuine industrial capitalism. The modes of accumulation of merchant capital, industrial capital and finance capital presupposed stage-specific economic policies advanced by the bourgeois state, which rendered the more intractable use values amenable to market regulation in each major historical period of capitalism.

If bourgeois economic policy cannot successfully 'internalize the externalities' present so that the logic of capital may begin to operate autonomously, then such an economy is no longer viably capitalist, no matter how desperately chrematistic activities are engaged in. Capitalism's flexibility is not great enough to effectively manage the production and circulation of heavy and complex use values on a global scale. Nor can the *law of value* operate when political considerations so greatly affect outputs, prices, investment, trade flows and the mobility of labour. Thus, contrary to appearances, both capital and capitalism have no future in the organization of real or substantive economic life.

After 1914, western societies could not successfully revive capitalism-II; thus, subsequent periods cannot be theorized as 'material types', or viable stages of capitalism, and are more properly viewed as phases in the transition away from capitalism. Societies in which capitalist activity is prevalent but in which capital is incapable of overcoming intractable use-value resistance (even with the assistance of the bourgeois state) have been characterized by Sekine (2001) as examples of capitalism-I. Presently, even the attempt to prop up capitalism-I has been called into question.

With the aid of the above concepts and definitions, I shall now describe the process of the disintegration of capitalism, or the phase of 'ex-capitalist transition', in similar terms to our earlier paper (Bell and Sekine 2001, pp.37–55), but with some understandable changes in emphasis, reflecting both the passage of time and subtle differences in the way we interpret this history.

THE AGE OF THE GREAT TRANSFORMATION

The phase of ex-capitalist transition is divided into three periods: (1) the age of 'great transformation' (the interwar period); (2) the age of 'consumerism–Fordism' (the three decades following World War II); and (3) the age of post-Fordism and casino funds (the past three decades). What distinguishes our approach from others who periodize similarly is that we regard each of these sub-phases (periods) as distinct steps in the *disintegration* of the genuine capitalism that Marx and Uno theorized. In the following section, therefore,

I wish to quickly review the main features of these two first sub-phases in the process of ex-capitalist transition.

No effort was spared during the 1920s to revive the pre-1914 imperialist order, but to no avail, as was made obvious by the failure to restore the international gold standard. The 'relative stability' of the latter half of the 1920s depended on the regular flow of American funds which, after irrigating Europe, went back to the United States. The abrupt cooling-off that occurred after the post-war reconstruction boom in Europe wound down resulted in serious debt and overproduction crises in light and heavy industry, agriculture and transportation, which the atrophied market could neither prevent nor overcome. Then a speculative boom in the United States cut off the international flow of money to Europe and left much of the world starved of funds. This was followed by the crash of share prices on Wall Street in the fall of 1929, which ushered in the Great Depression. The right remedy for the occasion was not part of the policy 'arsenal' of the bourgeois state; thus, capitalism could not subsequently be revived. So began the era of the 'great transformation'.

The rapid rise of the fascist regimes and internal class conflict began to pose threats to the bourgeois state. To avoid being engulfed, either from without or from within, it had to transform itself, both to re-establish its economic viability and to maintain its political–ideological legitimacy. Roosevelt's New Deal reforms marked the first step towards the reshaping of America from a bourgeois state that had sustained a viable capitalism to a social democratic welfare state that would support a mixed economy. Thus, capital was preserved, but operated within a restricted space that was subject to far greater state regulation. Roosevelt's administration brought banking and finance under government supervision and exerted regulatory authority over production, employment, sales, pricing and other areas of economic life which had previously been deemed the exclusive province of the private sector.

The New Deal did not succeed in establishing a fully developed welfare state in the United States. It was the expansion of arms production and the transition to an oil- and petrochemical-based economy that allowed the United States to recover from the Great Depression. Nevertheless, on the eve of World War II, all western countries, other than the fascist ones, had opted for some form of social democracy within the framework of a nascent welfare state. Here, 'social democracy' refers broadly to governments, parties and policies which implicitly or explicitly repudiated the classical liberal approach to the regulation of economic life in favour of decidedly more interventionist policies, because they intuited that the logic of capital was no longer capable of managing the prevailing use-value space. Only because they embraced social democracy (within the framework of the welfare state), dampened down class warfare within their borders and forged an alliance with the Soviets did the western powers emerge in such a strong position after the war. With this 'great transformation' the west took its first decisive steps away from capitalism.

FORDISM, CONSUMERISM AND THE WELFARE STATE

After World War II, the old bourgeois state indifferent (or hostile) to the working class could not be revived. The Cold War made it politically expedient to maintain industrial peace and social democracy. American corporate capitals, which to win the war had both accelerated their development of vastly more productive petro-technologies and had increased their output capacity dramatically, now had to avoid a post-war recession and the mothballing of their factories. These goals were accomplished thanks to Fordism, Keynesian economics and cheap oil.

The post-war welfare state committed itself to full employment and price stability and promoted the energy revolution, which revolutionized production methods and transportation. Its economic policies placed the 'planning principle of the state' alongside 'the market principle of capital' in the regulation of the national economy. Such policies were no longer restricted to preparing the ground for the self-regulation of the capitalist market by 'internalizing unwieldy externalities'. The state assumed responsibility for the macro-management of the national economy, in which it would cooperate extensively with capital. Managed currency, which had replaced gold-standard money, undermined the self-regulatory capacity of capitalism, while 'full employment' policies were incompatible with the maintenance of labour power as a commodity. The universal adoption of macroeconomic fiscal and monetary policies in the west thus accelerated capitalism's disintegration.

Although the United States was the only major industrial power that managed to preserve and develop its productive facilities throughout the war, the welfare state might not have become an enduring reality had not the 'Fordist' mode of production appeared, embodying a new industrial technology which, when applied, yielded a large enough value added to be amicably shared between capital and labour.[33] Fordism, or the Just-in-Case system, originated in F.W. Taylor's 'scientific management', which, with time-and-motion studies, etc., accelerated the mechanical processes of task completion. Taylorism, however, 'culminated in and was transcended by' Fordism (Brenner and Glick 1991, p.7), when the conveyer-belt assembly line was introduced. Fordism thus refers to the mode of mass producing consumer durables, such as automobiles, by combining simplified, disinterested, indifferent labour and standardized and interchangeable parts with heavy, single-purpose machines, connected in a series by an automated assembly line.[34] This was a transitional production system with no stable and enduring structure equivalent to capitalism's that would tend to prevent it from self-destructing. It was propped up by ad hoc, pragmatic and constantly evolving state economic policies.

Fordism supported the emergence of a voracious consumerism. Consumerism should, in this context, be understood as the mass consumption of heavy consumer durables that was promoted by the corporate institutionalization of planned obsolescence and the unprecedented mass manipulation of consumers by producers.

With the establishment of the 'mixed economy', money, and especially labour power, had became significantly decommodified; thus, the Juglar decennial cycles, which had characterized liberal capitalism in the previous century and which are shown by the pure theory or dialectic of capital to be necessary for the operation both of the *law of relative surplus population* and the *law of value*, and, therefore, for capitalism's survival, could not operate. Since oligopolistic corporations were not subject to the discipline of a competitive capitalist market, their decision making with regard to pricing and output, whether collusive or predatory (or both), became strategic, rather than market-responsive. Indeed, the economy did not tend to move towards equilibrium in successive prosperity phases of regularly recurring business cycles and, thus, could not provide capitalistically appropriate price signals in any case.

Governments in the United States and elsewhere found that it was expedient to implement programmes and support technological development in the oligopolistic, corporate (consumer durable and military–industrial) sectors, rather than to attempt to assist in maintaining the viability of a multitude of smaller capitalist firms. The post-war economies of the major western powers, and in particular the United States, thus became dominated by the upper echelons of the corporate, state and military managerial bureaucracies. Simultaneously, the United States also asserted its unchallenged leadership as the main architect and guarantor of the World Bank/IMF/GATT/Bretton Woods system, which established the US dollar as the reserve currency and ensured that the other western economies would develop along similar lines.

Because Fordist production expanded more rapidly than the labour–output ratio fell, the United States led the developed west with its unprecedented economic growth during the 1950s and 1960s. With the vast outpouring of mass-produced goods, the living standard of the population improved dramatically, albeit unevenly, in highly urbanized, industrialized and affluent mass-consumption societies.

PETRO-TECHNOLOGY, AGRICULTURE AND INDUSTRY

Whereas Polanyi focused on 'the disembedding of economy from society' in modern times, I follow Sekine (Bell and Sekine 2001, p.54) in believing that an even more fundamental 'disembedding' occurred when capitalist manufacturing or industry ceased to be part of agriculture. Even then, the presence in the leading capitalist countries of an independent class of non-capitalist landlords, whose income was derived not from moveable capital but from land rent, acted as a bulwark against capitalist rapacity and, thus, protected the soil for future generations. Capitalism inverted the relationship between agriculture and industry, but, because it employed only light, coal-based technologies that relatively small capitalist firms could afford to purchase and because it had to contend with a non-capitalist class of landlords, who acted as guardians of the soil and ground water, it did not create incremental entropy in excess of the absorbing capacity of the water cycle (Sekine 1985, p.1). Both of these barriers were removed over the course of the twentieth century.

The theory of rent reveals that a commodity-economically rational price for land must tend to gravitate towards the value of rental revenues in the light of a ruling rate of interest in a viable capitalist society. This could not occur once the fusion of oligopolistic corporate capital and a weakened landed property began to take place. There was no longer a level playing field among capitalists, which would permit the *law of average profit* to operate (Sekine 1985, p.54). This undermined the 'commodification' of land, necessary for capitalism's continued existence.

The productivity of material things remained relatively low up to and including the age of liberal capitalism. The mobilization and deployment of productive labour then constituted the primary concern of society. This fact lent credence to the first principle of historical materialism, according to which the organization of the production of material things (the economic base or substructure) determined the ideological superstructure of society. Capitalism, which essentially ran on coal, was the last society in which economics need have occupied a privileged place in the social sciences, because of its promise to assist us in 'economizing' or optimally allocating society's productive resources to provide most efficiently for its material needs.

Both Fordism and consumerism presupposed the age of petroleum. Although coal and oil (petroleum) are both fossil fuels, they have dissimilar economic effects. Coal mining is labour-intensive, physically demanding and dangerous, while oil is pumped out of the ground almost automatically, once the well is bored. Not only that; oil, unlike coal, can run internal combustion engines and can replace many natural raw materials with synthetic ones (such as fibres, detergents, fertilizers, etc.). Petro-technology accomplished a vast expansion of society's productive powers that would have been unimaginable in the previous age of coal and natural raw materials. Oil's predominance stimulated power revolutions in both production and transportation. Indeed, oil brought about the elimination of scarcity that coal could not quite achieve, because oil-based technologies dramatically raised productivity in both industry and agriculture.

If capitalism was the last human society with a superstructure that was dependent on the particular manner in which productive labour was mobilized and deployed, the advent of petroleum changed all this by finally liberating human society from the burden of the productive labour which produces material objects, at least in principle. Indeed, the mobilization and deployment of productive labour no longer determines the basic structure of human society. The productive powers at our disposal today are so great that only a small number of hours of human labour can produce what we require to live comfortably.

Affluent societies may believe that they have transcended the limits of the petrochemical civilization, but while it is clear that the world could do without coal, for example, albeit with some inconvenience, all societies today continue to be oil-dependent, either directly or indirectly, even if they generate much of their power from nuclear plants (which draw heavily on conventional forms of energy). Unfortunately, the corporate (and especially agribusiness) reliance on petro-technology has been not only radically labour-saving, but also environmentally destructive. In the first or Fordist phase of the petroleum age, it was the second of the above-mentioned properties that predominated. Indeed, what constrains the production of material wealth today is no longer human labour, but the declining stock of non-renewable resources, and environmental decay.

By the end of the 1960s the application of massively productive petro-technology had already produced an adequate stock of consumer durables, so the demand for their replacement no longer matched the existing supply capacity as the market in advanced countries grew increasingly saturated. Moreover, the necessarily elevated labour costs in the affluent western nations made them less competitive in the production of consumer durables. As the high-productivity Fordist sectors became much less profitable, the production of value added (v + s) could no longer grow rapidly enough to prevent conflict between labour and capital with regard to its distribution, and this undermined the foundation of the welfare state. The United States, in particular, continued to spend heavily in order to prevail in the military and space race even as its economic hegemony was challenged, first by Europe and then by Japan.

POST-FORDISM

When the Arab oil cartel dramatically increased the price of crude oil, the energy-intensive Fordist production system found itself at a dead end. The production of goods that were 'big-heavy-long-and-thick' (jukochodai), and hence relatively energy intensive, had to be de-emphasized in favour of the production of those that were 'small-light-short-and-thin' (keihakutansho), and, hence, relatively energy-saving. This accelerated the adoption in the leading industries, first in Japan and later in the west, of advanced technologies – notably in the areas of microelectronics, information technology, robotics, fibre optics, new carbon materials, genetics, etc. – as firms struggled to 'downsize' or to become 'lean' by reducing energy use, labour input, inventories, waste, defects, downtime and communication and financial costs.

Japan's Toyota or 'Just-in-Time' system, which had been adopted to permit that country to recover quickly through export-oriented growth in a difficult post-war economic environment in which energy and resources were scarce, was much better prepared to respond to the oil crises and to take advantage of the economic opportunities that computer-assisted design and manufacturing and numerical control offered. To the extent that Japanese, and later other firms, succeeded in this conversion, traditional Fordist labour (low-skilled, productive labour which had learned to endure the tedium of automatic production lines and to work in a 'thing-like' or 'robotized' fashion) quickly became redundant, as genuine robots and programmable automatic machinery, which were more precise, more flexible and more capable of operating autonomously than Fordist-era machinery, replaced most of them.

The leading firms in this post-Fordist or lean-production era required fewer workers for work which was increasingly knowledge-intensive and service-like because that was what was appropriate or fit for 'advanced manufacturing'. Since labour markets could not adapt to such a change overnight, high rates of unemployment plagued the United States and other western economies.

The subsequent reorganization of US industry did not restore America's competitiveness in consumer durables, nor did it reduce the trade deficit. It rather confirmed the 'hollowing-out' of American industry, in that many more firms became multinationals, shifting their production abroad to a few favoured developing countries that could supply workers at the lowest wages compatible with the provision of an infrastructure that supported such manufacturing, leaving only their 'nerve centers' or headquarters at home. In the IC (information and communications technologies) sectors, where the United States endeavoured to maintain a competitive edge, the production of hardware was also typically shifted abroad, while until recently the development of knowledge-intensive, high-value-added 'software goods' and services (research, development, design, innovation and engineering functions) remained at home. The United States today imports the bulk of the goods it requires to survive.

Considering the fact that capitalism's distinction as an economic system was due to its superiority in the production of material wealth, the deindustrialization of the United States and other developed nations must signify capitalism's disintegration as surely as the industrialization of capitalism signified its maturation. Although corporate capital has embraced globalization and blithely pits one nation against the other in a 'race to the bottom', with each nation surrendering ever greater control over the activities that take place within and across its borders, it is beyond capitalism's capabilities to develop either a planet-wide capitalist market or a bourgeois world state to support its operations. Production and circulation on a global scale favour oligopolistic, transnational corporations, but these institutions are inimical to the operation of the competitive capitalist market and can evade effective regulation by the post-bourgeois state. What corporate capital can do in its pursuit of higher profit rates is to shed millions of productive employees in the developed nations without creating enough employment in the developing nations to achieve a compensatory affluence there. For the global economy to grow enough to create employment for all those destined to be marginalized by radically labour-saving technologies, we would have somehow to stimulate a massive increase in demand, at a time when the affluent are already satiated and many others cannot maintain their current levels of consumption due to stagnating or declining incomes. The attempt would only exacerbate the ecological crisis.

The era when capitalist firms were drawing more and more workers into capital's orbit is definitively past. Even in China, the current 'factory of the world', the enormous export-oriented growth in manufacturing and industrial output has not been accompanied by a parallel growth of the labouring population employed in productive activities, because the attendant massive dislocation of workers formerly employed in state-owned factories or subsisting on land that has now been engulfed by the enclosure of the global commons cannot all be absorbed by factories utilizing advanced, labour-saving technologies transferred from the west. While production in China has lowered inflationary pressures in the global economy and increased profits for firms which invest there by providing a seemingly inexhaustible supply of cheap labour, the working class in China and globally really expands only when capital actually provides a net increase in employment.

Many employed in the primary and secondary sectors of the developed nations are really engaged in service labour, not productive labour. According to Drucker (1986), only 15–16 percent of manufacturing jobs still require manual labour. Thus, it is probably the case that about 20 percent of the workforce or about 10 percent of the population are actually engaged in productive labour. An increasing quantity of the labour that developed societies now demand has become more intellectual than manual, and should, therefore, be viewed as unproductive service labour, even if it is employed in the so-called productive (non-tertiary) sectors.

Working with data supplied by Miyazaki (1990), Sekine (Sekine and Bell 2001) estimates that of the cost of a typical integrated circuit (IC), the constant-capital component (c) of the output price accounts for 8 percent, the variable-capital component (v) for 12 percent and the 'surplus-value' component (s) for 80 percent. Yet about 75 percent of that 'surplus value' (to use the term loosely in this post-capitalist era) must be paid out for the knowledge-intensive services of unproductive workers who develop new products and new generations of products on an ongoing basis, leaving only 5 percent for the producer as profit. An enormous amount of 'surplus value' is thus produced by relatively few productive workers. It is then redistributed to a very large number who are employed in services, where productivity is bound to be lower, with the result that the economy as a whole has a relatively low growth rate. Today, when the production of material wealth has reached its limit, real investments can produce only a small value added.

Furthermore, even after western producers have embraced lean-production techniques they still have to confront the fact that affluent consumers became increasingly satiated with ordinary goods in the course of the Fordist era. Manufacturers can no longer simply mass-produce mundane goods and expect the market to absorb them without demur. They are under pressure to produce items that have novelty value and, thus, have to accept the necessity of heavy start-up costs, brief product life cycles, continuous improvement and the rapid obsolescence of their plants and equipment, which weighs heavily on their R&D and capital costs. Innovations in production methods take place continuously in the post-Fordist economy rather than periodically as in Fordism or as in mature liberal capitalism (which tended to introduce new generations of technology coming out of the depression phases of business cycles, just as we would expect from our examination of the business cycle in pure theory). The new generations of technology that firms must now introduce entail a *qualitative* departure from the prevailing technology and not merely a *quantitative* improvement in the existing technology, as occurred periodically during the liberal capitalist era. Thus, today it is far more difficult for firms to make the necessary investments to remain both competitive and profitable. The pressure on firms to supply innovative goods for narrow and fleeting markets has become intense. Market dogma notwithstanding, it requires considerable state intervention of the appropriate kind to ensure that a nation's firms remain competitive in the sectors where information technologies are being developed.

The dialectic of capital demonstrates that the absolute rent that landed property carves out of surplus value prior to its distribution as profits to different branches of industry has an upper limit, such that, if it is exceeded, the working of the *law of value* becomes adulterated and capitalism ceases to exist (please refer to the earlier discussion of rent or see the definitive account in Sekine 1997, II, p.122). This suggests that no matter how large the 'surplus value' (again, loosely speaking) that our own society produces, if too much of it accrues to rent, interest and the incomes of society's non-productive service providers, leaving little profit accruing to capitalist producers, the accumulation of capital will languish.

MONEY GAMES

Keynes was one of many who advocated the euthanasia of the parasitical *rentier*. Although US finance capital was involved from early on in speculative stock market activities, stringent regulations on banking and finance were maintained during the age of consumerism-Fordism. A large amount of popular savings entered the stock market, but it was held in check.

The new monetary regime that emerged in the United States in the 1970s greatly stimulated offshore banking. This type of banking was developed as a vehicle that would permit fund managers to avoid country-specific regulations that appeared to obstruct capitals engaged in the trading and banking of currencies internationally. These changes, together with the introduction of new information and communication technologies, which greatly increased the mass, mobility and velocity of capital movement across borders, added to the volatility of global markets, exposing firms, industrial sectors, nations and economic regions to undue risk and uncertainty.

Wall Street initiated this trend to seek profit from the speculative buying and selling of existing assets, financial instruments and currencies during the era of the oil crises, when American manufacturers were struggling. The declining demand for funds (money convertible into capital) on the part of large US corporations stimulated the search for financial investment opportunities elsewhere. As the economy remained sluggish under stagflation, corporations had little incentive to expand the scale of their operations, which meant that their demand for outside funds remained weak. Not only did they borrow less from banks and raise less money from capital markets, but they also supplied their own idle funds for investment in securities. Thus, capital markets and banks were flooded with idle money.

Monetary savings, which could not immediately be transformed into real investments, were typically held in diversified portfolios of securities or financial assets so as to earn 'rentier' incomes. Large institutional investors (such as pension funds, mutual funds, investment trusts, insurance companies, hedge funds) to whom individual and corporate savers entrusted their funds played a significant role in securities markets. They hired professional fund managers to valorize their holdings for the benefit of their clients. As long as production grew, funds were eventually converted into real capital.

The Reagan era restructuring of the US economy, which entailed deindustrialization/off-shoring and financial deregulation, stimulated a 'mergers and acquisitions' boom, the introduction of a host of financial innovations and the easing of monetarist constraints that provided enhanced opportunities to earn speculative incomes from unproductive investments, as the opportunities to profit from supporting capitalist production declined. This reactivation or resuscitation of moribund 'rentiers' and of the financial sector, which we shall refer to as 'financiarization', was possible, first, because the opportunities for industrial growth were limited by both social and ecological factors; second, because foreign central banks obligingly held so much of the U.S. debt; and, lastly, because of the presence of an abundance of idle money or 'loanable' funds that could not easily be converted into capital.

'Casino funds' seek opportunities to earn interest or rent from asset and property appreciation and from high risk, speculative gambles. What they do is to valorize long-term idle funds within the capital market without investing in the production of use values or useful services. If they are to be successful they must engage in activities which are expropriatory. They migrate from one economy to another, aiming to appropriate profits earned by others and, in the process, frequently destabilizing the global economy. Rather than rendering the production of 'surplus value' more efficient, they often hinder and disrupt it. 'Financiarization', or the hypertrophy of finance, is symptomatic of the disintegration of capitalism. Capital is retreating to the interstices or lacunae of the world economy, where it began, because there capital flows are less subject to regulation or control by any national authority. Thus, speculative money games and cross-border capital flows now dwarf the movement of goods.

Capital now focuses more attention on asset appreciation than it does on the production of use values for profit. The 'enclosures' which are taking place today, whereby capital attempts to establish proprietary interests, intellectual property rights, patents, copyrights, and so on over everything and anything (for example, the genetic inheritance of plants and animals) that can provide rental earnings (or the prospect of future earnings), are substitutes for vigorous capitalist activity, whereas the original enclosures of productive land were preludes to it.

Casino funds may be deemed to have played a positive role during the mergers and acquisitions boom of the 1980s, which promoted the restructuring of the American economy. Yet casino funds can also engineer an illusory prosperity before abruptly departing from economies, building and then deflating speculative bubbles before migrating elsewhere. The activity of casino funds, though they are not directly tied to the real economy, can seriously disrupt it, together with stock and financial markets.

Hedge funds of a global or macro-type are blamed for seriously destabilizing international financial markets, with their highly leveraged, 'off-the-balance-sheet' gambles in colossal amounts. They have also contributed to an increase in liquidity, by whetting investors' appetites for reckless risk taking. Indeed, they have been implicated in the 1992 British pound crisis, the 1994 Mexican peso crisis, the 1997 Thai baht crisis and the 1998 Russian rouble crisis. Options, which played a part in the dramatic yen appreciation of 1994, have exacerbated the volatility of foreign exchange markets. Derivatives were implicated in the Enron collapse. The recent bailout of Fannie Mae and Freddie Mac may have been undertaken to rescue those who had entered into credit-default swaps that required them to make good on the defaulted bonds of these lenders. The issuing of credit default swaps was AIG's nemesis.

Currently, currency speculation far exceeds the volume of trade and thus plays more of a role in determining exchange rates than the latter. In this era of massive, unregulated and instantaneous capital movement, only the strongest nations with the largest currency reserves can defend themselves against frequent speculative attacks on their currencies.

It is understandable that firms would employ derivatives, options, swaps, futures and other financial innovations to hedge against the imposing market risks in the post-Fordist era. Unfortunately, although hedging aims at self-protection, it cannot be separated from speculative gambles, which tend to greatly magnify risk. Even the largest firms can get into trouble due to the high leverage involved in these transactions. Moreover, hedging raises what were unit or sector risks to the status of systemic risks.

When large stakes crumble, financial authorities must arrange bailouts with public money to avoid exposing the international financial system and, therefore, the world economy to a deadly 'systemic risk'. Yet individual states cannot regulate this 'industry'. Even the leading states acting in concert find it difficult to do so, because they are simultaneously competing to attract investment and because the products, transactions and operations involved are so complex and opaque.

During the 1990s, when Japan was trapped in a long, post-Plaza Accord recession, the Americans demonstrated their acumen at financial speculation and at seizing the much hyped commercial opportunities presented by internet commerce, high technology stock offerings and the removal of real and psychological barriers to global investment that occurred after the collapse of the Soviet Union. The United States used its dominant position in the IMF and WTO to press for a global liberalization of financial services. The global liquidity boom, the growth of financial transactions that far outstrip the growth in the production and trading of goods, and the concomitant debt-fueled asset and property inflation were accelerated by the dramatic expansion of the US dollar supply, initiated by the Greenspan-era Federal Reserve, which encouraged reckless financial speculation with its policy of easy money and low interest rates. Such a policy was facilitated because China and Japan produced so much of what America consumed, while holding much of the US debt. The repeal of Glass–Steagall in 1999 by the Clinton administration, which permitted the merging of commercial and investment banks, accelerated this trend.

When the dot-com euphoria ended, the Bush-era Federal Reserve and US tax laws facilitated the inflation of an unsustainable bubble in the real estate and home mortgage markets. This led to reckless lending at rates that did not adequately price the risks entailed. Because banks and related financial institutions were no longer required to hold adequate collateral to back loans extended or reserves sufficient to cover losses from loan and mortgage defaults, they evolved into loan and mortgage brokers, lending borrowed money, while Wall Street financial markets became heavily involved with the financing of home mortgages by a process known as 'securitization'. These mortgage-backed securities were in turn used as collateral by private equity firms and hedge funds engaged in highly leveraged buy-outs and gambles. Market capitalization increased markedly, thus leading to an escalation of share prices, while profits languished.

Although the inevitable deflation of the real-estate bubble, the subsequent failure of major financial institutions, and hastily arranged rescues were initially US phenomena, the financial havoc created by highly leveraged and speculative gambles is global in scope. Deregulated financial firms have not closely scrutinized the value of the dubious assets they have bought, sold, held or insured and have not maintained sufficient capital to cover sudden and significant rises in defaults, because behaving prudently would have interfered with their goal of keeping the maximum amount of capital in play. Because both the market for asset-backed securities and inter-bank lending were paralyzed and major financial and insurance firms were insolvent, a US-government-sponsored 'bailout' was instituted to restore confidence. Nevertheless, America's status as a financial superpower has been progressively diminished as the contagion has spread, as have its 'financiarization' and 'securitization' models of wealth 'creation'.

The dialectical theory of pure capitalism explains the necessary presence of two unproductive forms of capital, loan capital and commercial capital, but in the pure theory (or definition) of capitalism there is no room for 'casino funds', a chrematistic operation in money games which does not support either the activities of industrial capital or the reproduction of substantive or material economic life. In mature, market-regulated capitalist societies, accumulation funds were converted into capital when they attained a certain magnitude, so as to participate in the industrial production of surplus value. While merchant capital and moneylending capital flourished in history prior to the appearance of industrial capitalism, casino funds becomes dominant only after its enfeeblement. The increasingly prominent casino funds, which share with money-lending capital the property of Hegelian *measurelessness* (Sekine, 1997, I, p.103; 1984, p.209), in that their operations tend to disrupt real economic life, are not part of the self-definition of capitalism and signify rather that capitalism has disintegrated.

US GLOBALIZATION

There are fundamentally two types of money. One is commodity money, such as gold, which arises automatically from commodity exchanges in capitalist society in order to regulate them. The other is fiat money or legal tender, which the state issues. This money is not an asset, but a pure debt. The state has the power to 'debase' it or to devalue its original liability. The distinction tends to be blurred, since real money often combines elements of both. Thus, for a long time, the US dollar was gold money, then it became a 'managed currency' that retained an indirect connection with gold. In the end, gold was demonetized and became a pure liability. 'Globalization' was made possible only because the dollar became an uncontested reserve currency, though it was not backed by any commodity value.

Because of a steadily worsening balance of payments and the consequent loss of confidence in the dollar, President Nixon was forced to terminate the convertibility of the dollar into gold in 1971, which meant that the dollar became a non-capitalist fiat currency unrelated to gold. The fall of the IMF regime (the international currency system based on the gold-dollar standard and fixed exchange rates) and the shift to flexible exchange rates did not undermine the dollar's reserve-currency status, in part because so many western and oil-producing nations depended on the United States for protection in the era of the east–west rivalry, because global finance was comfortable employing the dollar as a vehicle currency and because the United States had the most sophisticated money and capital markets. The consequence of this acceptance was that the United States would owe its ever increasing debt to foreign creditors in its own currency, which was no longer backed by any commodity value, while unfettered American casino finance could continue to be a dominant force in finance and foreign investment even if American industry lost its pre-eminence and even if the United States regularly ran budgetary and balance-of-payment deficits.

In 1974 the United States renewed the agreement with the House of Saud (and, subsequently, with OPEC generally) whereby the Saudis would continue to receive US protection while their oil would continue to be priced and traded in dollars. The dollar's purchasing power with regard to that oil would also continue to be protected. Since both the price of and the demand for oil would tend to increase, the dollar's status as the reserve currency would be strengthened. The OPEC nations conveniently recycled much of their oil earnings into the US stock market and financial institutions (and were thus frequently saddled with poorly performing investments). Moreover, the world's dominant oil markets, the NYMEX and the IPE, also insisted that oil transactions be made in US dollars; so poorer nations, which typically lacked large oil reserves, had to sell goods so as to acquire and hold US dollars or securities, which would provide protection should their own currencies be devalued against the dollar.

Because demand-side Keynesian macroeconomic policies only fueled stagflation, Reagan embraced deregulation in order to eliminate supply-side rigidities and to promote the swift adaptation of post-Fordist technologies and forms of organization, but, unfortunately, 'military Keynesianism' combined with Volcker's monetarist policies to generate far higher interest rates than intended, a large influx of foreign, and especially Japanese, funds and a dramatic 'crowding out' phenomenon in the US bond market. US budget and current account deficits rose dramatically and US industry had to endure the burden of high interest rates and a strong dollar.

During his second term, however, Reagan concluded the Plaza Accord, which led to a substantial devaluation of the US dollar, together with lower interest rates in the United States and still lower interest rates among the other G5 nations, especially Japan. During this era and subsequently Japan maintained a large trade account surplus with the United States and, in turn, purchased US treasury bills, thus financing US budget and balance-of-payments deficits. This stimulated a spectacular mergers and acquisitions boom in the US stock market, which was accompanied by the restructuring of the American, western and global economies.

Reagan's success in revitalizing the American economy, even as the 'twin deficits' were constantly rising, hinged crucially on the dependable inflow of foreign funds, especially of Japanese money. The mergers and acquisitions boom would not have been so spectacular if the only funds mobilized had been American casino funds. Industrial and managerial reorganization required funds far in excess of the US domestic capacity to save. Reagan, thus, unwittingly introduced a new international division of labour, whereby the United States proclaimed to its trading partners, 'you save what I spend'. The twin deficits of the United States would be financed by the savings generated in other advanced industrial nations. For this to be possible, it was essential that these powers continue to accept the American dollar as their international currency. Although the concept of 'globalization' did not exist in Reagan's time, international 'cooperation' with regard to interest rate policy gave shape to it. This ensured that American deficits would henceforth be financed by foreign surpluses.

The United States, which had been the leading creditor nation in the post-1945 era, had by 1985 become the leading debtor nation, and yet it could still print more money to purchase imported goods and oil, while, at the same time, any fall in the value of the dollar was cushioned by the dollar's privileged status. While the poor nations struggled, the oil-producing nations, Japan and later China, lent massively to the far more affluent American debtor in its own currency. The developing nations, which were subject to the harsh discipline of the neoliberal-informed and US-dominated Washington Consensus, would not have been in such dire straits if they, like the Americans, could have arranged to have their debts denominated in their own currency.

Japan and West Germany were the two main targets of America's financial 'diplomacy' from the Carter era onward. Germany, like the rest of western Europe, derived some protection from its membership in a developing common market, while the Japanese, who were either less experienced or more influenced by geopolitical considerations, did not realize the danger of buying into dollar-denominated securities (or of lending in the borrower's currency). In the early 1980s Japan, which had become an economic superpower with a large trade surplus, believed itself capable of purchasing a large chunk of American federal bonds; but that nation did not foresee the spectacular exchange losses which would befall Japanese investors after the Plaza Accord caused the dramatic appreciation of the yen. When Black Monday struck the US stock market in 1987, the Bank of Japan did not raise the interest rate, even though the Japanese economy was dangerously overheating, because it wished to protect Japanese investors. That promoted an 'economic bubble' that hurt Japanese industry. Nevertheless, the two nations have continued to harmonize their monetary policies in such a way as to assure the smooth flow of Japanese money into the United States. The Bank of Japan with its zero interest rate policy has ensured that all the dollars that that country earns through its trade surplus will quickly return to the American capital market for minor rentier incomes.

I concur with Sekine that the essence of 'globalization' lies in America's success in establishing economic 'partnerships' with those nations that have trade surpluses with the United States similar to those established with Japan, though the term 'globalization' only became popular with the collapse of the Soviet Union. In this type of arrangement the principle of 'you save what I spend' securely applies, because the Americans are allowed to borrow in their own currency. Felicitous terms for this kind of economic relationship are 'monetary imperialism' or 'super imperialism', the latter being the title of Michael Hudson's quite prescient book, which was first published in 1972. (Hudson also speaks of a Treasury Bill standard as underlying the dollar.) These terms draw attention to the novel type of US state-engineered imperialism that evolved in the post-Fordist era and that differed so radically from the capitalist variety that arose in the late nineteenth century. So long as the dollar continues as the reserve currency, even though it is no longer backed by gold, the US government is in the position of being able to print dollars and to issue more treasury bonds without restraint. It is not necessary to 'dollarize' all currencies. The US government need only contrive a situation in which all the dollars earned by the foreigners return to the United States, not to buy its goods, but to buy its securities, in order to fully 'globalize' the world economy and put an end to capitalism. The necessity to hold depreciating American dollars and low-yield US treasury bills constitutes a type of appropriation by seignorage fee, tax or tribute.

Consumption and investment by low-cost debt financing has been possible for US households, businesses and government as the dollars earned by foreigners as trade surpluses with the United States have returned to that nation to purchase low-yield public and private securities and, in the process, have helped to make US bond markets the world's largest. The central banks of America's major trading partners, which receive depreciating dollars from their domestic exporters and commercial banks, can do little but exchange them for US treasury bills, which have yielded comparatively low rates of interest. In this fashion, they have financed US budget deficits. These banks have no interest in seeing the US dollar as reserve currency decline precipitously in value even if the US economy is not performing well, because of their large US dollar holdings and because of the negative effect of such a slide on those of their domestic firms that compete with US firms. Failure to lend the dollars earned from trade surpluses would raise the value of their currencies relative to the dollar making their producers less competitive. Because foreign central banks have held so much of the growing US debt for the last three decades, American investors and American financial, commercial and industrial firms employing ever plentiful American dollars have been free to seek higher-yield investments in stocks, real estate and mineral rights both at home and abroad.

The United States has also benefited because its trading partners have funded America's military adventurism and post-colonial-era empire building. The US military budget is reputed to be larger than all of its serious rivals combined, and its trading partners and debt holders are made accomplices – albeit often unwillingly – of US unilateralism.

The 'globalization' of the world economy is not a technological imperative to which we all must conform. It is an American initiative that aims to dominate the world by means of their dollar, which is fully disconnected from gold. Perhaps the deepening global financial and economic crises that began to emerge in 2007 will alert China, Japan and Europe to the dangers of acting as America's providers and creditors.

In these twilight years of the petro-chemical civilization, when the global economy is possessed of a systemic malaise, we face an uncertain future, because we still aspire to be capitalist, though capitalism cannot manage prevailing use-value spaces. The reinvigoration of the Keynesian legacy and the revival of social democracy, which aimed to humanize rather than to replace capitalism, are also non-starters, because globalization has deprived the nation state of the power to opt for an internal, at the expense of an external, equilibrium. The corporate 'goose', which can take flight much more easily today, is much less inclined to lay golden eggs that social democratic governments may redistribute to their citizens. It is high time then that we set about the task of creating vibrantly democratic, socialist societies, which have made peace with nature.

Notes

1. As goods embodying value, all commodities can and must be priced. This does not imply that whatever is positively priced must necessarily possess value. The commodity form can attach to goods such as works of art, which are not capitalistically produced. Such prices are arbitrary, since they do not reflect the underlying allocation of society's resources; by contrast, the equilibrium prices of genuine commodities do. It is necessary to suppose, therefore, that no non-capitalist goods are produced in pure capitalism.

2. Though it may be counterintuitive, it can be argued that categories which are appropriate to present the natural world as it appears to unreflective perception are appropriate in the doctrine of circulation because, although capitalism is a social institution, it initially presents its social relations as thing-to-thing commodity relations. The commodity economy seems reducible to matter in motion, when viewed externally. Thus, as Dunne has observed, bourgeois society, as a commodity exchange system, behaves like a natural system and must initially correspond to the categories relating to natural change or transition in Hegel's doctrine of being (Dunne 1977, pp.69–70).

3. If the purchasing power of money becomes doubtful in a capitalist society (for example, if, for some contingent reason, hyperinflation becomes rampant) a more primitive expression of value, such as 'this bottle of wine is yours for three pounds of butter', will return to the clearing house of commodities.

4. While it is a broader social expression of value than the simple value form, this form, in which the value of A is expressed alterably by many finite limits, can degenerate into what Hegel calls *bad infinity*. The bad infinite, which results from the transcendence of one finite something in another, merely reinstates the contradiction inherent in finite, limited being, repeating it endlessly as one finite gives rise to another indefinitely. This non-encompassing infinite does not meet the demand for a coherent determination of the nature of finitude. Similarly, in the dialectic of capital, the potentially infinite series of exchange proposals never yields the desired effect, which would be the exchange of any commodity owner's commodity for any other commodity he might wish. In Hegelian terms, the commodity is still a commodity *an sich* rather than a full fledged commodity *für sich*.

5. Underlying the market equilibrium is a specifically capitalist division of labour or productive organization. In order to determine the value of a commodity *substantively*, we must know the conditions under which the socially necessary (equilibrium) quantity of the commodity is produced. The formation of equilibrium prices cannot be adequately discussed until the prevailing technological basis of commodity production, the level of the general rate of profit and the structure of social demand are made explicit. Here, at this early and much more abstract point in the dialectic, equilibrium prices must appear in a less specified or 'emptier' form as normal prices.

6. A genuine commodity is *capitalistically reproducible*, that is to say, it can, in principle, be supplied in any quantity (in any number of interchangeable samples) demanded. The economic theory of capitalism does not deal with goods such as antiques or art objects which are only accidentally traded in the commodity market. These cannot be reproduced in any quantity in a capitalist factory in response to demand. Their supplies are absolutely limited, and their prices tend to be quite arbitrary, depending on many contingent factors.

7. In the theory of a self-contained or purely capitalist economy, foreign trade must be left out of consideration, since domestic and foreign trade cannot be distinguished in such an abstract context. Therefore, the only way in which society's stock of gold can be increased, in preparation for economic expansion, is by the conversion of non-monetary gold, or

the production of new gold in greater quantity than what is lost through the abrasion of existing monetary gold. This discussion will be resumed when we reach the doctrine of production.

8. The history of mercantilism illustrates the collusion of established merchant houses with the political powers of the absolutist monarchy. Since merchant capital could not overcome use-value restrictions on its chrematistic operations without assistance, it tended to depend on extra-economic powers. Large firms, specializing in particular lines of trade, developed into powerful institutions, thanks in no small part to the privileges and protection granted by the state. So long as commerce remained an economic activity external to the prevailing mode of production, however, the unification that the society-wide market heralded could not be fully realized.

9. Moneylending is not entirely risk free. Debtors do become insolvent, in which case, even with the foreclosure of their assets, lenders may lose not only the interest owed to them, but part of their principal as well. A risk of this kind, however, is insurable or convertible statistically into the cost of lending, which the lender can charge over and above the interest. *Risk premiums* offset the costs of lending which arise from bad loans. They are normally distributed in such a way that less creditworthy borrowers pay the greater share of it and fully qualified borrowers none.

10. Because of the emptiness of its chrematistic and its indifference to use values, moneylending capital possessed no internal check on its predatory and expropriatory nature. Since its nature was akin to that of a loan shark, it posed more of a threat to traditional society and its mode of production than did merchant capital. In order to fend off moneylending capital, feudal lords were often forced to raise rents and kings to impose heavier taxes, which strained an already impoverished agriculture.

11. Even after the disappearance of the professional moneylender, capital continues to seek an ideal form of moneylending capital that will achieve a self-enhancement of value not entangled with use values. This ideal is realized in the form of interest-bearing capital, the highest, and therefore most 'fetishistic', form of capital.

12. Granted, capital's access to land, through a rental contract rather than by its purchase as a commodity, is never free from impediments. It must be presupposed, until later in the development of the dialectic, however, that capital somehow obtains free access to land of uniform quality. Thus, for the present, industrial capital may be assumed to be unrestrained as it undertakes to produce all use values as commodities by means of commodities.

CHAPTER 2

13. See Sekine 1984, pp.250–8 for an extended discussion of the correspondences between the two parallel doctrines.
14. See Sekine 1984, pp.264–7.
15. See Sekine 1984, pp.266–7.
16. For a more detailed discussion of this topic, together with numerical examples, see vol.I of Sekine's *Outline of the Dialectic of Capital* (1997), especially pp.136–7.

CHAPTER 3

17. See Sekine 1984, pp.454–7 for a more detailed discussion of the correspondence.

CHAPTER 4

18. See Sekine 1986, pp.17–20.
19. See Sekine 1986, pp.11–16.
20. In the simplest model of the capitalist market, in which there exists only one wage good, Y, it is as if all workers were paid a physical wage in terms of Y. In reality, when money wages,

w, are paid, individual workers are free to spend them on various wage goods according to their needs, which can differ from one worker to another. What is important, in this case, is that the money value of all wage goods produced must equal the total wages bill paid in the system.

CHAPTER 8

21. For an interesting discussion of this topic, see Albritton 1991 (pp.69–77).
22. Monopolies do not make an appearance in the theory of a pure capitalism, not only because they would interfere with the operation of the law of value, but also because it cannot be demonstrated that a capitalist society governed by that law would of necessity generate such monopolistic enterprises. We deal with monopoly and oligopoly at the level of stage theory, in which capital must confront varying degrees and kinds of use-value resistance that it cannot overcome through its autonomous operation. One would, of course, expect to see more monopoly or oligopoly in the eras of mercantilism and of imperialism, when capitalism was either developing or declining, than in the period of mature liberal capitalism, when competitive industrial capitals confronted more of the light, relatively simple use values that they were best equipped to produce autonomously.
23. For more on this important topic, see Albritton 1991, ch.4.
24. The preceding analysis draws upon Uno's unpublished manuscript, *Types of Economic Policies Under Capitalism*, II, 'The Stage of Liberalism', ch.2.
25. The limited liability joint-stock company, which facilitates the rapid centralization of capital and ultimately encourages the separation of ownership and control, began to play a more important role in the economy late in the stage of liberalism, but it did not develop to the point that it altered the competitive and entrepreneurial character of cotton manufacturing. It was only in the imperialist era that the joint-stock corporate form came into its own as an instrument for the centralization of capital in heavy industry.
26. Ordinary shareholders no longer functioned as real capitalists, for they differed little from depositors with the banks (except that they expected greater returns due to the greater risks involved). Indeed, they were often made to bear a major part of company losses, while large shareholders, who were in charge of the running of business, could escape with less financial hardship than if they were individual proprietors (Uno unpublished, III, ch.1, sect.2).
27. Banks were not constrained by specific use values as industrial firms were. This made them less prone to mutual competition and more inclined to mutual accommodation. Hence, they typically worked together to pursue monopoly profits. Banks frequently promoted mergers, monopolies and cartelization and restrained destructive competition, since this enhanced stability and profitability, while minimizing the risks of losses from such large loans and investments.
28. The close ties between large banks and large business enterprises generated benefits in which small regional banks and firms could not participate. A small number of large banks, headquartered in the major financial centers, tended to dominate the whole nation by means of networks of branches. These large banks often syndicated themselves in such businesses as the issuing of stocks. Their presence was particularly extensive in international banking, which developed together with overseas investment (Albritton 1991, p.185).
29. Because of the precipitous fall in profit rates and the cost of technological innovation in heavy industry, fixed capital was not cyclically renewed to launch a new phase of prosperity by means of innovations introduced towards the end of the depression phase of a regularly recurring business cycle. Indeed, innovations could occur at any time. Thus, business cycles, which formerly regulated growth in liberal capitalism, were seriously deformed by the hypertrophy of fixed capital in heavy industries. Even the working of the law of average profit, one of the fundamental laws of capitalism, was irrevocably distorted. The market was thus incapable of correcting the lopsided growth of the economy (Uno unpublished, III, ch.1).
30. For a discussion of ideology in the imperialist era, see Albritton (1991, pp.214–20).

CHAPTER 9

31. Please refer to the previous chapter for an extended discussion.
32. Here, I follow Sekine in employing terms borrowed from neoclassical economics (Bell and Sekine 2001, p.54).
33. The term 'mode of production' is used loosely here, because Fordism, unlike capitalism, is not, strictly speaking, a mode of production.
34. I follow Sekine in using the term 'Fordism' to describe, from the supply side, a major aspect of this post-capitalist era, whereas the French Regulationist school includes in its conception of Fordism the demand side as well. Our definition of Fordism is closer to that of Brenner and Glick (but see also Womack, Jones and Roos 1990).

Bibliography

Albritton, Robert (1984), 'The Dialectic of Capital: A Japanese Contribution', *Capital and Class*, Spring, 157–76.

—— (1986), *A Japanese Reconstruction of Marxist Theory*, London: Macmillan.

—— (1991), *A Japanese Approach to Stages of Capitalist Development*, London: Macmillan.

—— (1992), 'Levels of Analysis in Marxian Political Economy: An Unoist Approach', *Radical Philosophy*, 60.

—— (1998), 'The Unique Ontology of Capital', *Poznan Studies in the Philosophy of the Sciences and the Humanities*, 60, 55–98.

—— (1999), *Dialectics and Deconstruction in Political Economy*, London: Macmillan.

—— (2001), 'Capitalism in the Future Perfect Tense', in Robert Albritton et al. (eds.), *Phases of Capitalist Development*, London: Palgrave.

—— (2004), 'Theorizing Capital's Deep Structure and the Transformation of Capitalism', *Historical Materialism*, 12(3), 73–92.

—— (2007), *Economics Transformed: Discovering the Brilliance of Marx*, London: Pluto Press.

—— and T. Sekine (eds.) (1995), *A Japanese Approach to Political Economy: Unoist Variations*, London: Macmillan.

—— and John R. Bell (1995), 'Introduction', in Albritton and Sekine (eds). *A Japanese Approach to Political Economy: Unoist Variations*, London: Macmillan, pp.1–10.

——, M. Itoh, R. Westra and A. Zuege (eds.) (2001), *Phases of Capitalist Development*, London: Palgrave.

Bell, John R. (1995), 'Dialectics and Economic Theory', in Albritton and Sekine (eds.) *A Japanese Approach to Political Economy: Unoist Variations*, London: Macmillan, pp.107–39.

—— (2003), 'From Hegel to Marx to the Dialectic of Capital', in R. Albritton and J. Simoulitis (eds.) *New Dialectics and Political Economy*, London: Palgrave.

—— (2004), 'Marx's Anti-Authoritarian Ecocommunism', in R. Albritton, J.R. Bell, S. Bell and R. Westra (eds.) (2004), *New Socialisms: Futures Beyond Globalization*, London: Routledge.

Bell, John R., and Thomas Sekine (2001), 'The Disintegration of Capitalism: A Phase of Ex-Capitalist Transition', in Robert Albritton et al. (eds.), *Phases of Capitalist Development: Booms, Crises and Globalizations*, pp.37–55.

Brenner, R. and Glick, M. (1991), 'The Regulation Approach: Theory and History', *New Left Review*, 188.

Drucker, P. (1986), 'The Changed World Economy', *Foreign Affairs*, 64(4).

Duncan, Colin (1983), 'Under the Cloud of CAPITAL: History vs. Theory', *Science and Society* 47(3), 300–22.

—— (1996), *The Centrality of Agriculture: Between Humankind and the Rest of Nature*, Montreal and Kingston: McGill–Queens University Press.

—— and Makoto Maruyama (1986), 'The Significance of the Japanese Counterpart to Karl Polanyi: The Power and Limitations of Kozo Uno's Perspective', in Kari Polanyi Levitt (ed.), *The Life and Work of Karl Polanyi: A Celebration*, Montreal: Black Rose Press, pp.221–8.

Dunne, P. (1977), 'Hegel's doctrine of Quality in Reference to the Theory of the Commodity-Form in the Dialectic of Capital', unpublished manuscript.

Hegel, G.W.F. (1969), *Science of Logic*, trans. A.V. Miller, London: Allen & Unwin.

—— (1975), *Hegel's Logic*, trans. W. Wallace, Oxford: Oxford University Press.

Hilferding, R. (1981), *Finance Capital*, London: Routledge & Kegan Paul.

Labergott, S. (1996), 'Labour Force and Employment, 1800–1960', in National Bureau of Economic Research, *Output, Employment, and Productivity in the United States after 1800*, New York: Columbia University Press.

228   CAPITALISM AND THE DIALECTIC

Lenin, V.I. (1965), *Imperialism: The Highest Stage of Capitalism* Peking: Foreign Languages Press.
Marx, Karl (1970), *A Contribution to the Critique of Political Economy*, New York: International Publishers.
—— (1969), *Capital*, vol.I, Moscow: Progress Publishers.
—— (1969a), *Capital*, vol.II, Moscow: Progress Publishers.
—— (1969b), *Capital*, vol.III, Moscow: Progress Publishers.
—— (1972), *Theories of Surplus Value*, vols.I–III, London: Lawrence & Wishart.
—— (1973), *Grundrisse*, Harmondsworth: Penguin.
—— (1975), *Texts on Method*, ed. T. Carver, Oxford: Basil Blackwell.
—— (1977), *Capital*, vol.I, New York: Vintage Books.
—— (1978), *Capital*, vol.II, New York: Vintage Books.
—— (1981), *Capital*, vol.III, New York: Vintage Books.
—— and Frederick Engels (1951) *Selected Works* Moscow: Progress Publishers.
—— (1975), *Collected Works*, Moscow: Progress Publishers.
—— (1965), *The German Ideology* London: Lawrence & Wishart.
—— (1973), *Political Writings*, ed. D. Fernbach, Harmondsworth: Penguin.
Miyazaki, Y. (1990) *Kawariyuku Sekai-Ketzai* [The Changing world Economy] Tokyo: Yuuhikaku.
Polanyi, Karl (1944), *The Great Transformation*, Boston: Beacon Press.
—— (1977), *The Livelihood of Man*, New York: Academic Press.
—— (1968), *Primitive, Archaic and Modern Economies*, ed. G. Dalton, Garden City: Doubleday.
Schumpeter, J.A. (1937), *The Theory of Economic Development*, Cambridge, Mass.: Harvard.
Sekine, Thomas (1972), *Keizaigaku no Kouyou* [The Usefulness of Political Economy: A Dialogue with Professor Kozo Uno], Tokyo: University of Tokyo Press.
—— (1973), 'Method of Marxian Political Economy and Modern Economics I', *Methods of Social Sciences*, 6, 1–8.
—— (1974), 'Method of Marxian Political Economy and Modern Economics II', *Methods of Social Sciences*, 7, 1–9.
—— (1974a), 'Economics and the Modern Economy', in Shigeto Tsuru (ed.), *In Pursuit of Political Economy*, vol.IV, pp.121–203.
—— (1974b), 'On Ex-Capitalist Transition', *Keizai Seminar*, 227(2), 22–34.
—— (1974c), 'Towards a Rejuvenation of the Uno doctrine', *Asahi Journal*, 14(4), 59–61.
—— (1975), 'Uno-Riron: A Japanese Contribution to Marxian Political Economy', *Journal of Economic Literature*, 13(3), 847–77.
—— (1975a), 'Ex-Capitalist Transition Once Again', *Keizai Seminar*, 245(6), 106–14.
—— (1980), 'The Necessity of the Law of Value', *Science and Society*, 44(3), 289–304.
—— (1980a), 'An Essay on Uno's Dialectic of Capital', in Kozo Uno, *Principles of Political Economy, Theory of a Purely Capitalist Society*, trans. T. Sekine, Sussex: Harvester Press, pp.127–66.
—— (1981), 'The Circular Motion of Capital', *Science and Society*, 45(3), 288–305.
—— (1983), 'The Law of Market Value', *Science and Society*, 46(3), 420–44.
—— (1983a), 'A renewed Interest in Marx' (as Part 5 of 'Special Contributions on Marx, Keynes and Schumpeter'), *Nihon-Keizai Shimbun*, January.
—— (1983b), 'The Dialectic of Capital and the Logic of Hegel', *Keizaigaku Hihan*, 14, 81–101.
—— (1983/4), 'The Present-Day Significance of Marxian Political Economy', *Keizai Hyouron*, pp.32–46.
—— (1984), *The Dialectic of Capital: A Study of the Inner Logic of Capitalism*, vol.I, Tokyo: Yushindo Press (republished 1986).
—— (1984a), 'An Uno School Seminar in the Theory of Value', *Science and Society*, 48(4), 419–32.
—— (1984b), 'Marx's View on the Liberation of Man', in M. Itoh and M. Iida (eds.), *Ima Marx wo Tou*, Koyou Shuppan, pp.187–206.

—— (1984c), 'Political Economy and the Entropy Problem', *Keizai Kenkyuu*, 35, 97–106.

—— (1986), *The Dialectic of Capital: A Study of the Inner Logic of Capitalism*, vol.II, Toshindo Press, Tokyo.

—— (1986a), 'The Structure of the Tamanoi Riron', *Keizai Seminar*, special issue on ecology and entropy, 1986, pp.246–52.

—— (1987), 'Kozo Uno' in *The New Palgrave: Marxian Economics*, ed. J. Eatwell, M. Milgate and P. Newman, London: Macmillan, pp.384–5.

—— (1990), 'Socialism as a Living Idea', in T. Sekine and H. Flakierski (eds.), *Socialist Dilemmas: East and West*, pp.128–51.

—— (1990a), 'A Change of Paradigm in Political Economy', in *The Legacy of Political Economy*, vol.I of the collected works of Tamanoi, Tokyo: Gakuyou Shobou, pp.343–59.

—— (1993), *Marxian Theory of Value* (unpublished manuscript).

—— (1994), 'The World Economy in Transition: Beyond Post-Fordism', *Keizai Seminar*, 476(9), 38–45.

—— (1995), 'Fordism, Casino Capital and the Current Japanese Recession', in Dennis J. Dicks (ed.), *Communicating with Japan, Images Past, Present and Future: An Interdisciplinary Anthology*, Montreal: Concordia University, pp.168–98.

—— (1995a), 'Uno School Seminar on the Theory of Value', in T. Sekine and R. Albritton (eds.), *A Japanese Approach to Political Economy*, pp.13–33, London: Macmillan.

—— (1995b), 'The Necessity of the Law of Value, Its Demonstration and Significance', in T. Sekine and R. Albritton (eds), *A Japanese Approach to Political Economy*, pp.34–43.

—— (1995c), 'Uno's Method of Marxian Economics', *Chiiki-Bunseki*, 33(2), 73–80.

—— (1995d), *Keizaigaku no Houkou Tenkan* [Towards a Paradigm Change in Economics], Tokyo: Toshindo Press.

—— (1995e), 'Is the Concept of Entropy Indispensable to Economics?' *Entoropii*, 33, 2–14.

—— (1997), *An Outline of the Dialectic of Capital*, 2 vols., London: Macmillan.

—— (1997a), 'Dialectic of Capital and the Analysis of the Current Economy: From the Point of View of the Uno doctrine', *Shougaku Kenkyuu*, 41(1), 1–20.

—— (1998), 'The Dialectic of Capital: An Unoist Interpretation', *Science and Society*, 62(3), pp.434–45.

—— (1998a), 'General Economic Norms and Socialism: From Uno to Tamanoi', *Chiiki-Bunseki*, 36(2), 105–12.

—— (1998b), 'Rediscovery of Karl Polanyi: From the Point of View of the Uno doctrine', in two parts, *Keizai Seminar*, 26(11), 108–14; and 27(12), 95–101.

—— (1999), 'Une réflexion sur les tendances actuelles de l'économie mondiale', *Chiiki-Bunseki*, 37(1), 17–25 (an earlier version appeared as 'Le capitalisme a déjà été aboli', in Bernard Stéphan (ed.) *Le Manifeste communiste aujourd'hui*, Paris: Les éditions de l'atelier, 1998, pp.199–209).

—— (1999a), 'Polanyi, Marx et Uno', *Shougaku-Kenkyuu*, 42(1.2), 53–78.

—— (1999b), 'Marxian Theory of Value: An Unoist Approach (I)', *Chiiki-Bunseki*, 37(2), 99–136.

—— (1999c), 'Marxian Theory of Value: An Unoist Approach (II)', *Chiiki-Bunseki*, 38(1), 43–90.

—— (2000), 'Marxian Theory of Value: An Unoist Approach (III)', *Chiiki-Bunseki*, 39(1), 9–54.

—— (2000a), 'L'<Economie au sens large> conçue par Karl Polnyi et Yoshiro Tamanoi', *Shougaku-Kenkyuu*, 43(1), 1–21.

—— (2000b), 'How Did the Twentieth Century Appropriate Hegel and Marx? From the Point of View of the Dialectic of Capital', in S. Furihata and M. Itoh (eds), *Reconstructing Marx's Theories: What to Learn from Uno's Economics*, Tokyo: Shakai-Hyron-sha.

—— (2001), 'Economics in the Broad Sense: The Environmental Issues in the Process of ex-Capitalist Transition', in Entropy Society of Japan, *Junkan-gata Shakai wo tou*, Tokyo: Fujiwara Shoten, pp.165–83.

—— (2001a), 'Farewell to Capitalism: A Production-Centered Society', *Chiiki-Bunseki*, 40(1), 9–15.

—— (2001b), 'La Vie économique d'une société et les valeurs humaines', *Chiiki-Bunseki*, 40(1), 17–20.

—— (2001c), 'Beyond Globalization and Capitalism: Towards an Environment-Friendly Economy', in Denzaburo Yui and Yasuo Endo (eds.), *Framing the Pacific in the 21st Century: Coexistence and Friction*, Center for Pacific and American Studies, University of Tokyo, pp.320–5.

—— (2003), 'The Dialectic, or Logic that Coincides with Economics', in Robert Albritton and John Simoulidis (eds.), *New Dialectics and Political Economy*, London: Palgrave Macmillan, pp.120–30.

—— (2003a), 'What Do We Learn from Value Theory?' in Richard Westra and Alan Zuege (eds.), *Value and the World Economy Today*, London: Palgrave, pp.188–204.

—— (2004), 'Socialism Beyond Market and Productivism', in Robert Albritton et al. (eds), *New Socialisms: Futures Beyond Globalization*, London: Routledge, pp.231–44.

—— (2007), 'Globalization of the World Economy in Ex-Capitalist Transition', in *Neo-Liberalism, Japan and the Dynamics of Global Capitalism: Theory, History and Methodology*, proceedings of the Third Conference of the International Forum on the Comparative Political Economy of Globalization, Musashi University, Tokyo, 1–2 September.

—— and H. Flakierski (eds.) (1990), *Socialist Dilemmas: East and West*, New York: M.E. Sharp.

—— and R. Albritton (eds.) (1995), *A Japanese Approach to Political Economy: Unoist Variations*, London: Macmillan.

Strange, S. (1998), *Casino Capitalism*, Manchester: Manchester University Press.

Uno, Kozo (1980), *Principles of Political Economy*, trans. T. Sekine, Brighton: Harvester Press.

—— (1971) *Keizai Seisakuron* [Types of Economic Policy Under Capitalism], Tokyo: Kobundo Press (also translated into English by T. Sekine, publication pending).

Westra, Richard (2003), 'Globalization: The Retreat of Capital to the "Interstices" of the World?', in Richard Westra and Alan Zuege (eds.), *Value and the World Economy Today*, London: Palgrave.

Womack, J.P., Jones, D.T. and Roos, D. (1990), *The Machine that Changed the World*, New York: Rawson Associates.

Index

industrial capital
  circulation process of, 45, 82–91
  circulatory phases of, 44–5
  form of, 43–6
  production process of, 44
industrial reserve army, *see* law of relative
  surplus population
Industrial revolution, 186–7
information and communication technologies
  (IC), 211, 214
inner laws or logic of capitalism, 2, 3, *and
  see* dialectical logic
innovation, 76, 138
  continuous innovation in post-Fordist era,
    211–12, 214
  and see business cycle
input-output process, 57
institutional investors, 215
integrated circuit, cost of production, 213
intensification of labour, 76
interest, 41, 163, 169, 172, 174
interest rate, 41, 43, 163–4
inter-industrial differences in the profit-rate,
  117, 119, 122–8, 133
interlocking directorship, 197
internal combustion engine, 210
International Monetary Fund (IMF), 209,
  216, 218
internet commerce, 216
investment banks, 194
iron and steel industry in imperialist
  Germany, 192–3

Japan, 211, 214, 219, 220
joint production, 131
joint-stock corporation, 174–5
  in imperialist era, 194–5

Keynesian, 208
knowledge intensive, 212–14

loan capital, 41–3, 161–4, 169, 170–3
loanable funds, 162–4, 172
labour, 79
labour-and-production process, 56, 62
labour cost, 120–1
Labour-output ratio, 209
labour-power, 43, 56, 65–6
  as a commodity, 44–5, 125
  as a time commodity, 45–6
  conversion into a commodity, 48–9, 150,
    176
  decommodification of, 209
  reproduction of, 94–7
  value of, 80–1, 96, 108, 111

labour process and production process, 56
labour theory of value, 66–75
  and the labour theory of price, 70
  and the viability of capitalism, 71
  grounded on the law of population, 105–8,
    111
  necessity of, 68
  validity of, 71
laissez-faire, 190
landed property, 149–50, 169, 180, 182, 209
  fusion with oligopolistic corporate capital,
    210
  teleological coexistence with, 160
landlordship, 74, 150
lean production, *see* Fordism
law(s) of
  average profit, 128–30
  falling rate of profit, 138, 146–8
  market value, 130–4
  relative surplus population, 105–8, 111
  value, 66–70
levels of analysis, vi, 11–12
Leninist, 202
leveraged gambles, 216–17
liberal ideology, 189–90
liberalization, 217–18
liquidity, 216
Luxemburg, Rosa, 202
luxury goods, 179

machines, power, transmission, working, 78
macroeconomic fiscal and monetary policies,
  208
managerial revolution, 196
manufactory, 181
mapping or mathematical function, 127
marginal productivity (declining), 154
marginal suppliers/producers, 132
marginal technique, 132
market (or price) mechanism, 208
market production price of an agricultural
  commodity, 153
market principle, 208
market regulating production price, 131, 135
market value (or market production price),
  136
Marx, Karl, vi, vii, 1–5, 10, 11, 151
Marxist, 197
mass production, 208
material (substantive or real) economic life, 17
means of circulation, 33
means of labour, 56
means of payment, 36
means of production, 43, 73–5
  natural forces, 48–9, 74–5

protectionism, 182–4, 201–2
pure capitalism (or purely capitalist society)
 dialectical theory of, 213
 movement towards and away from, 192,
  294
putting-out-system, 11, 39, 180–2

Reagan, Ronald, 215, 219
real estate bubble, 217
realization of value, 82, 86
reification, 2, 6, 9, 11, 21, 60, 118
relative surplus value, 75
relative value form, 25
rent, 150
 absolute, 156–60
 differential rent of form I, 153–4
 differential rent of form II, 155
 monopoly, 159–61
rentiers, 194, 214–15
reproduction process of capital
 and fixed capital, 104
 condition of reproduction, 102, 105, 125
 condition of self-replacement, 100
 reproduction schemes (circular flow),
  100–5
 simple and expanded reproduction, 83,
  89–90, 93–100, 103
research and development,191, 212
reserve currency, status of, 209, 218
restructuring, 212, 213–15
Robinson Crusoe(s), 58, 61, 71–3
robotics, 211
Roosevelt, F.D.R., 207
royal charter, 182

Samuelson, P., 129
'satisficing' (Simon, H.A.), 160
scarcity, 210
scientific management or Taylorism, 191–8,
 208
 time and motion studies, 208
securitization, 217
Sekine, Thomas T., vi, vii, 5, 12
services, 21–60
 knowledge intensive, 213
shareholders (large and small) in imperialist
 era firms, 194–5
simplification of labour, 58
simple commodity production, 44, 46, 59, 70
single-purpose machines, 208
slavery, slave trade and slave labour, 45, 61,
 183, 191
social democracy, 207
social division of labour, 57
socialism, 221

socially necessary labour, 67–8, 101, 134
'Socialpolitik', 202
software and hardware, 212
Soviet Union, 216, 220
specialized production with mutual trade, 72
speculation, 39, 214–15
speculative capital flows, 215
stage(s) theory, see capitalist development
stagflation, 214
standardized/standardization, 77
 of parts, 208
stationary state (Ricardian), 159
steam engine, 187
storage, 86
store of value, 33
sub-structure and superstructure, 14, 210
supplementary materials, see accessory
 materials
super imperialism (monetary), 220
supply and demand, 34
supply price, 30
surplus labour, 184
surplus (pure economic) profit, 135
surplus value, 44, 65, 75, 121
 absolute and relative, 75–6, 188
 extra, 76, 136
 rate of, 120–2
surpluses, 179
synthetic materials, 210
systemic risks, 216

tariffs, 201
technical composition of capital (roundaboutness), 106
technical progress, 108–9, 137
technology
 radically labour saving, 212
 quantitative an qualitative advancements
  in, 213–14
technological complex, 117, 124
teleology, 7, 10
territorial expansion in imperialism, 203–4
time deposit, 163
trade credit, see commercial credit
trade in mercantilist era, foreign and
 domestic, 179–80, 182–4
trade bills, 36, 162
trade surpluses, 221
trading firms, 183
transformations (dialectical and
 mathematical), of values into prices and
 of surplus value into profit, 123, 126–30
transnational corporations and the disintegration of capitalism, 212
transportation, 86, 186